I0803103

IMAGES
of America

AROUND CRESSON AND THE ALLEGHENIES

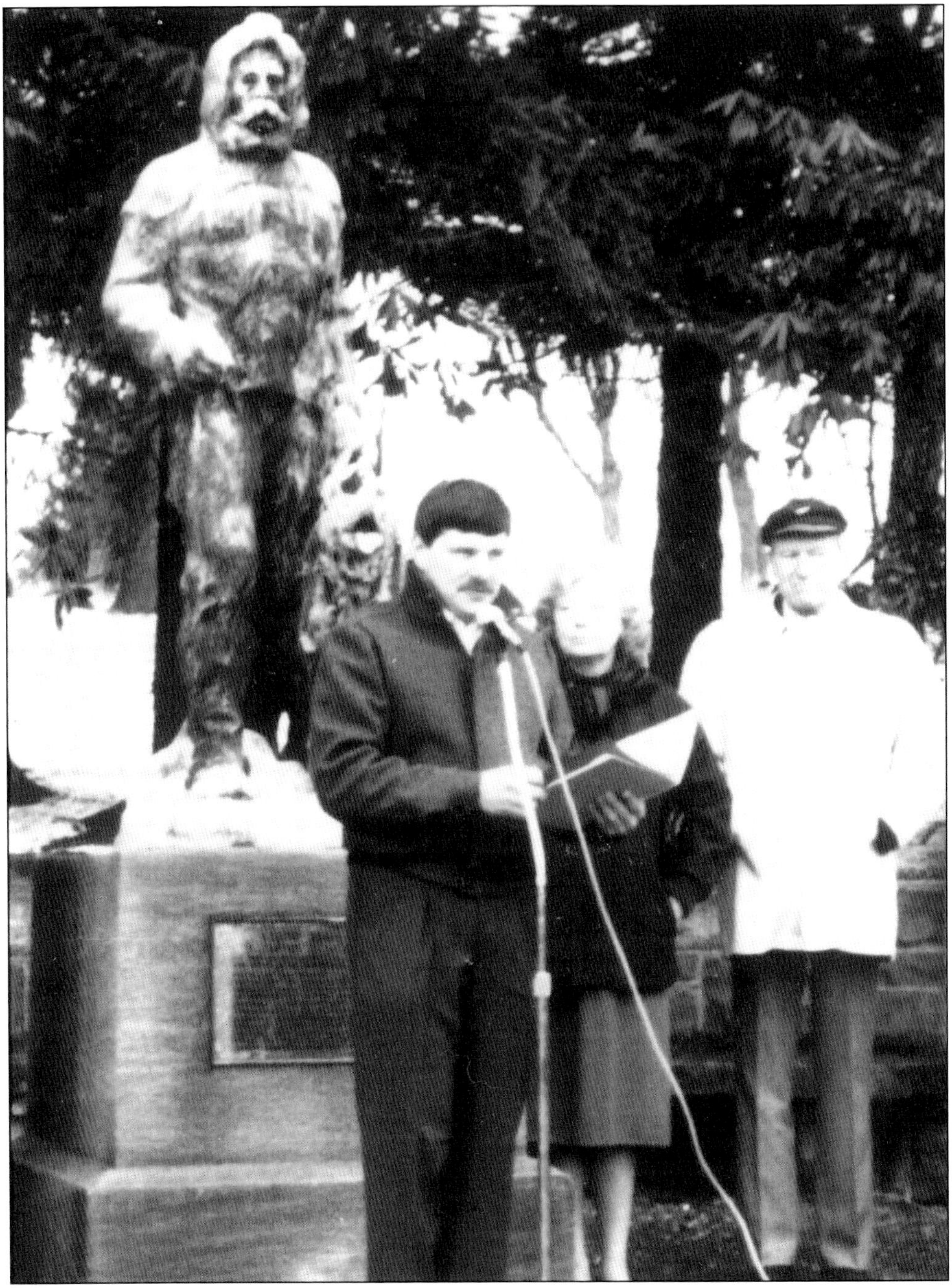

Charles Miller, president of the Cresson Historical Association, reads a proclamation declaring April 1, 1989, to be Peary Day. Edward Stafford (the son of Snowbaby and the grandson of Admiral Peary) visited Cresson with his wife Charlene in celebration of the 80th anniversary of his grandfather's historic discovery. Stafford retired from the Navy in 1963, and is now a speech writer for the Secretary of the Navy. A bronze statue of Admiral Peary with his Eskimo dog was unveiled by Snowbaby in 1937, when Peary Park was established. Charles Miller, a native of Cresson, is the assistant manager of Miller's Hunting and Fishing Shop in Cresson.

IMAGES
of America

AROUND CRESSON AND THE ALLEGHENIES

Sr. Anne Frances Pulling

ARCADIA
PUBLISHING

ISBN 978-0-7385-9040-0

Published by Arcadia Publishing
Charleston, South Carolina

Printed in the United States of America

For all general information contact Arcadia Publishing at:
Telephone 843-853-2070
Fax 843-853-0044
E-mail sales@arcadiapublishing.com
For customer service and orders:
Toll-Free 1-888-313-2665

Visit us on the Internet at www.arcadiapublishing.com

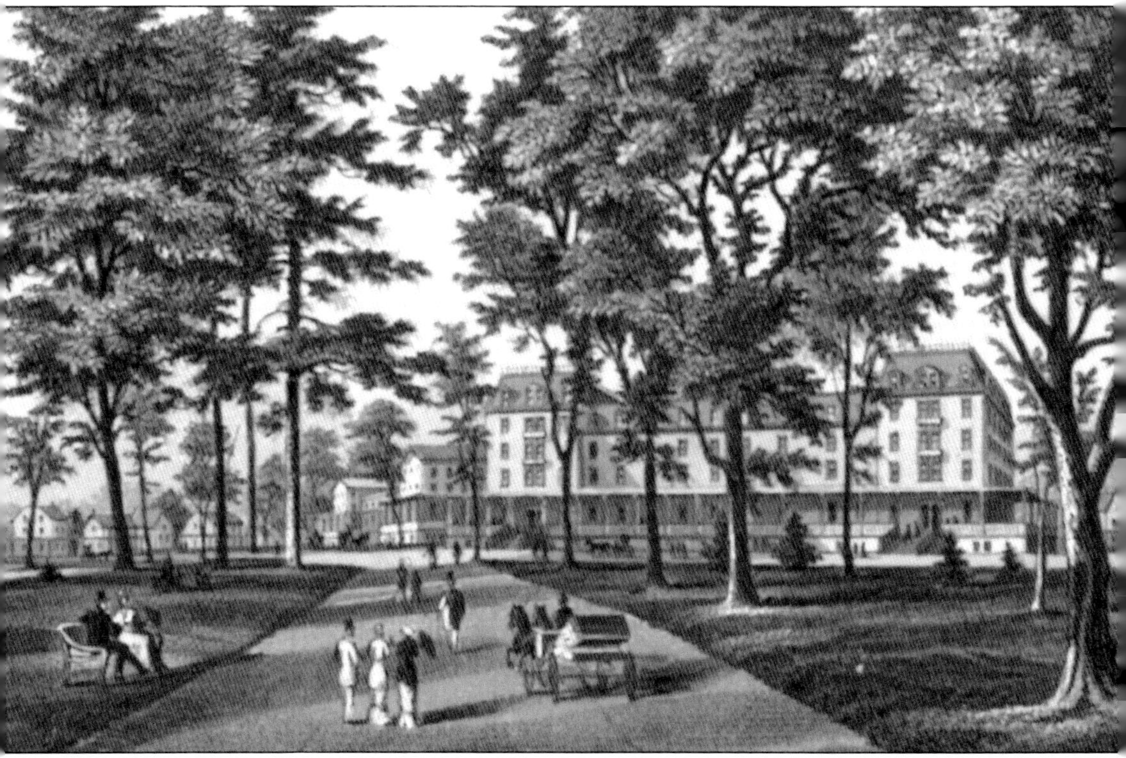

The original Mountain House, like so many notable to follow, arrived in Cresson via the Pennsylvania Railroad. Dismantled, it made the trip around Horseshoe Curve, through Gallitzin's Allegheny Tunnel, and was reconstructed in Cresson, where its lurid career as the playground of the illustrious began. It drew the affluent to the powerful, attractive, invigorating springs surrounding it, and all 300 acres were pressed into service as natural or man-made amnesties. Additions were added to the building until 1880, when a four-story Mountain House accommodating nine hundred guests was erected. Three years after its completion ocean front resorts began to have a noticeable impact on the area.

Contents

Acknowledgments

This publication is based on research, records, periodicals, documents, newspapers, and interviews with townsfolk knowledgeable on local history, many of whom graciously supplied information and offered constructive suggestions. A special thank you goes to John C. Adams, for sharing many photographs and for his wealth of knowledge and encouragement in the earliest stages of this publication.

A word of gratitude goes to Reid Miller on the Allegheny Portage Railroad, Robert Boland, Gerald Criste, Clifford Gailey, Fred Connacher, Roslyn Miller O'Neill, Robert Sanders on the Orphanage, Claudia Reed, Linda Lewis, Arthur Julian, Michael and Audrey Krumenaker, and Frank Seymour of Loretto. I wish to thank Charles Miller, President of the Cresson Historical Association, for the opportunity to select from his collection; coupled with his expertise he was most helpful. I also wish to acknowledge T.C. Ketenheim, Lyman Photographers of Altoona, *The Mainline Dispatch* of Cresson, the St. Francis College Archives, the Mount Aloysius College Archives, and The Sisters of Mercy Archives for their constructive assistance.

A prayerful gratitude goes to all who helped by supplying photographs, assisting with captions, and proofreading, and to my own religious community, The Sisters of Mercy of the Dallas Regional Community, for their support and encouragement in this project.

Introduction

The Allegheny Mountains presented an unique challenge to westward expansion. Creativity, initiative, and technical skill combined with natural resources created a transformation that conquered an almost insurmountable barrier and developed historic masterpieces along the way. An engineering triumph of the age was accomplished when the Pennsylvania Railroad climbed the steep incline on an all-rail route that took it around the now famous Horseshoe Curve, through the illustrious Gallitzin Tunnels and over the Crest of the Alleghenies.

The Summit (called Summitville) became a prominent village when the predecessor of the Pennsylvania Railroad, the Old Portage Railroad, was established. This was the last link of the canal railroad. Canal boats had been placed on railroad flatcars and hauled over the mountain on a series of ten inclined planes. Plane # 6 was at the summit. With the coming of the Pennsylvania Railroad the canal era was over and Cresson, a half mile down the mountain slope, became a center of commerce. Tracks were laid through the town and its colorful career as "The Healthy Place" began.

Cresson became a popular and prestigious health and recreational resort when its springs were discovered to have medicinal value and holiday seekers discovered the "pure mountain air." The town evolved into a mecca for notables when the Cresson Springs Company was incorporated as a place for recreation and convalescence featuring a library and other facilities for the promotion of natural science. This was housed in the Mountain House which dominated the landscape. The panorama was complete when individual dwellings sprang up, built by the wealthy businessmen of Pittsburgh. Andrew Carnegie's summer home, Bramar, has survived the ravages of time. President Benjamin Harrison vacationed here. This prominent resort phased out with the rise in popularity of the seashore as a resort and the decline in popularity of the railroad. Carnegie had bought land at the summit and later donated it to the state for a sanitarium which served western Pennsylvania for many years.

Our first settler was Ignatus Adams, a Revolutionary War veteran who was granted a tract of land at the summit by the federal government. "The Pike," constructed through his mountain domain, was the first stage link between Philadelphia and Pittsburgh. Jacob Troxel was among the many settlers the Pike brought to the area. He seized the opportunity to establish "Laurel Swamp Inn," later called "Troxel's Tavern," along the Pike, a mile west of the summit. This afforded accommodation for pioneers and horses traveling over the mountain. In 1830 the inn was bought by Dr. Robert Jackson, who capitalized on the naturally healthful and invigorating atmosphere of the mountains.

Jackson's friend, noted Philadelphia philanthropist John Elliot Cresson, recognized great potential in the area both as a resort and as a thriving town that attracted industry. Jackson named the settlement in Cresson's memory.

The surrounding area became a hub of commerce when the PRR established headquarters here with a round house, machine shops, and branch lines. Hotels, banks, churches, schools, and a variety of businesses sprang up as Cresson entered an era of industrial prosperity. A coal shaft was established which spanned four decades. History was made again when a native son, Admiral Robert E. Peary, discovered the North Pole in 1909.

It was to this setting that The Sisters of Mercy relocated Mt. Aloysius Academy for Young Ladies in 1897. Established earlier in nearby Loretto, access to the railroad became essential for adequate transportation. The Academy has evolved into Mt. Aloysius College, has weathered a full century, and continues to serve as a seat of quality education.

The little hamlet of nearby Loretto was founded by a prince/priest, Demetrius Gallitzin, whose father was Russian Ambassador to The Hague. The prince originally came on a two-year tour of the United States, then, following his dream, he became a missionary priest. His chapel house and residence remain intact and attract fascinated tourists year-round.

In 1847 the Franciscan Friars brought education to the mountains when they established St. Francis College in Loretto. This eminent school has kept pace with changing times and continues to flourish successfully!

Early in the century Charles Schwab of Loretto, once a poor hack driver, became the illustrious president of the Carnegie Steel Corporation. His magnificent estate in Loretto became a Franciscan monastery. Through his intervention a Carmelite monastery was established in Loretto as was a science hall on St. Francis College campus. His affluence went into the basilica-like Church of St. Michael for his home parish in honor of the centenary of Prince Gallitzin. A life-size statue of the prince rises over his tomb.

Portage retains the epithet of yesteryear. Its dense woodlands gave rise to numerous sawmills, and a vast coal-mining industry eventually developed here. The original bridge that carried the Old Portage Railroad is now an entrance to town.

Trends constantly emerged as immigrants from all parts of Europe settled here to work the railroads, mines, and sawmills. They brought innovations and transformations that have shaped our history. It is hoped that this rendition of our past recaptures and preserves an era that conquered the western frontier and affords a glimpse of yesteryear high up in the Allegheny Mountains of Western Pennsylvania.

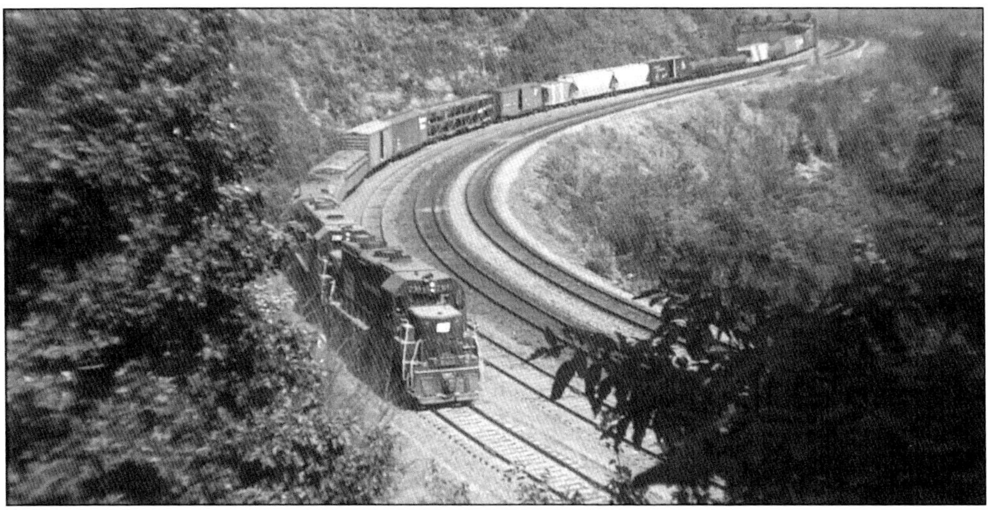

The Pennsylvania Railroad winds it way around the picturesque terrain of Horseshoe Curve. The golden age of railroads led to a successful career on the mountain where the railroad became king, the area played host to worldwide notables, and a little settlement became prosperous! For many years the economy of the railroad was the economy of Cresson. The Pennsylvania Railroad (now Conrail) continues to make many daily trips along this route.

One

Surmounting the Alleghenies

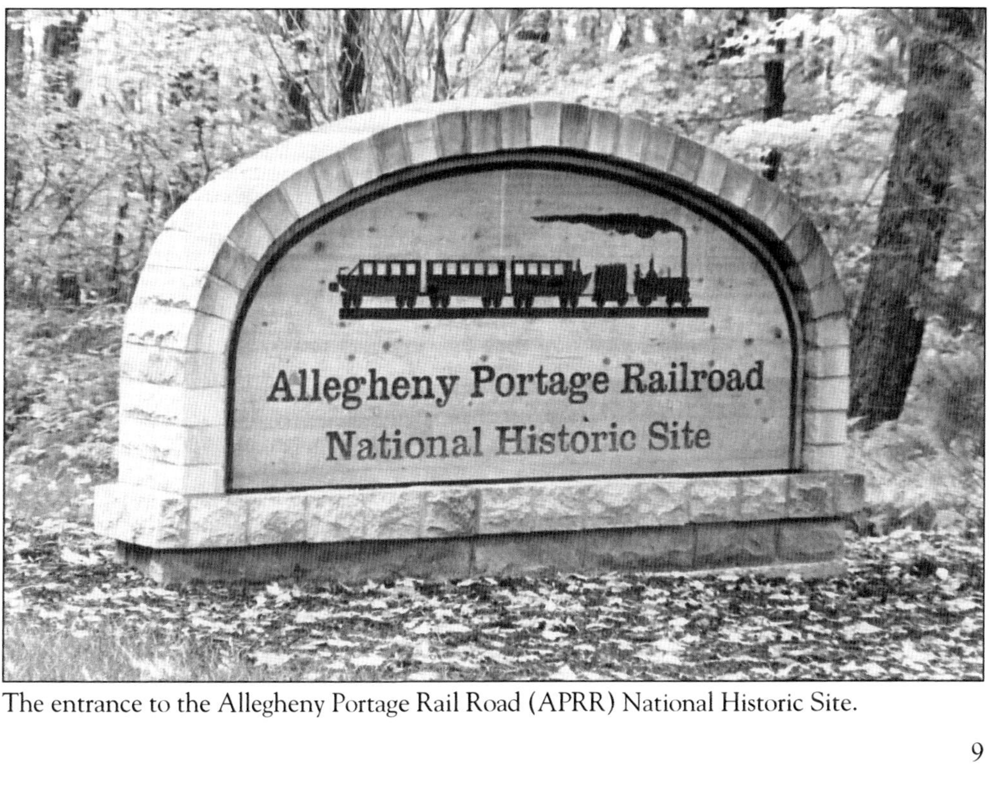

The entrance to the Allegheny Portage Rail Road (APRR) National Historic Site.

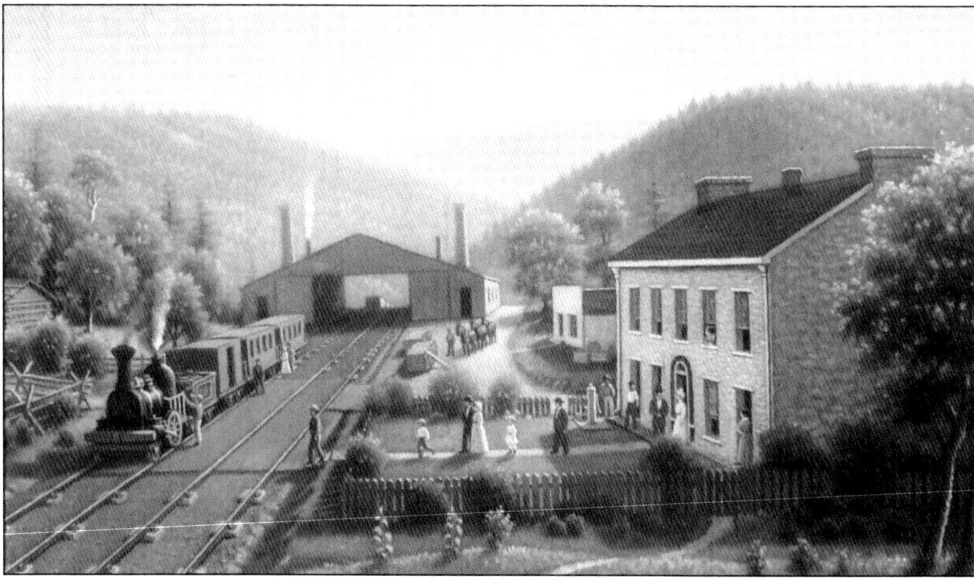

Plane #6 on the APRR. Rail cars are descending the incline plane while others are linked to a locomotive, which replaced horses, on the level section. Passengers emerge from the Lemon House to board the train and continue their journey. There were ten such inclines on the APRR, which operated over the Alleghenies from 1834 until 1854.

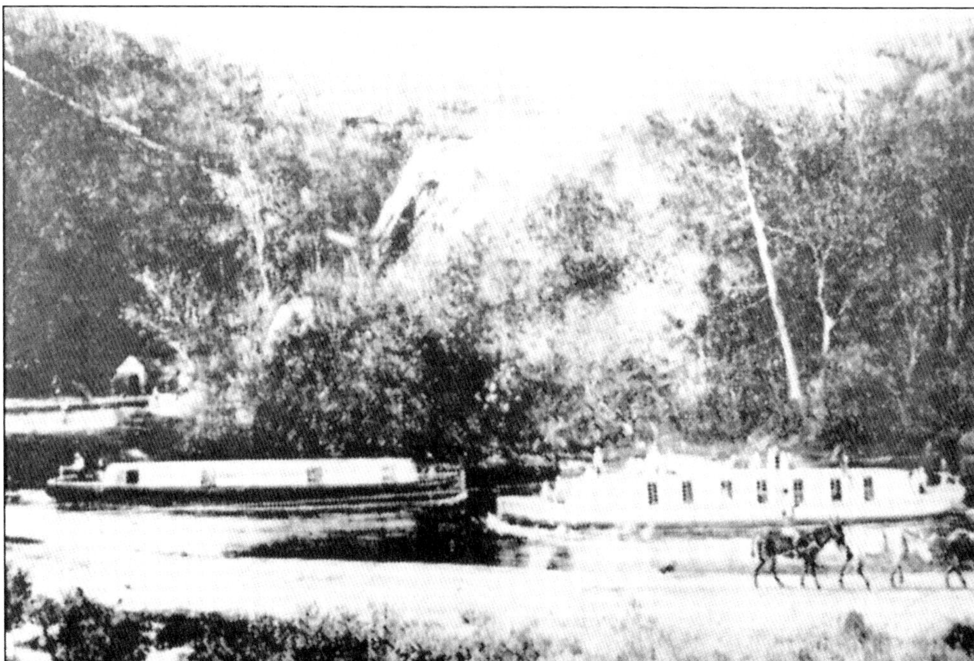

Canal boats. These boats were loaded on the APRR for the 36-mile trek over the Allegheny Mountains. Charles Dickens derived impressions for his *Life on A Canal Boat* following such a journey with a sojourn at Cresson Summit. He wrote of this experience ". . . The rails were laid on the extreme verge of a precipice; looking from the carriage window the traveler gazes sheer down, into the mountain depths below".

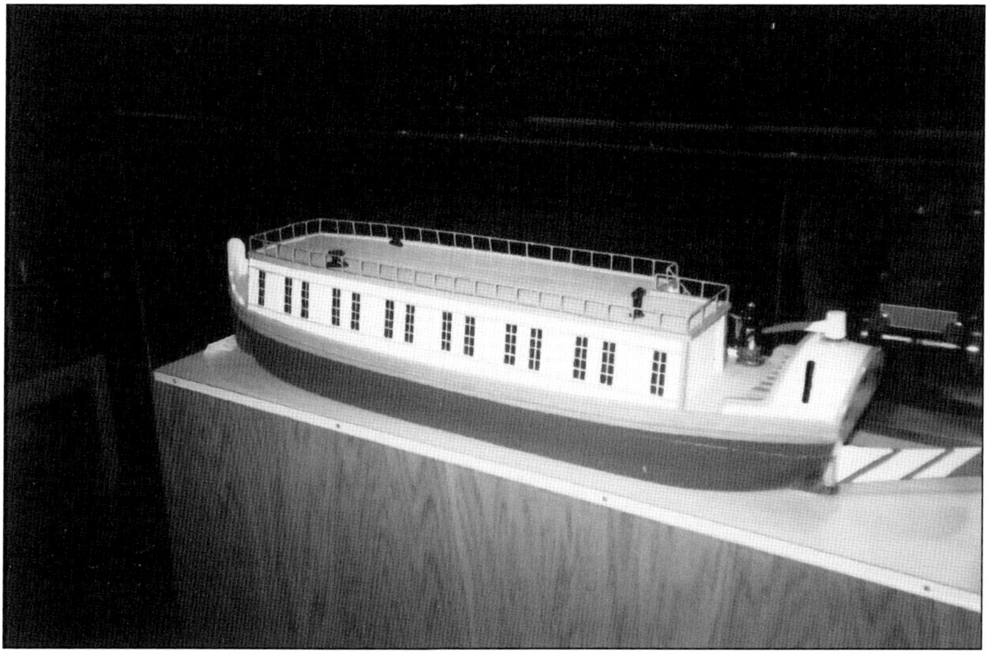

A passenger boat on the Main Line Canal System, established in 1826 to link Philadelphia and Pittsburgh. Westward expansion via the Pennsylvania Canal was feasible until it reached the mountain barrier. The APRR connected the canal basin of the Juniata River at Hollidaysburg on the east with the Conemaugh River canal basin near Johnstown on the west. Here canal boats were floated back into the water.

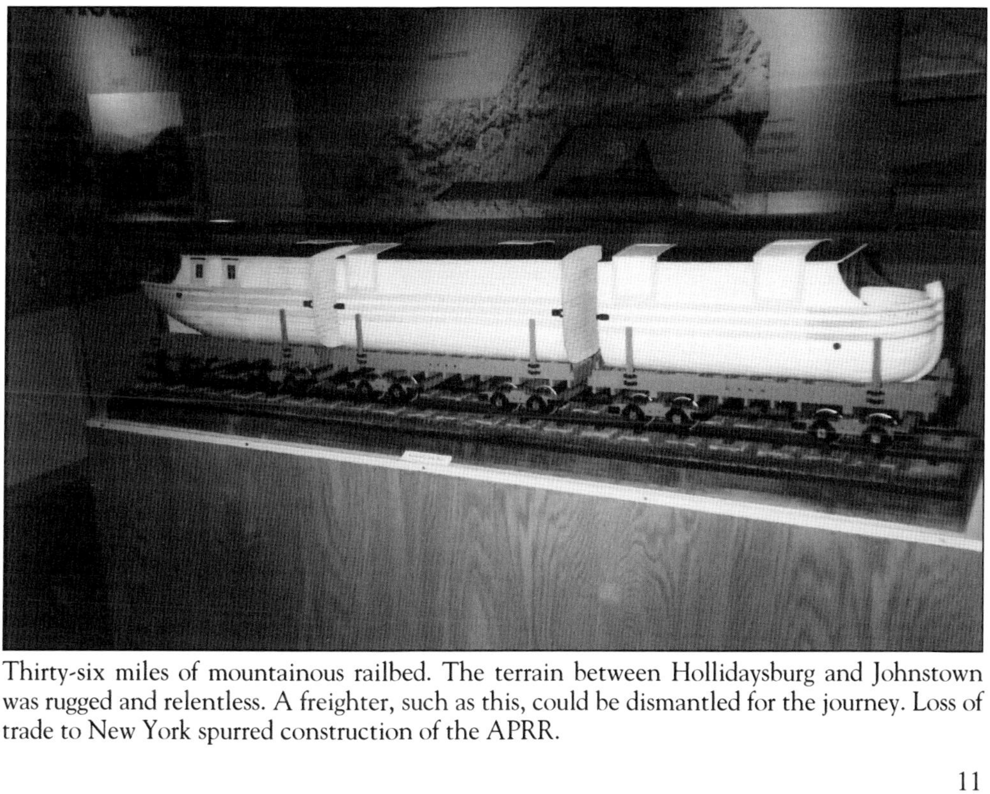

Thirty-six miles of mountainous railbed. The terrain between Hollidaysburg and Johnstown was rugged and relentless. A freighter, such as this, could be dismantled for the journey. Loss of trade to New York spurred construction of the APRR.

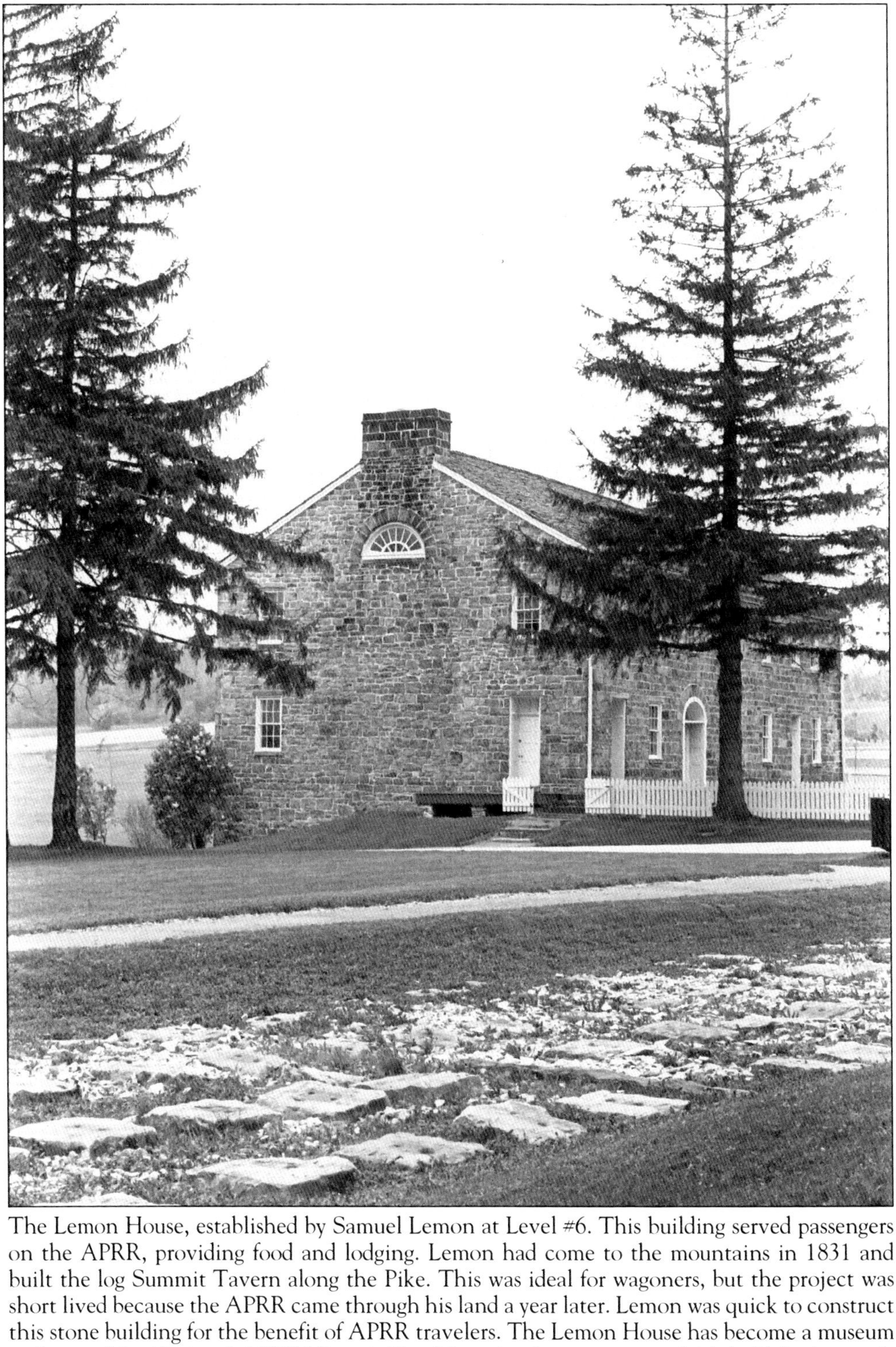

The Lemon House, established by Samuel Lemon at Level #6. This building served passengers on the APRR, providing food and lodging. Lemon had come to the mountains in 1831 and built the log Summit Tavern along the Pike. This was ideal for wagoners, but the project was short lived because the APRR came through his land a year later. Lemon was quick to construct this stone building for the benefit of APRR travelers. The Lemon House has become a museum and part of the National APRR Historic Site. Note the sleeper stones, which held the iron rails in place.

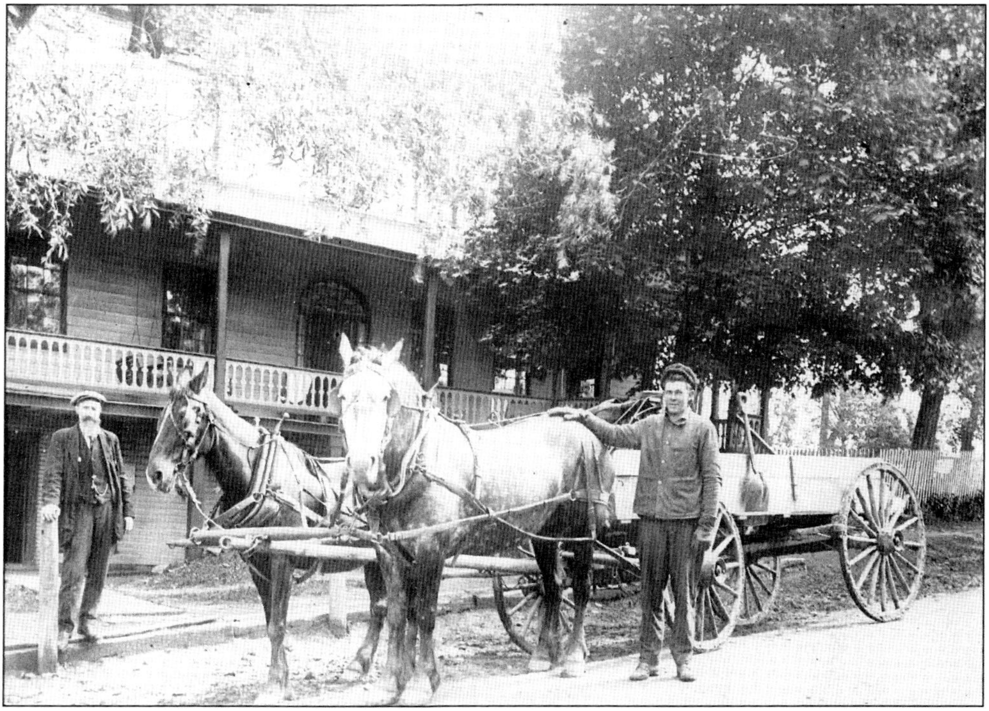

The Summit Mansion House. Charles Dickens stayed at this house, which was built in 1830 for travelers on the APRR. Located on the present William Penn Highway, it had forty-two guest rooms. A later owner, Simon Fisher, is on the left. It was destroyed by fire on March 18, 1980.

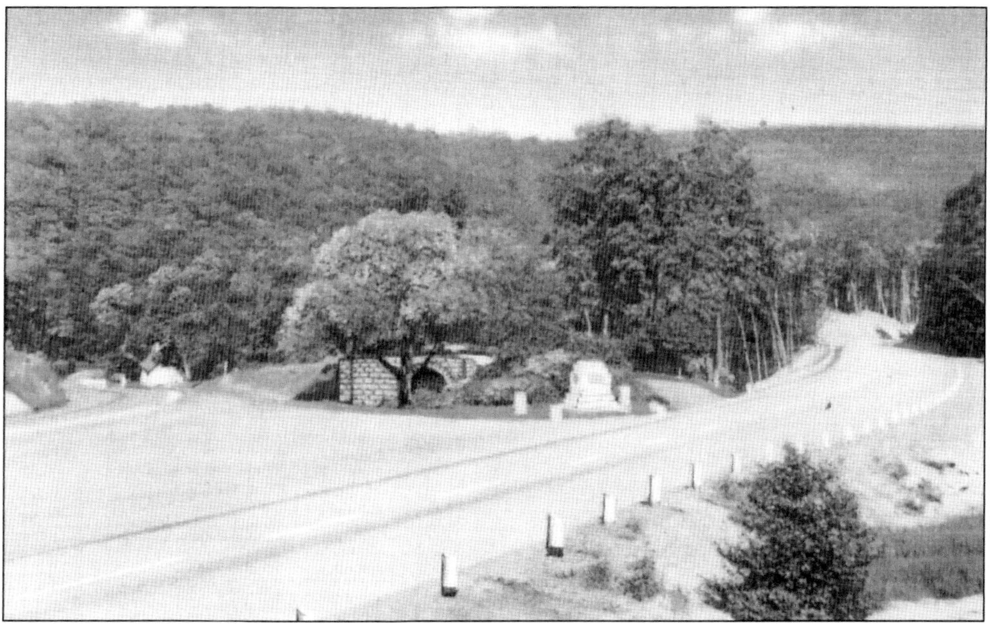

The Skew Arch Bridge. Built in 1832, this bridge was located where the Huntingdon, Cambria, and Indiana Pikes intersected the APRR. Stones were laid diagonally and held in place by keystones. The monument in the foreground commemorates the opening of the APRR on March 18, 1834.

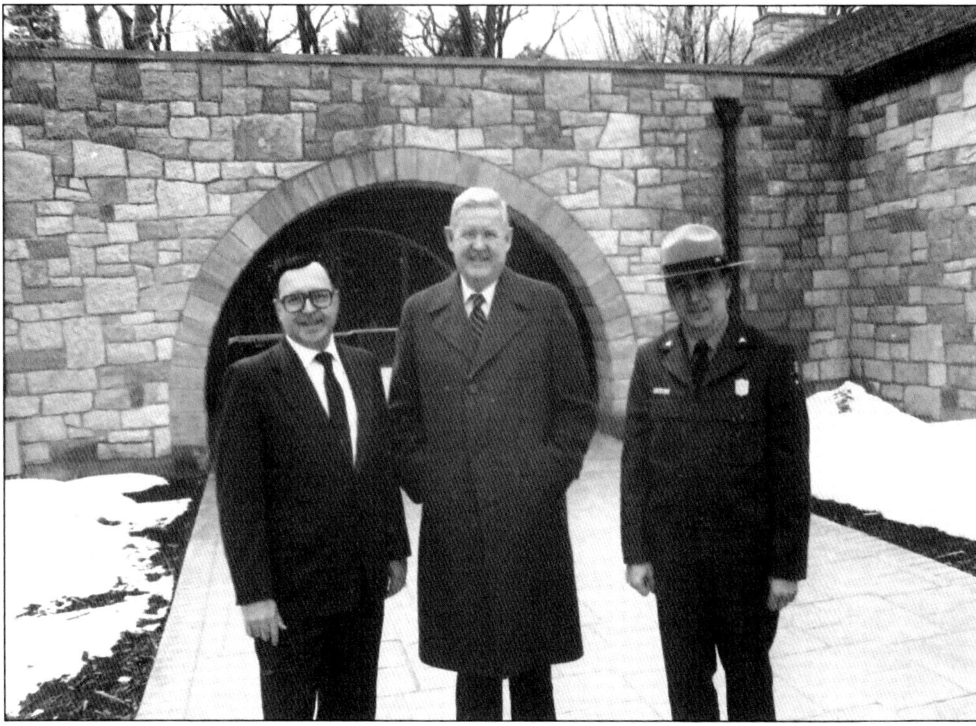

The new Visitor's Center at the APRR Historic Site, completed and dedicated on April 4, 1992. Present for the occasion were George Minnuci (a former president of the Eastern National Park and Monument Association), Congressman John Murtha, and Ranger Peter Nigh (a former superintendent of the APRR Historic Site).

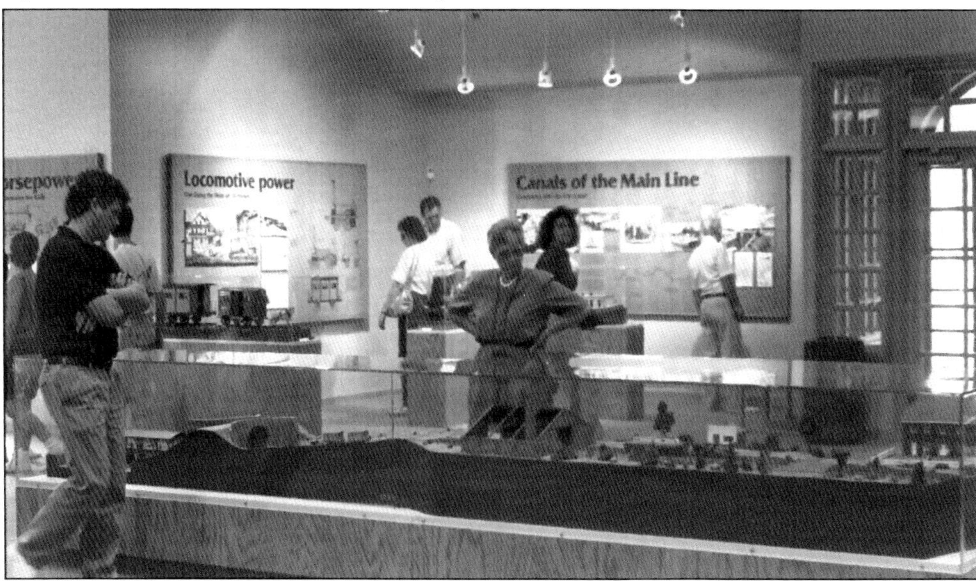

Visitors at the center. A glimpse into yesteryear is provided through a miniature reproduction of the APRR with canal boats on flat cars emerging from the engine house. The Skew Arch Bridge is on the left, the engine house is in the middle, and the Lemon House is on the right. The background displays trace the workings of the APRR.

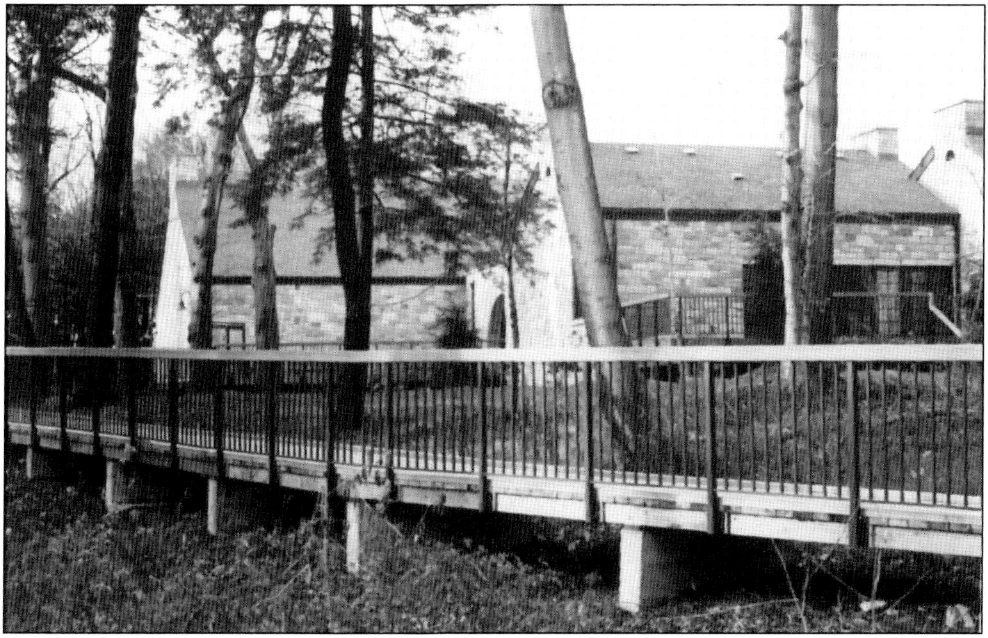

The Visitor's Center, with museum and offices at the APRR! A plank boardwalk takes one down through a picturesque forest to the Lemon House Museum and Engine House with its observation deck.

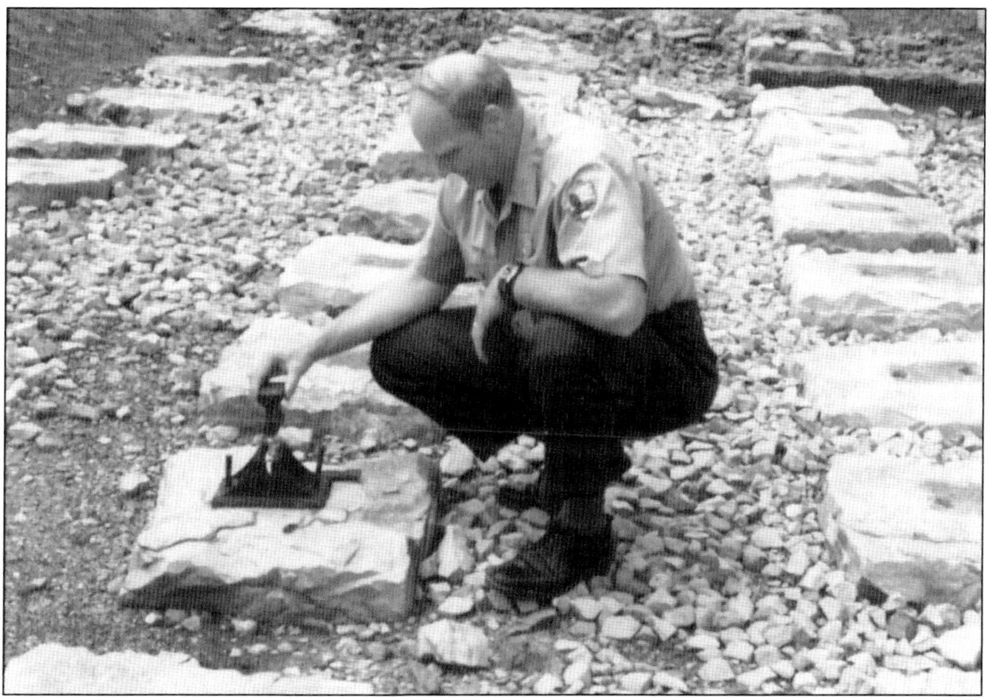

John C. Adams of Cresson, a park ranger and an instructor at Penn Cambria High School. Adams is shown here demonstrating how rails were attached to sleeper stones.

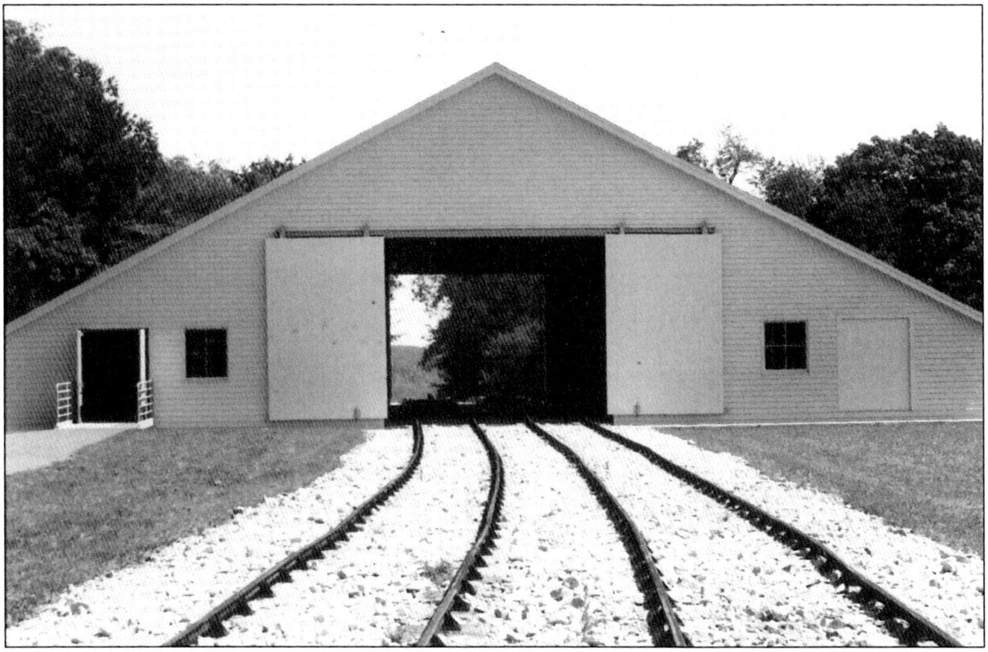

The reconstructed engine house, #6 shelter, an exhibit building and a vital part of the railroad story. It occupies the same site as the original engine house and demonstrates the workings of APRR in a bygone era.

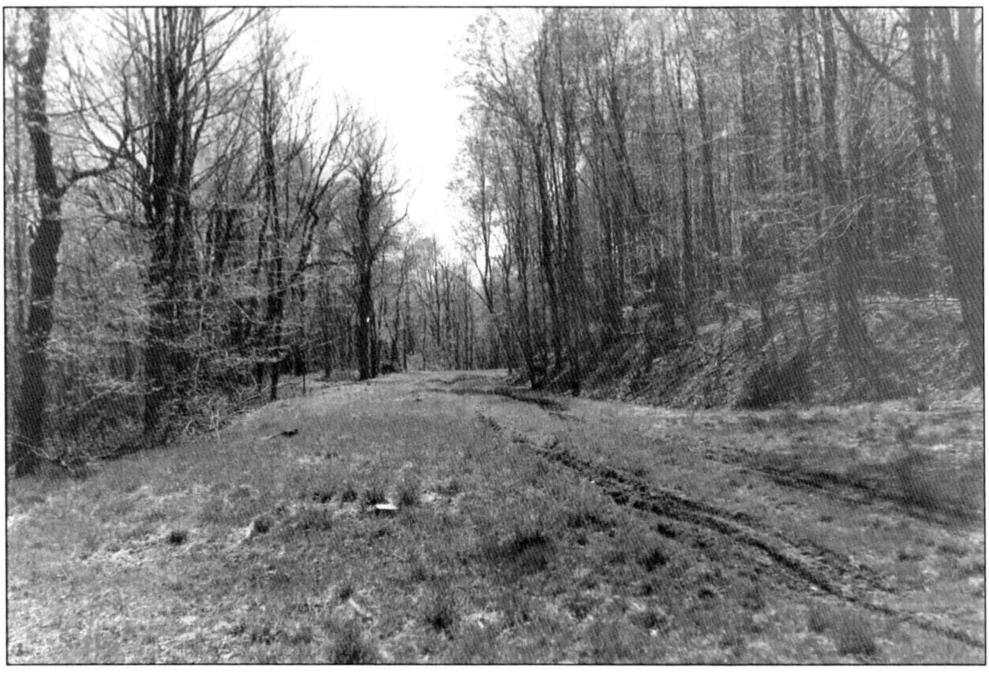

Verdant woodlands just west of Plane #6, once the roadbed of the APRR. This site no longer hums with activity, but affords a nostalgic reflection into the past.

Two

Steel Rails Wind Around, Through, Over

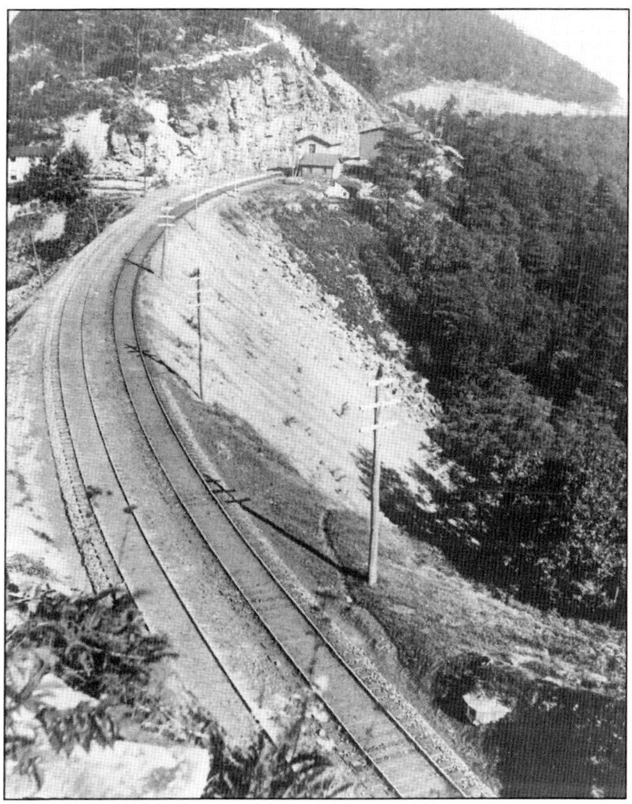

Horseshoe bend from the east, where a passenger station was located at the curve known as Kittaning Point. The curvature sweeps gracefully around the rugged terrain of the Allegheny Mountain. A deep chasm splits Kittaning Point—hence a loop was carved around the mountainside by Irish immigrants. It was called " The Amphitheater of the Alleghenies" and continues to delight spectators who watch trains circle the curve in opposite directions.

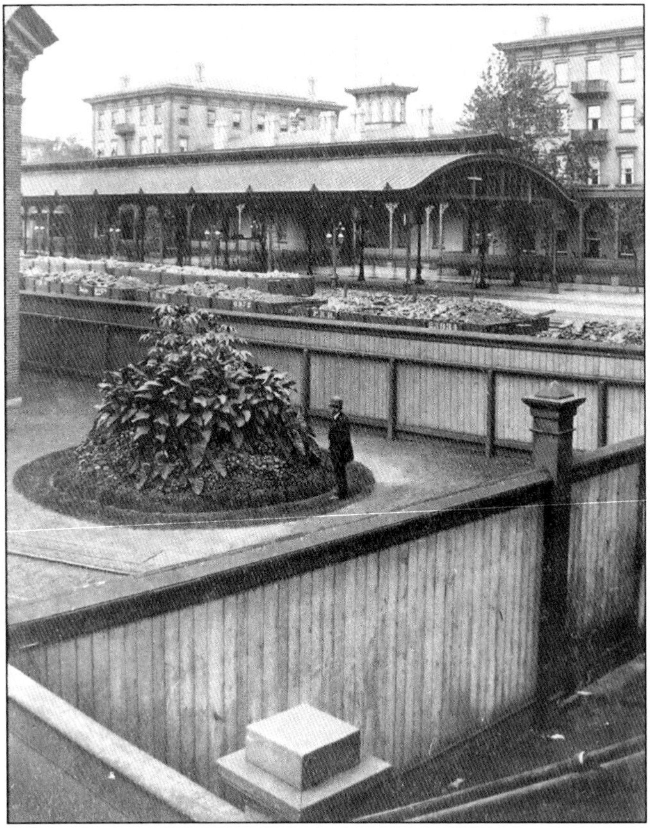

"The Mansion in the Wilderness." Slender rails of steel reached Altoona, at the eastern base of the Allegheny Mountains, in 1849. The Pennsylvania Railroad established the largest railroad yard in the country at the site! The Logan House was constructed as an office and boarding house for railroad personnel in Altoona. It became a hotel for passengers, and stood for a long time on the corner of 11th Avenue and 12th Street.

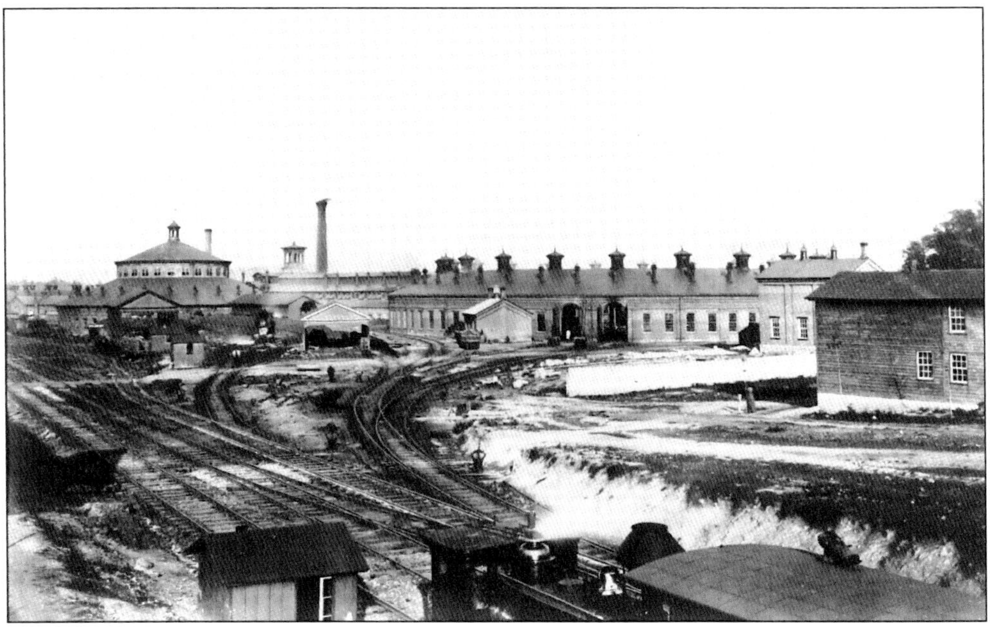

The Pennsylvania Railroad, *c.* 1896. The railroad expanded rapidly during the last half of the nineteenth century, creating a vast network of car shops nestled beneath the mountains. Many new innovations in rail travel originated here.

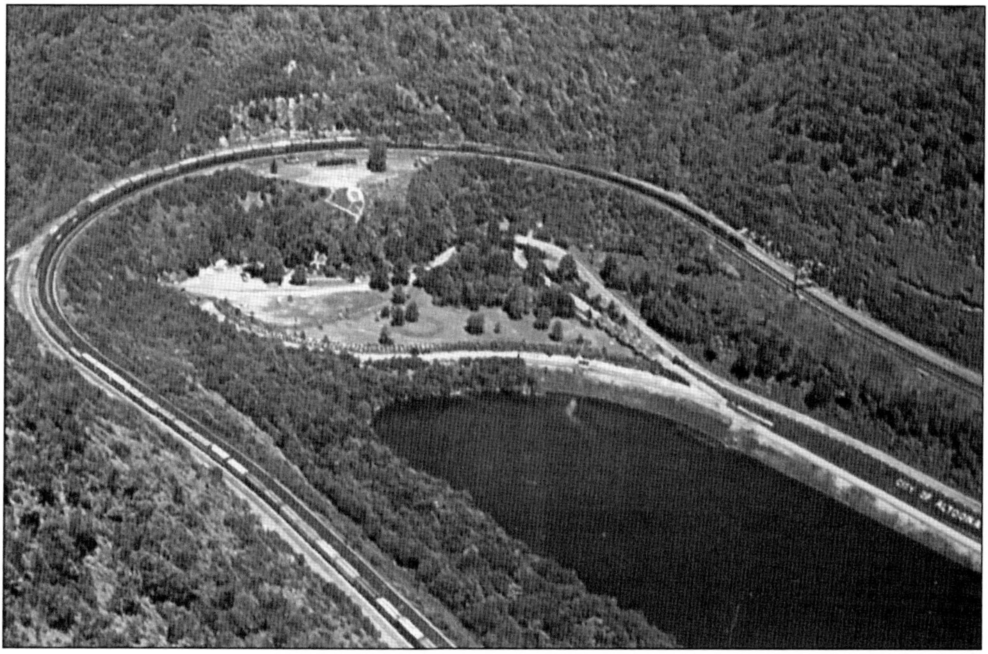

Horseshoe Curve, an engineering triumph that conquered the mountain barrier. A railroad line was folded around the ridge of a valley, into a half circle or horseshoe, linking the east with the west. J. Edgar Thompson, the chief engineer on the PRR, conceived the idea. Begun in 1851, it was built entirely by hand with primitive tools. Nearly fifteen decades later Horseshoe Curve continues to meet the needs of the railroad industry.

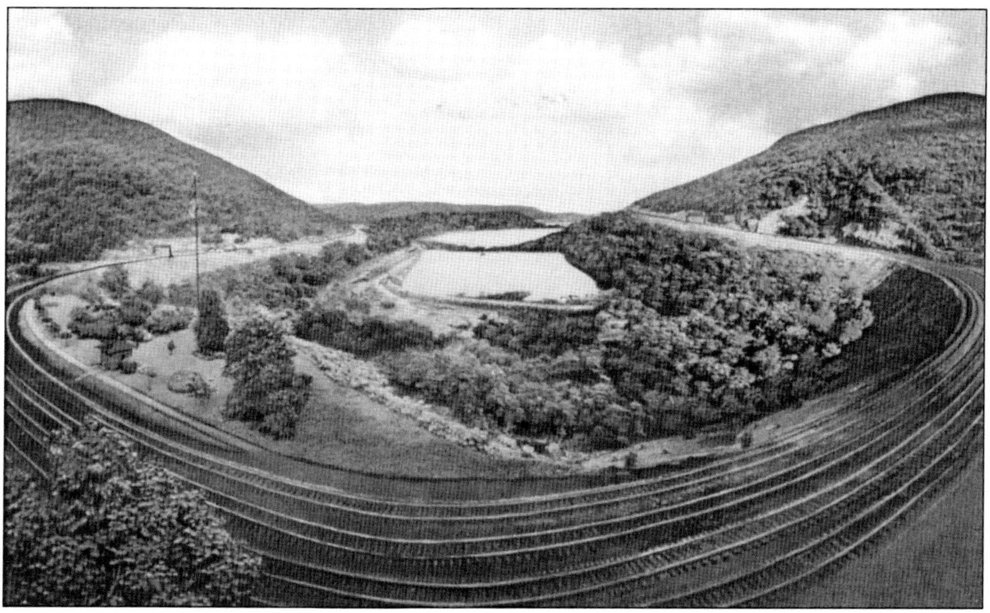

The 2,375-foot-long curve, at an elevation of 1,594 feet above sea level. Opened on February 15, 1854, on the eastern slope of the Allegheny Mountains, Horseshoe Curve gracefully circles Altoona Reservoir in a panoramic view of scenic vistas. It gave access to steam locomotives and cut travel time between Philadelphia and Pittsburgh from four days to eight hours.

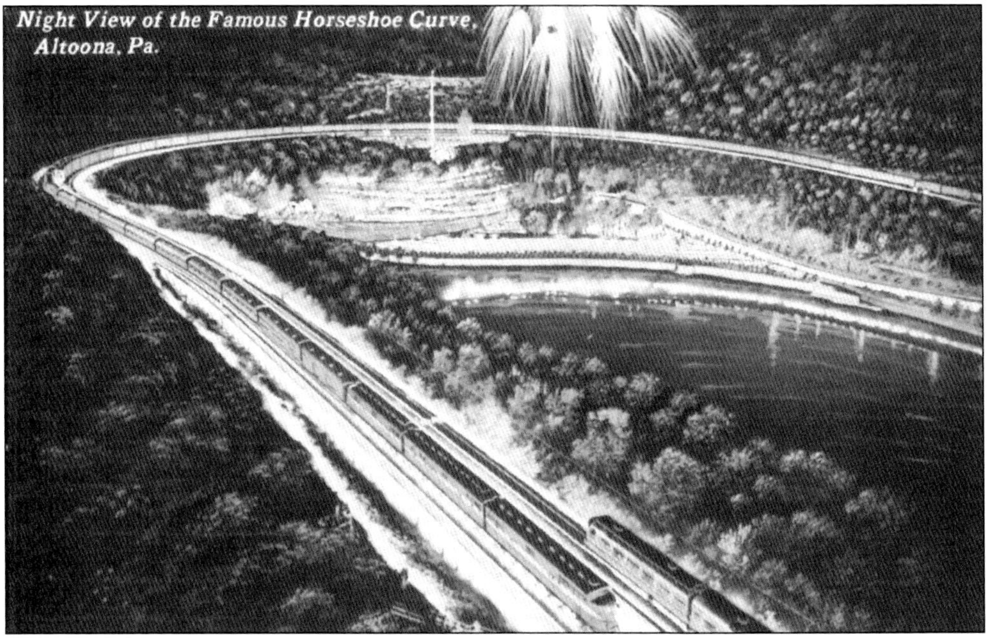

A night view of the curve. The railroad ascends from Altoona toward a mountain chasm which divides into two steep ravines. Here the railroad curves into a semi-circle, or horseshoe, then continues a gradual climb toward the Gallitzin Tunnels and the crest of the Allegheny Mountain.

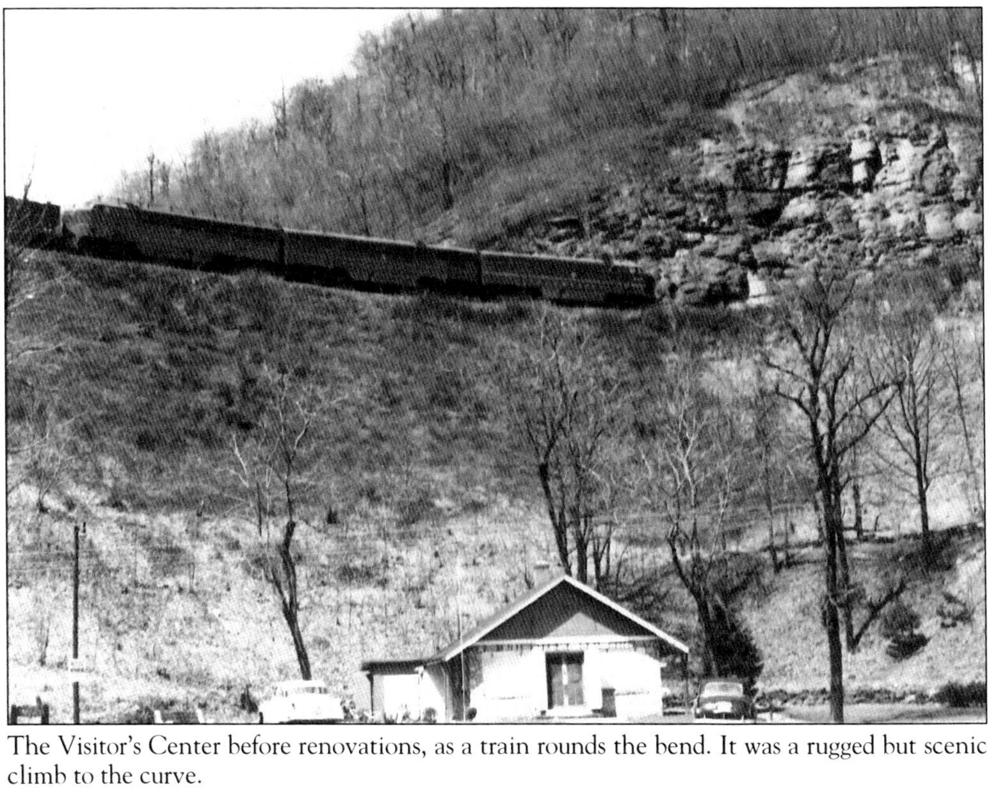

The Visitor's Center before renovations, as a train rounds the bend. It was a rugged but scenic climb to the curve.

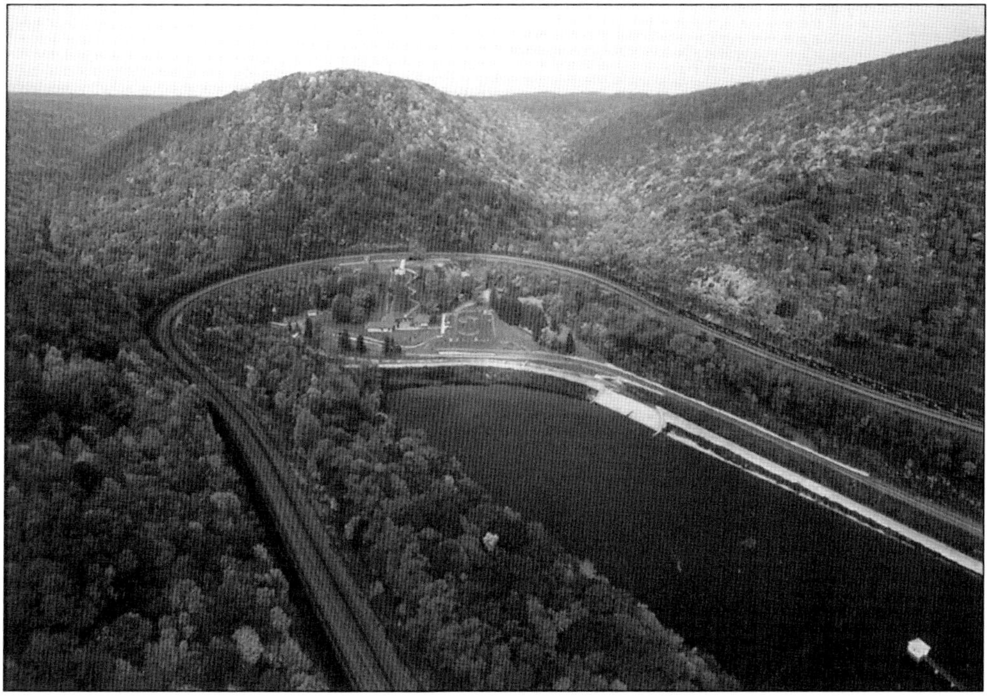

Another view of the curve. Conrail circles the curve many times daily. The new Railroad Memorial Museum and Visitor's Center with funicular lift and stairway can be seen nestled beyond Altoona Reservoir. Opened in 1992, the museum attracts many visitors year-round.

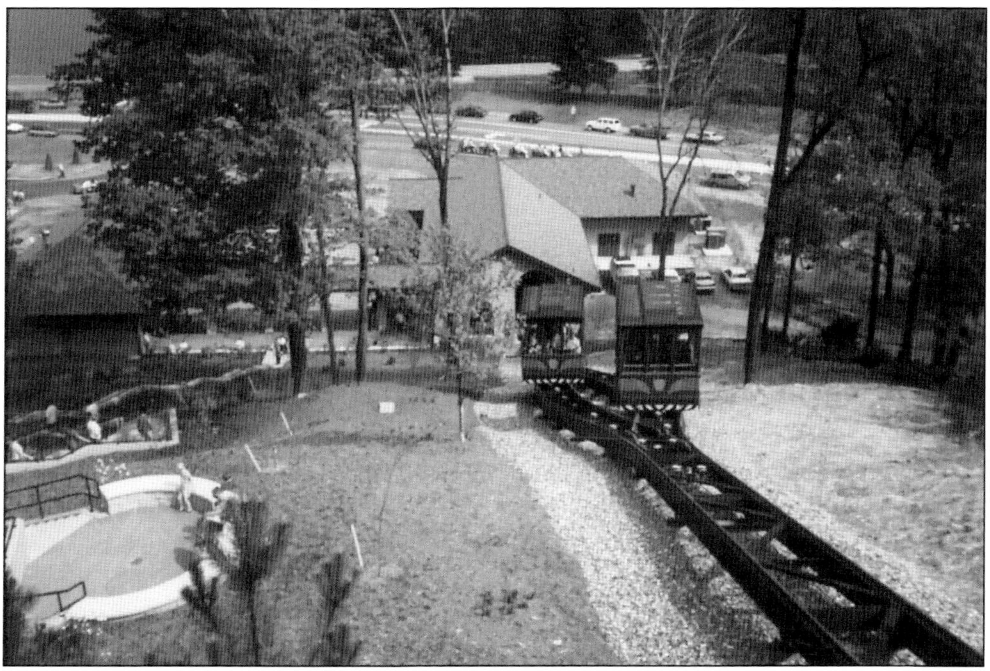

The funicular (or incline) that carries passengers from the Visitor's Center to the curve, where trains frequently travel in opposite directions. A scenic stair route and gift shop are on the left; the museum and funicular are on the right.

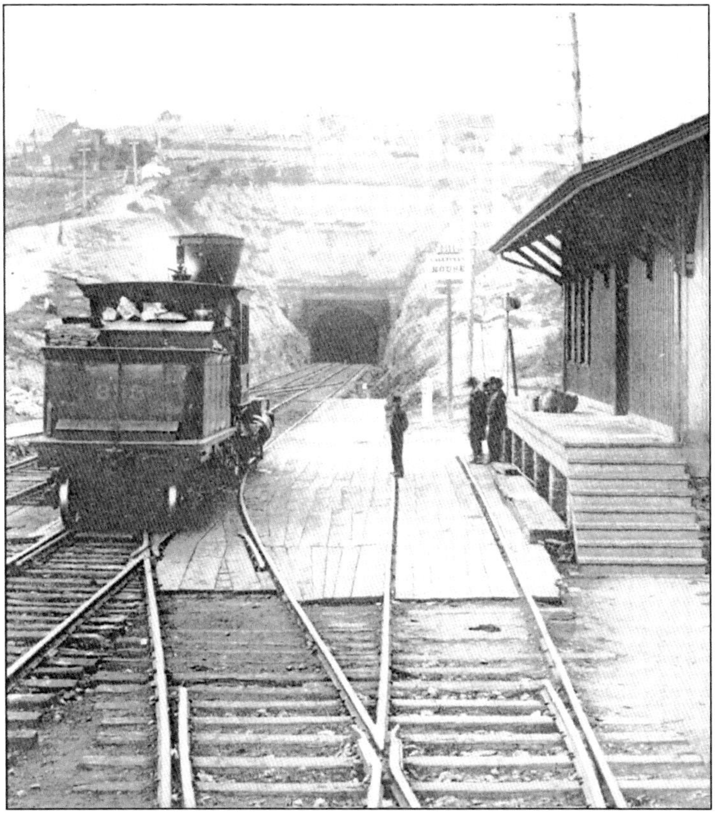

The Allegheny Tunnel, completed in 1854. High elevation necessitated the construction of tunnels through the mountain at Gallitzin. The Allegheny Tunnel, along with Horseshoe Curve, provided an all-rail route over the mountain. The tunnel is 3,612 feet long, and was originally 22 feet wide and 24 feet high, with an elevation of 2,167 feet. A narrower Gallitzin Tunnel was cut through on the left in 1904.

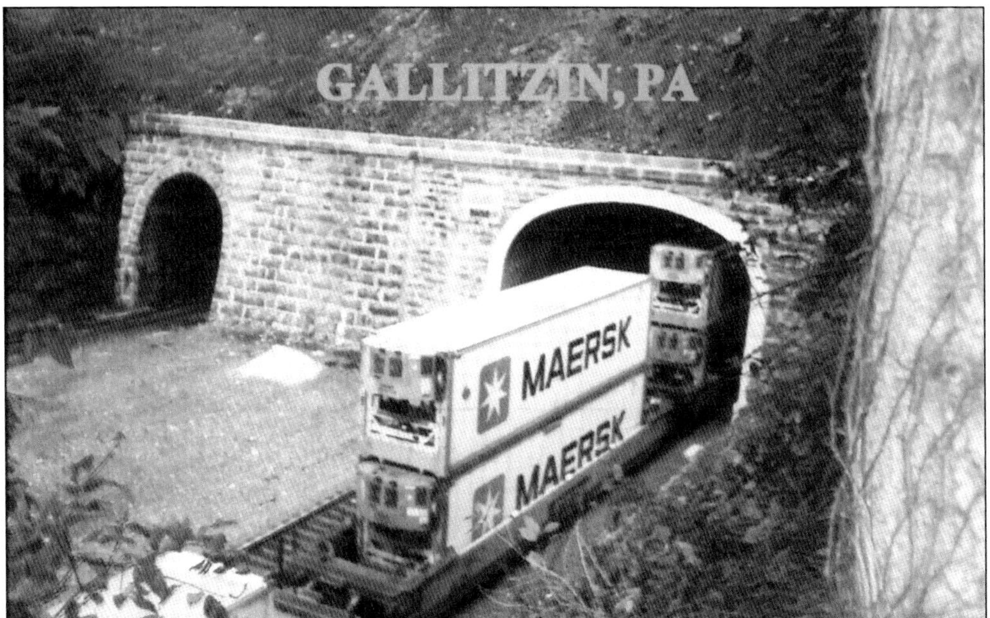

Modifying the Allegheny Tunnel. In 1994 the Conrail Pennsylvania Clearance Improvement Project modified the Allegheny Tunnel enlarging and lowering the track bed to accommodate the double stack freightcars now used by Conrail. The project took nearly two years.

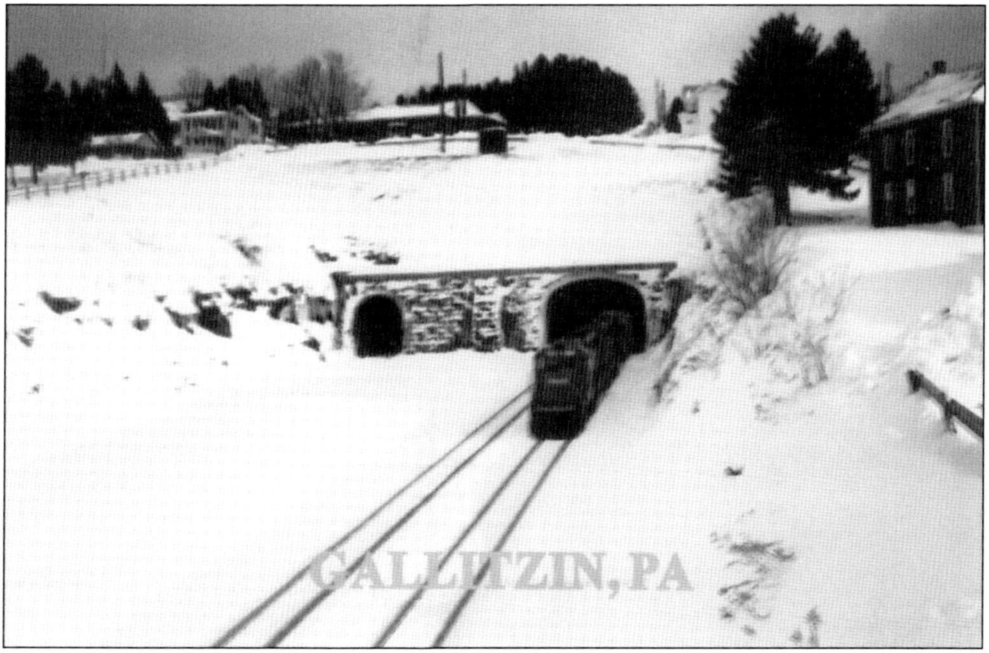

The expanded tunnel. Completed in 1996, the Allegheny Tunnel now houses two sets of tracks for the double-stack trains of the 90s. A covering of snow emphasizes the absence of tracks through the Gallitzin Tunnel.

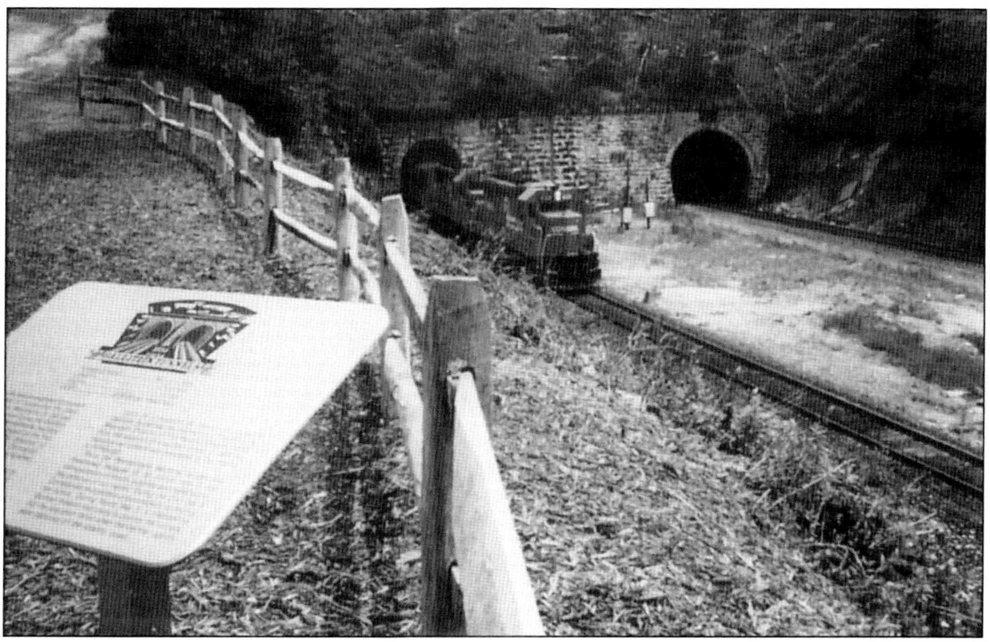

The last locomotive through the Gallitzin Tunnel before removal of the tracks.

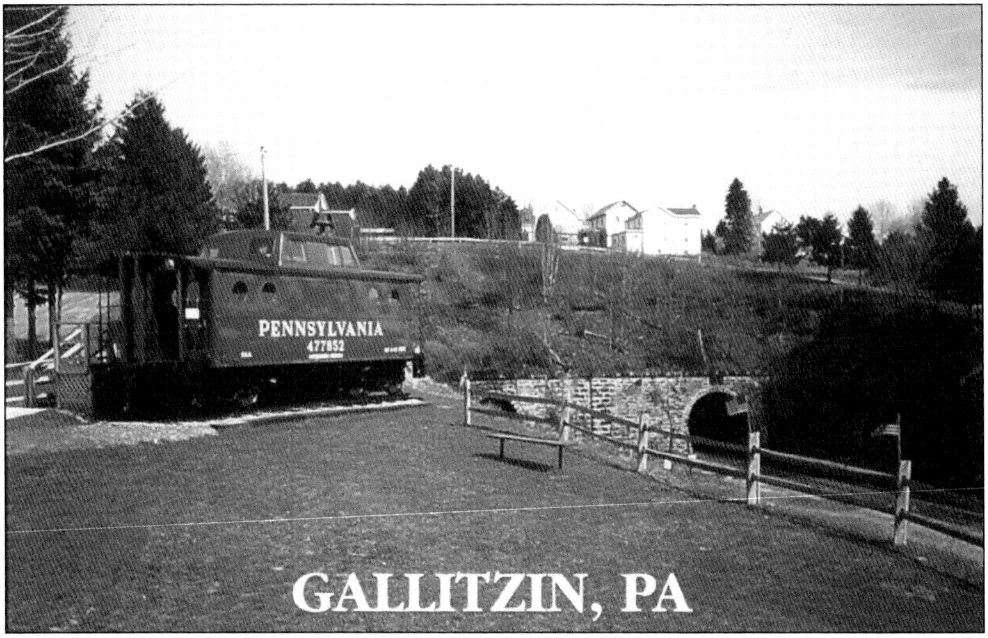

The Visitor Center at the adjacent Tunnel Park. A 1942 NC5 caboose is exhibited here! Reached by way of ramp or steps, one can climb aboard this caboose and enjoy a fascinating glimpse into a railroader's home away from home a century ago. The park also features a Gallitzin Station and train exhibit located nearby.

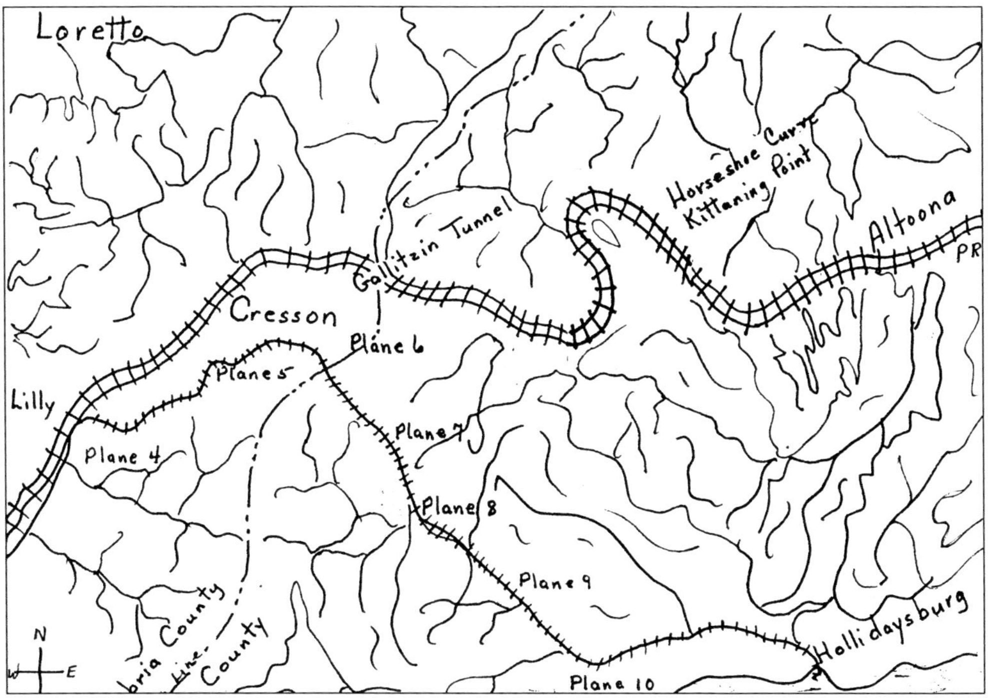

The route of the Old Portage Railroad (demonstrated by a single track), and later the Pennsylvania Railroad (double track), as it travels around, through, and over the rugged mountain terrain.

Three

The Mainline Comes to Cresson

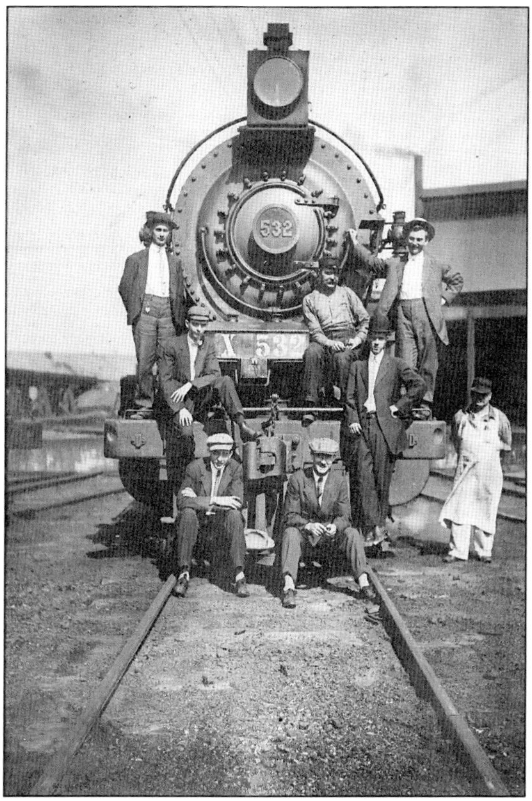

An engine and crew, photographed before World War I beside the engine house. Cresson became a hub of commerce when the Pennsylvania Railroad established headquarters here with a roundhouse (also known as an engine house), machine shops, and branch lines.

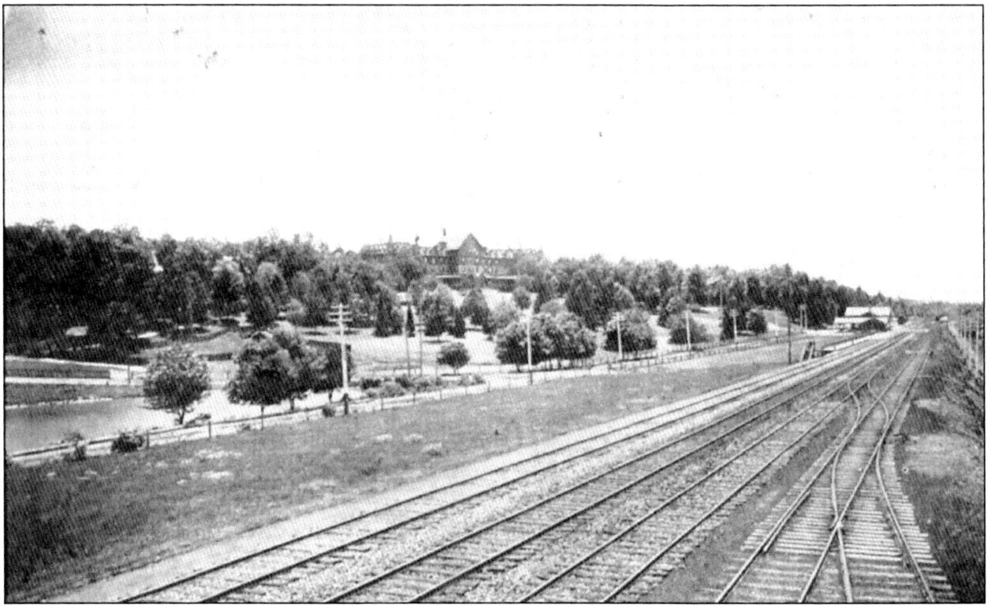

Looking east in 1908. The mainline of the railroad is responsible for Cresson becoming a successful resort. Tracks were laid with provision for branch lines to remote mountain settlements. The Mountain House in the left background.

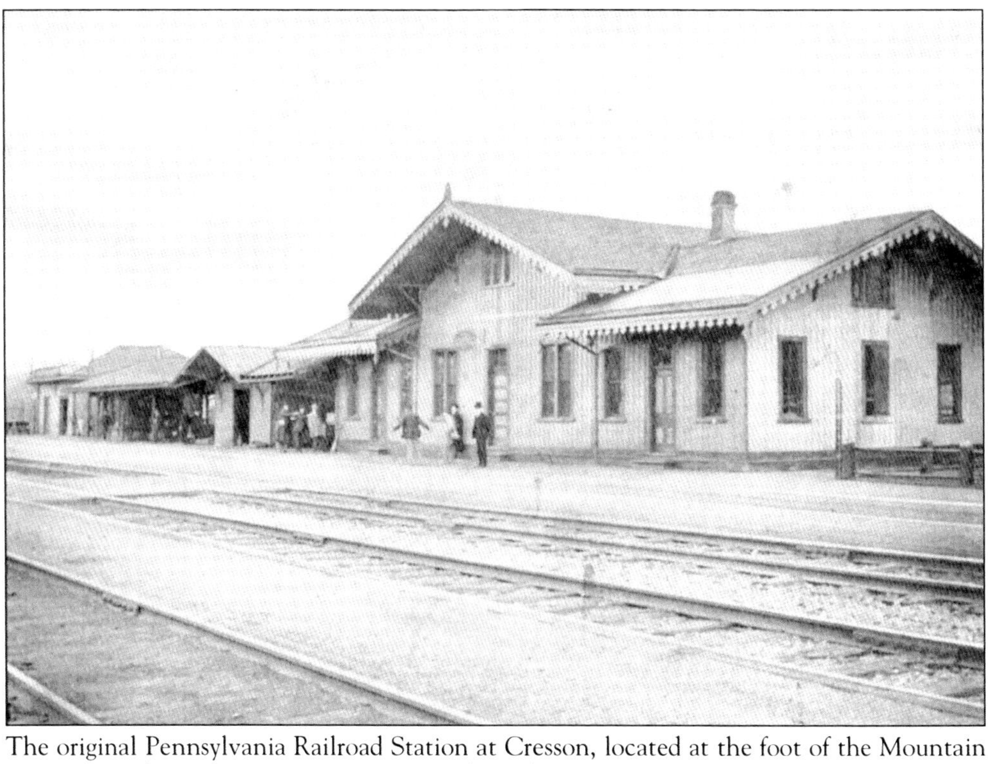

The original Pennsylvania Railroad Station at Cresson, located at the foot of the Mountain House. President Benjamin Harrison arrived via this station, which made Cresson accessible to vacationers.

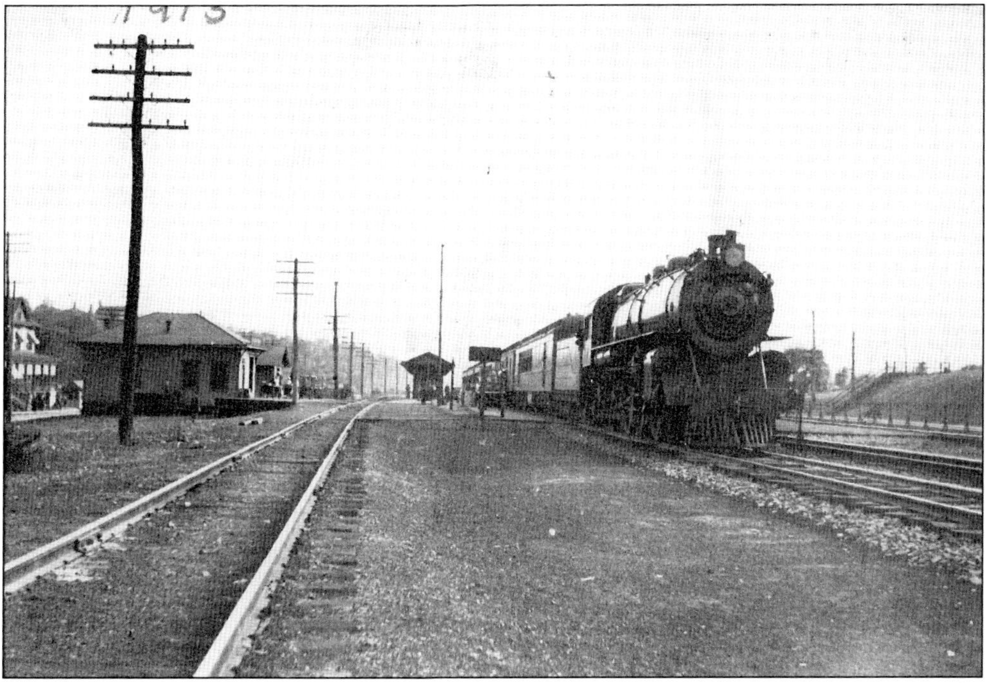

A passenger-freight train at Cresson in 1913. Note the spires of the Mountain House in the left background.

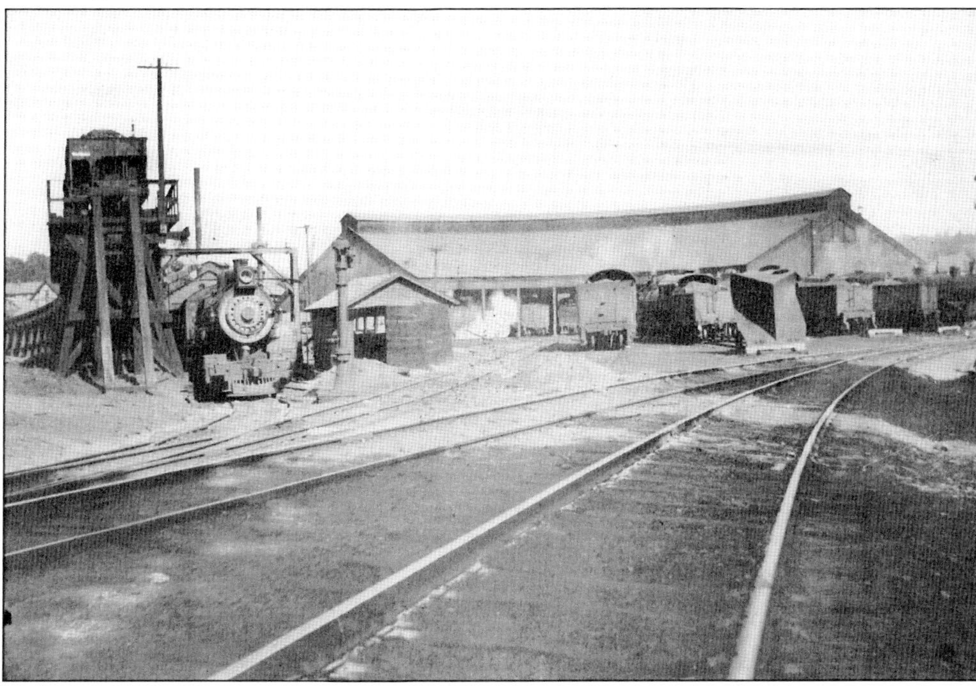

Returning to Cresson from the Hinterlands on a branch line in 1913. The sound of birds and the rustle of wind in the trees were broken only by the shrill whistle of a train as it made its way into secluded little settlements on the mountain. Among these were Munster, Bradley Junction, Winterset, and Ebensburg.

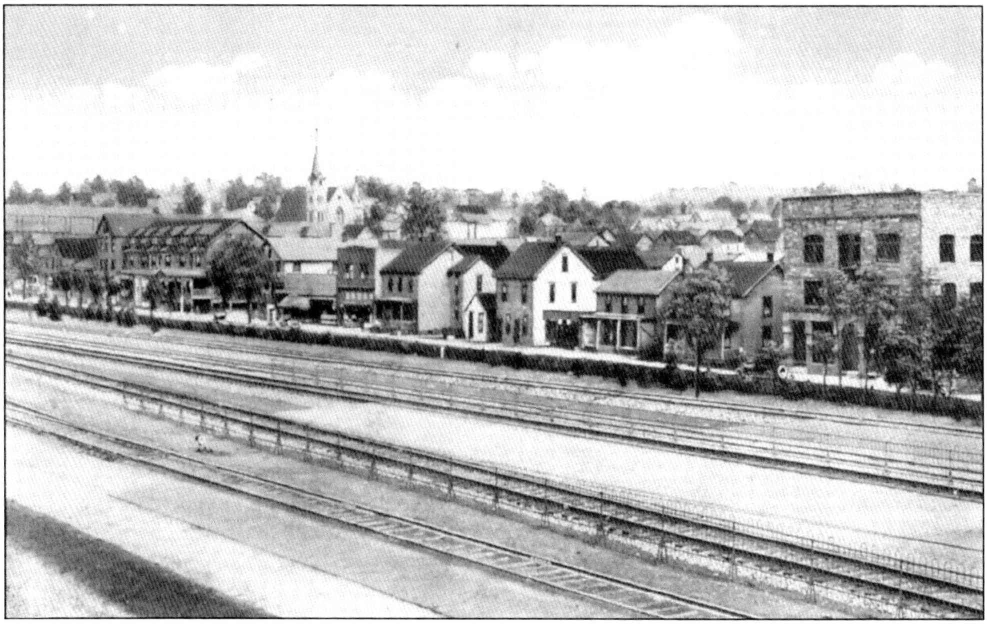

The business section of Cresson along Front Street, *c.* 1920. The Anderson House is on the left, the First National Bank is on the right, and St. Francis Church is in the background.

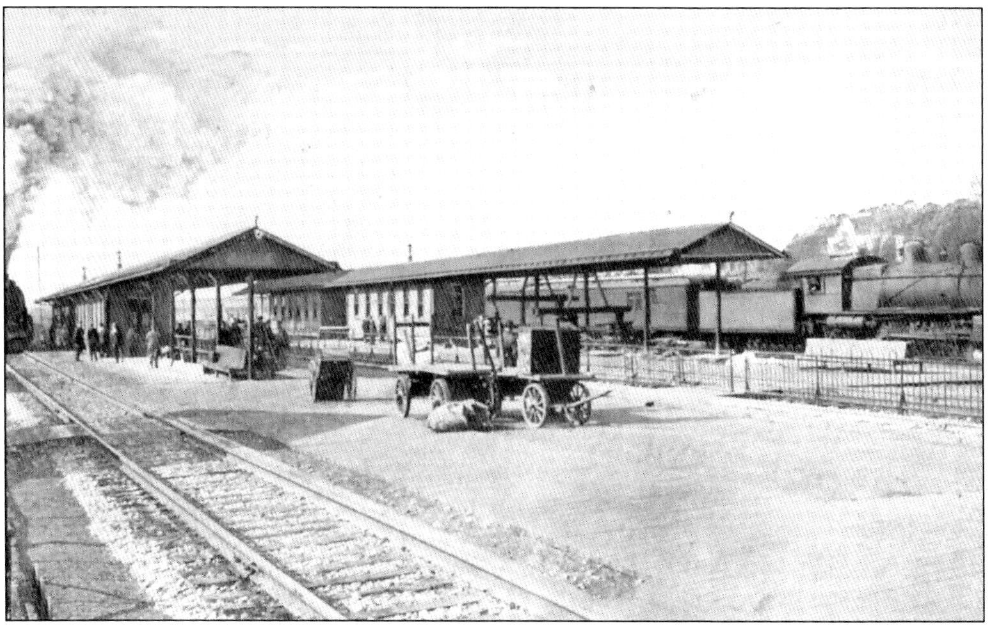

The junction and Pennsylvania Railroad yards at Cresson in 1913. The new station at Cresson was relocated east in 1910 and is nestled between the eastbound and westbound tracks. It is reached by underground passageways.

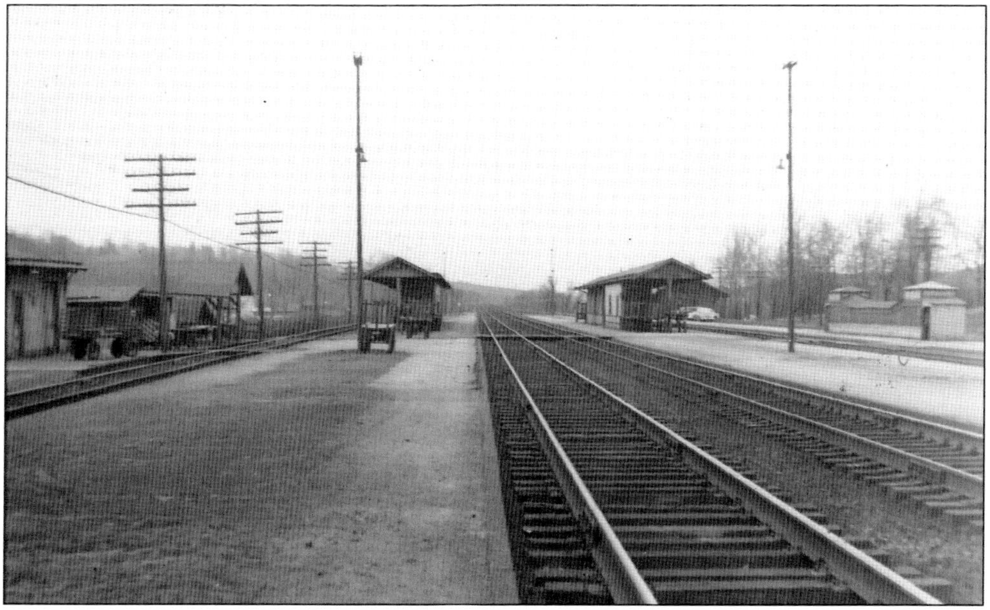

A glance westward along the ribbons of steel. Note the entrance to the underground passageway on the extreme right. The Pennsylvania Railroad served vacationers to the Mountain House, visitors to the San, and students to the academy.

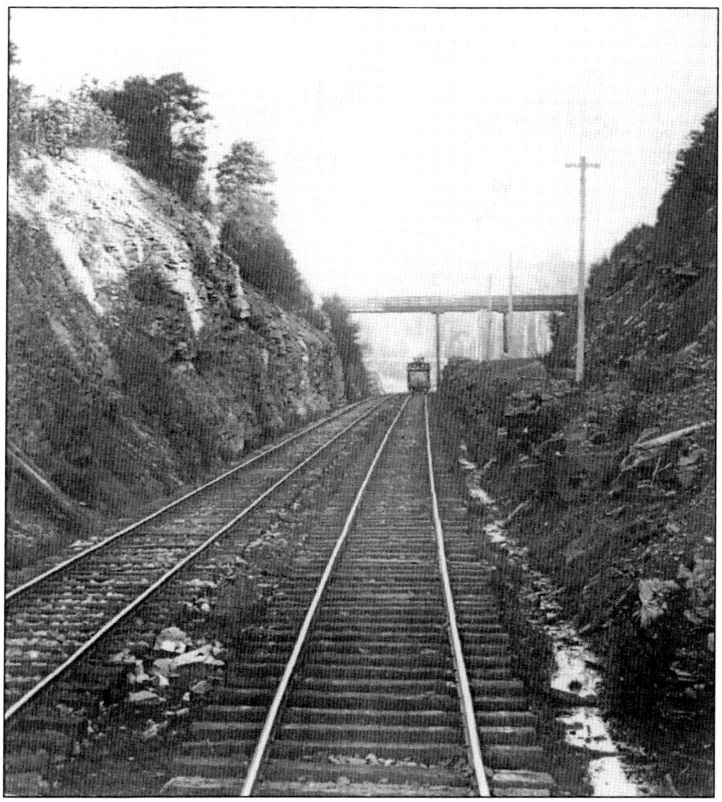

Cresson's High Bridge, located along Route 53 between Cresson and Gallitzin. This bridge spanned the railroad across a deep gorge carved through the mountain, with a depth akin to a canyon.

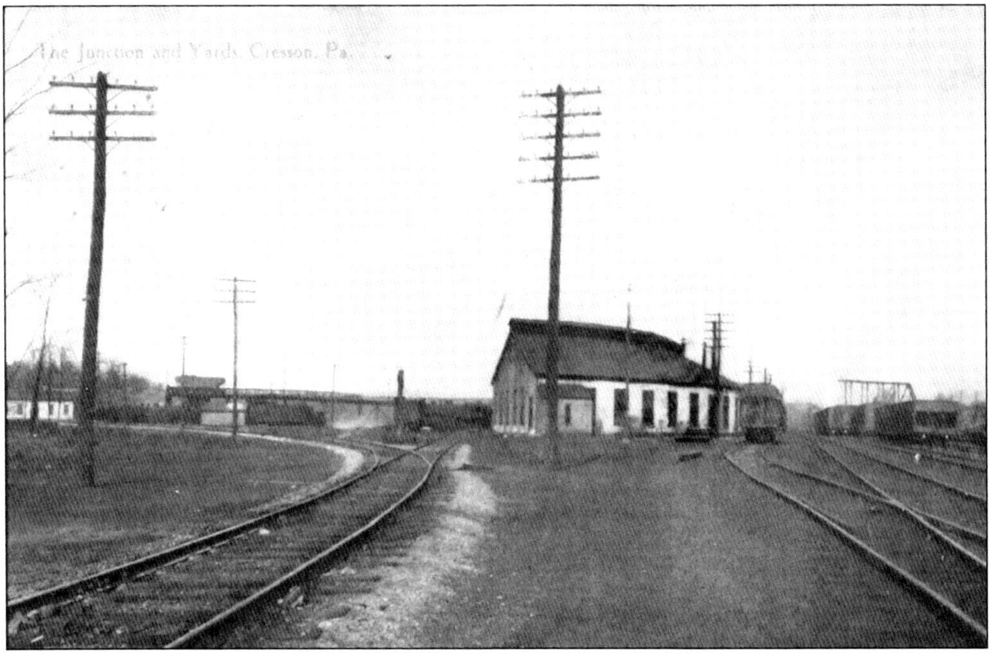

The engine house. Forty engines in a twenty-four-hour period were served here with a huge turntable. Water towers and coal storage bins fed the steam engines.

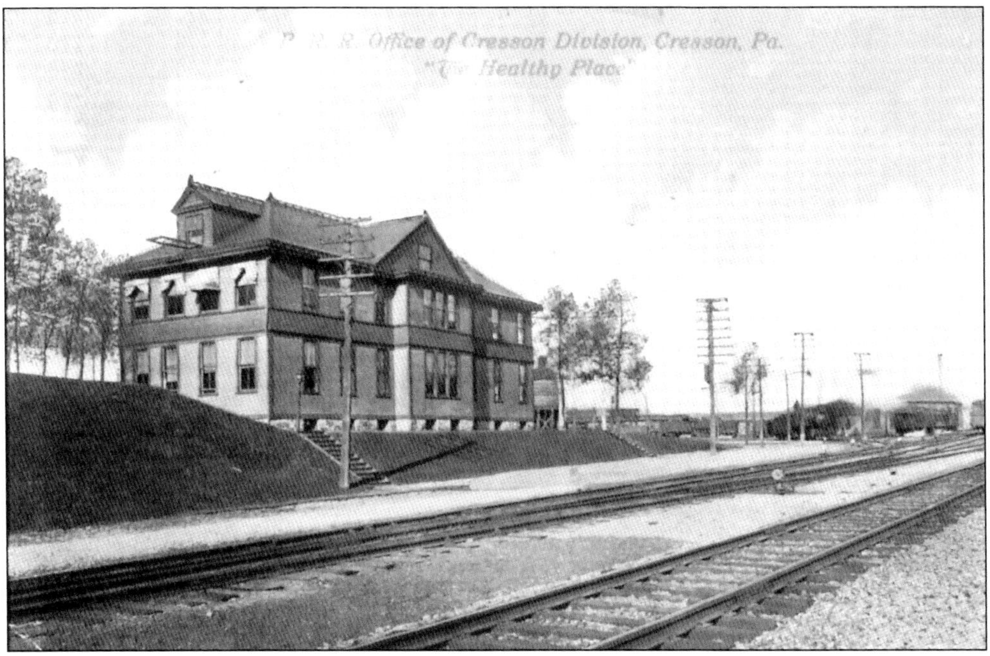

The Administrative Office Building of the Pennsylvania Railroad, Cresson Division. This building stands today as a monument to an era when the railroad was not only the fashionable mode of travel but the most accessible, comfortable, and convenient.

The MO Tower, a communications block station. The rugged mountain terrain necessitated the use of dispatch centers such as this one, which began directing railroad traffic in 1855. Presently rail traffic is controlled from Harrisburg, which moves trains through "The Cresson Bloc."

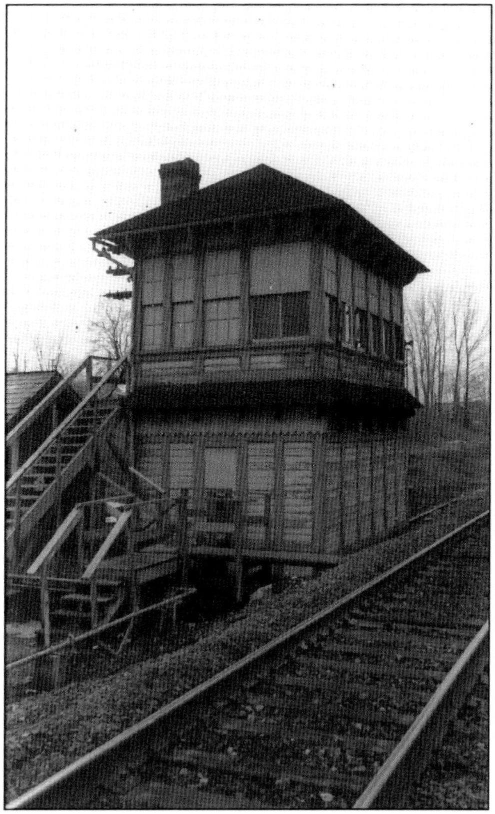

The north end of Front Street with the pedestrian bridge to Sankertown and the MO Tower in the background about 1900. This is the site of today's culvert under the railroad.

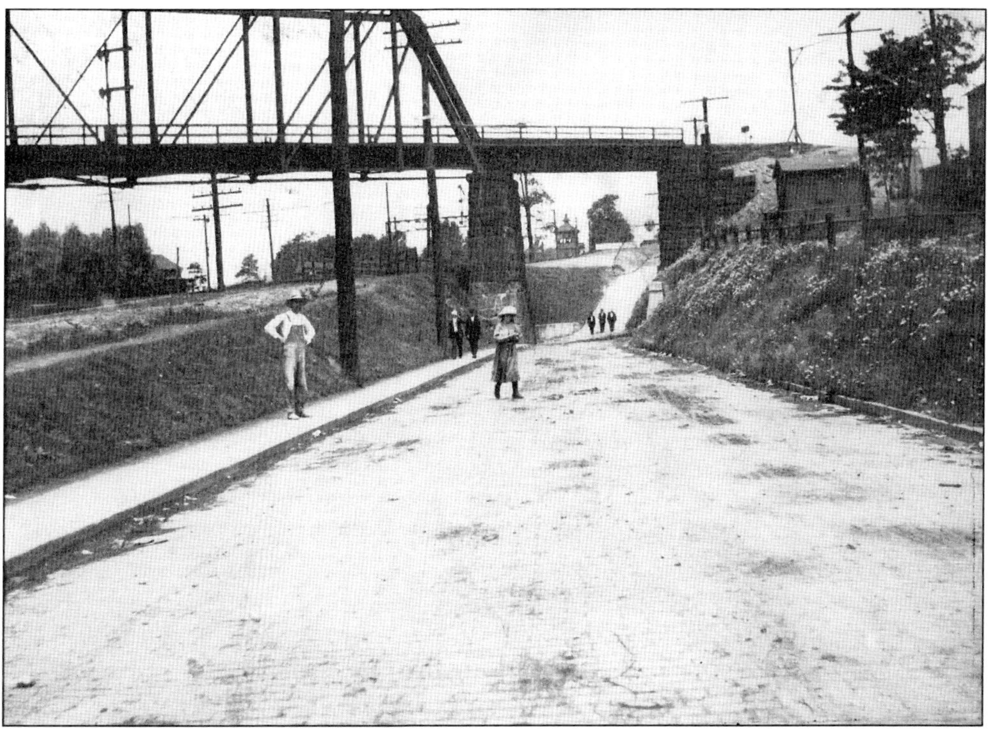

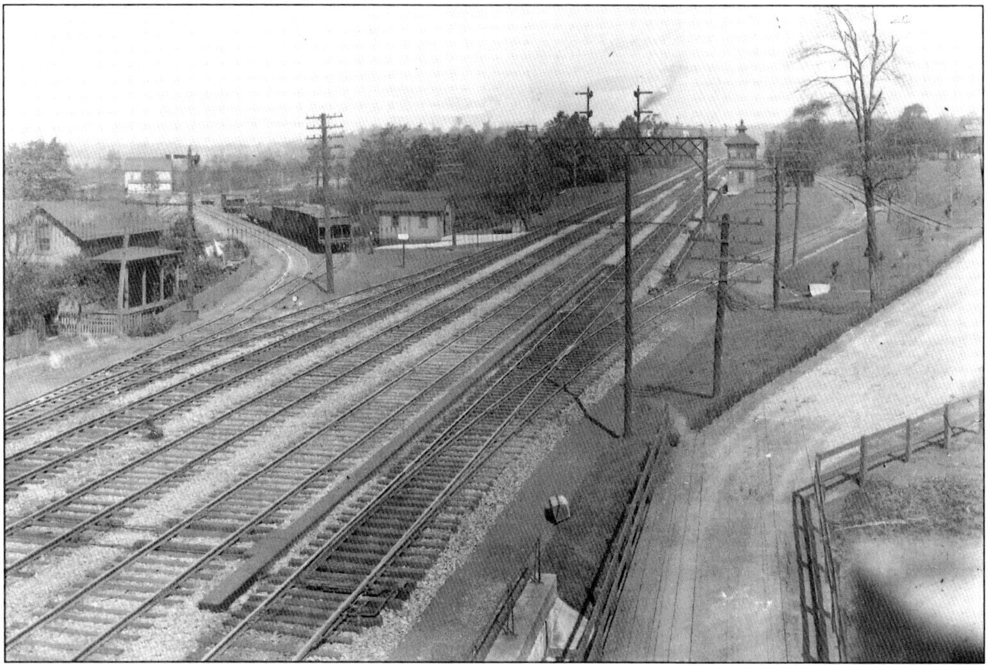

The mainline in 1915 facing east! Note the underpass in the center foreground with the MO Tower on the right and coal cars on the side track.

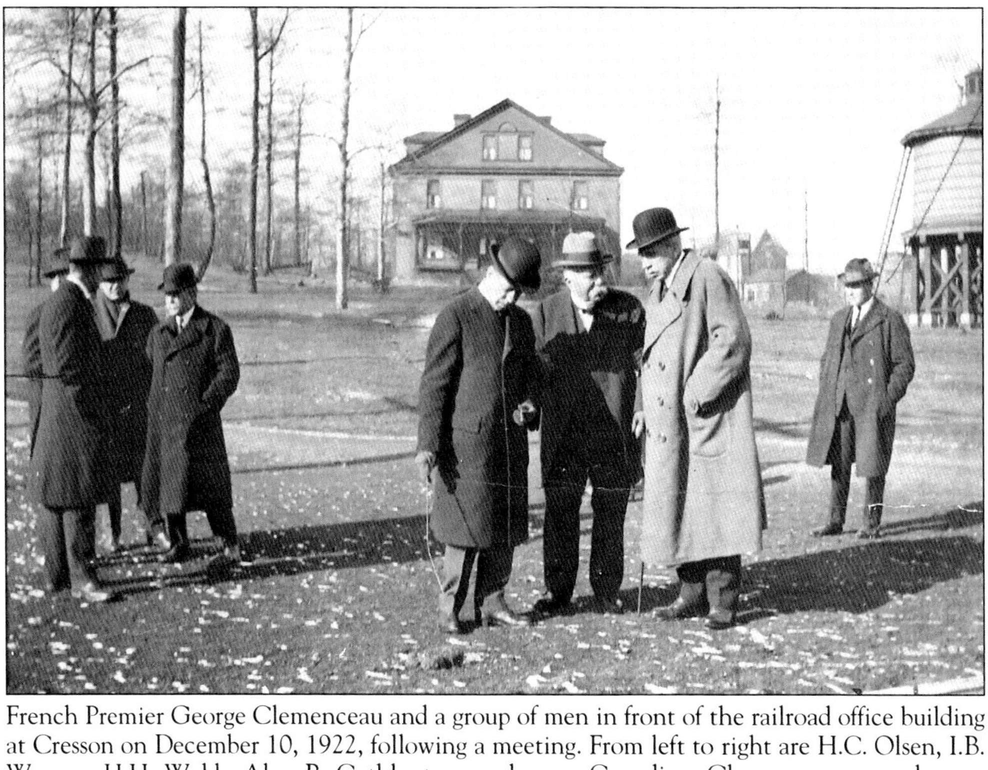

French Premier George Clemenceau and a group of men in front of the railroad office building at Cresson on December 10, 1922, following a meeting. From left to right are H.C. Olsen, I.B. Wagner, H.H. Webb, Alan B. Cuthbert, an unknown Canadian, Clemenceau, an unknown English visitor, and George Ketenheim.

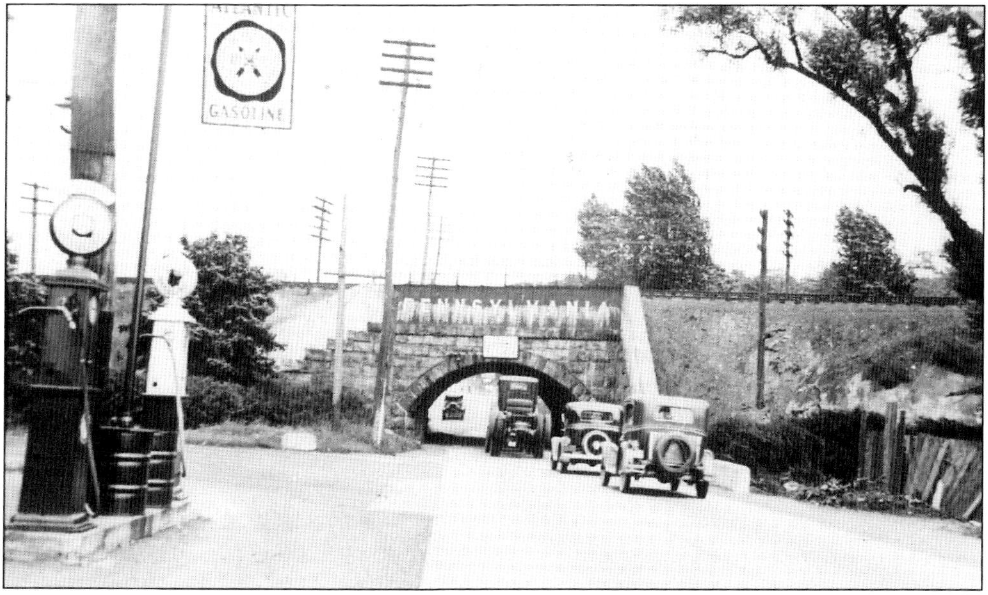

The culvert along Route 22 in an early view facing west. Erected in 1908 when the railroad station was relocated, the culvert permitted uninterrupted access for traffic.

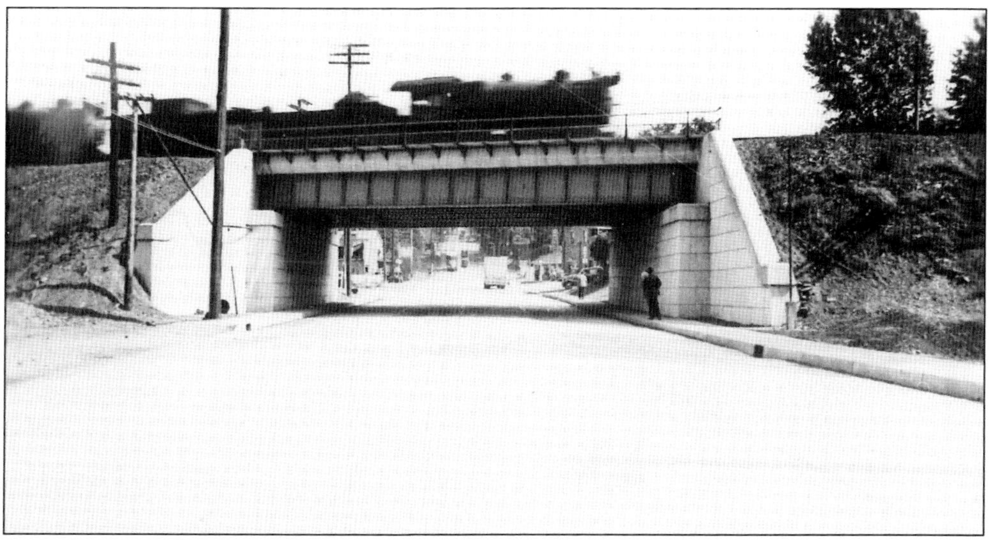

Travelling west through the new culvert on Route 22. The original culvert was replaced by this larger one in 1936.

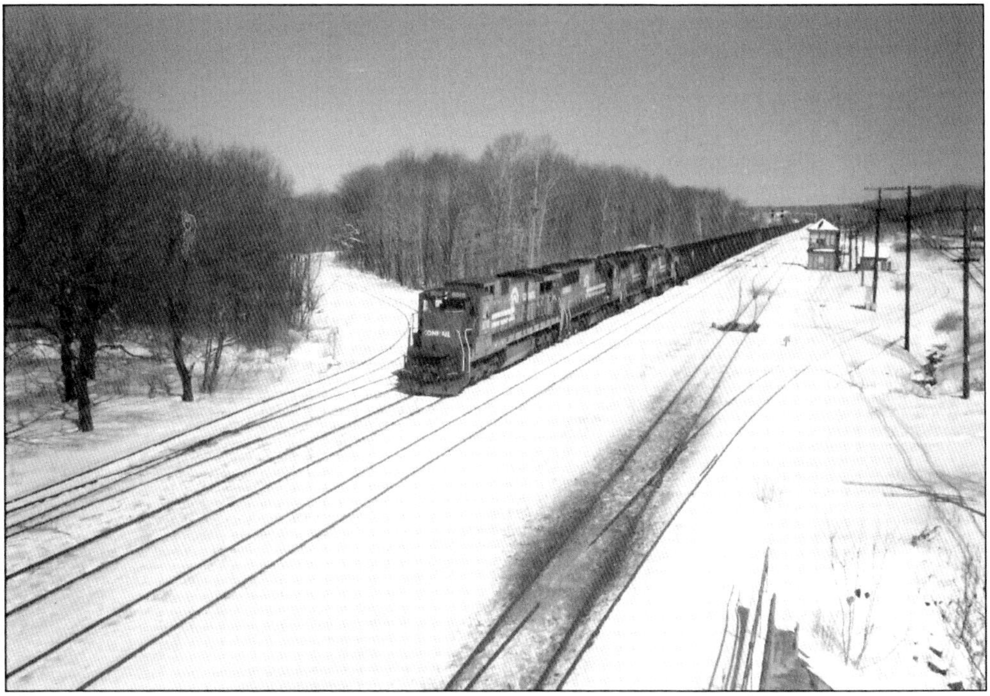

Coal cars continue to rumble through Cresson. These Conrail freightcars have just rounded Horseshoe Curve and emerged from the Gallitzin Tunnels as they continue their journey westward.

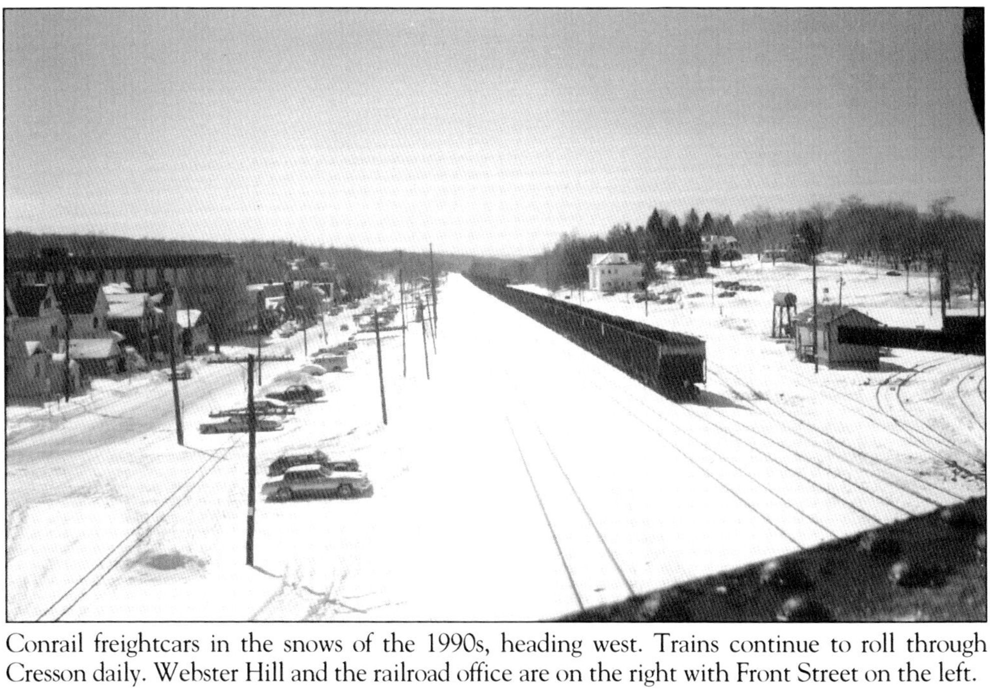

Conrail freightcars in the snows of the 1990s, heading west. Trains continue to roll through Cresson daily. Webster Hill and the railroad office are on the right with Front Street on the left.

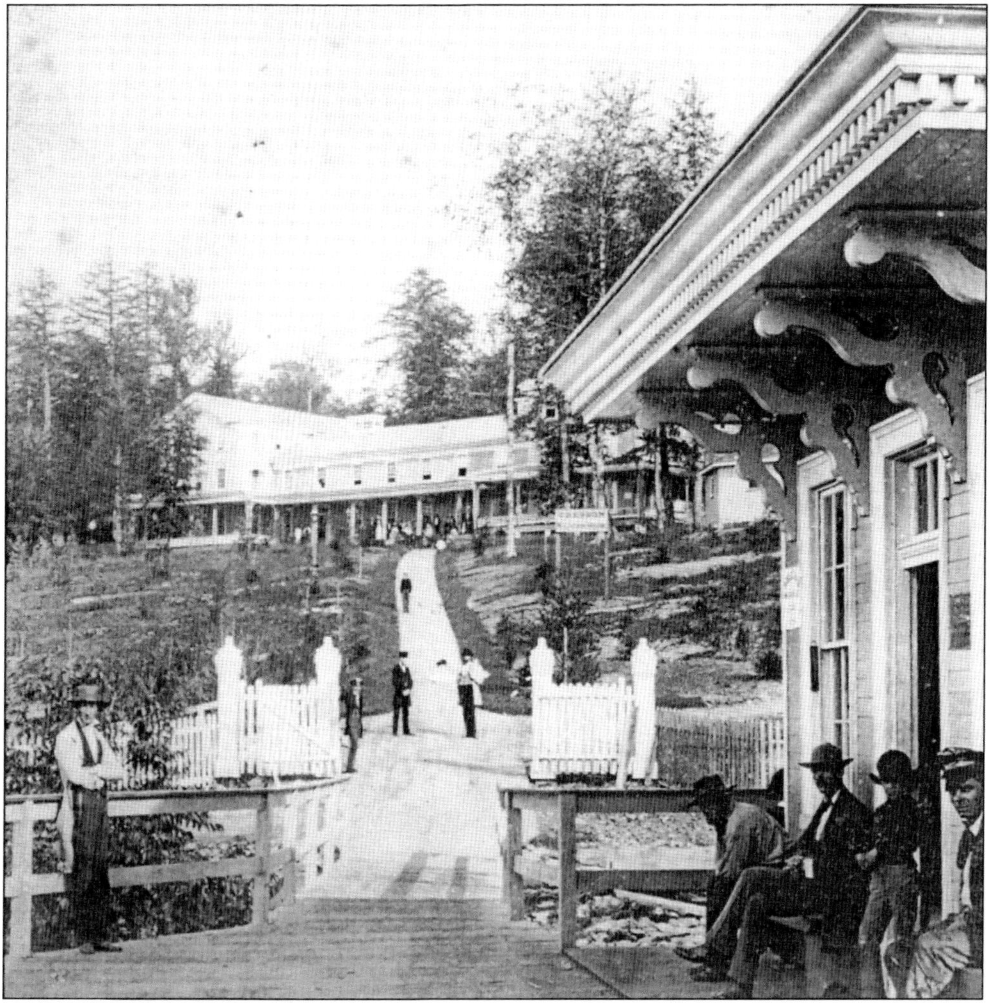

The Mountain House. This structure was originally built in Duncansville near the site of the Wye Switches by the Pennsylvania Railroad. In 1854, after Dr. R.M.S. Jackson established the Allegheny Mountain Health Institute at Cresson Springs, the building was moved to Cresson and became the Mountain House. Nestled among the pines of Cresson, the famed resort is linked to the railroad by a plank boardwalk. Many celebrities and dignitaries, including Abe Lincoln, vacationed here.

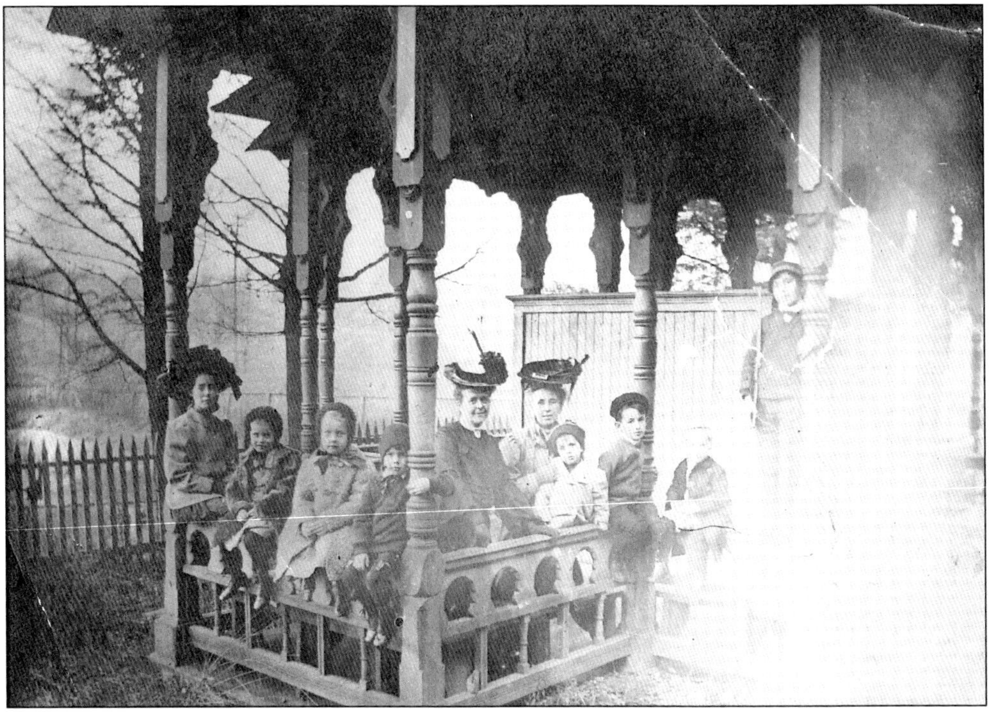

One of several spring houses that made the area famous. This gathering at the Mineral Spring in 1905 consisted of Mrs. Charles (Ella) Buck, Mrs. W.W. (Della) McAteer, Elizabeth, Faber, Elwood, Eugene, and Victor.

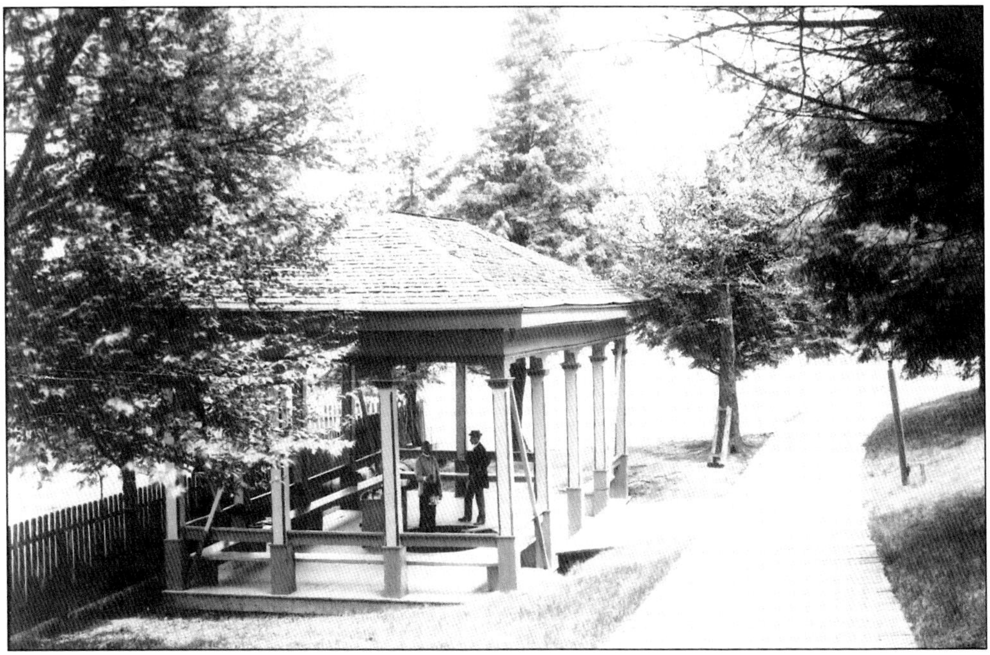

Spring houses, the gathering place for a refreshing, cool drink on a summer's day. These structures dotted the Mountain House grounds. The main spring was near the present site of Cresson Springs Restaurant.

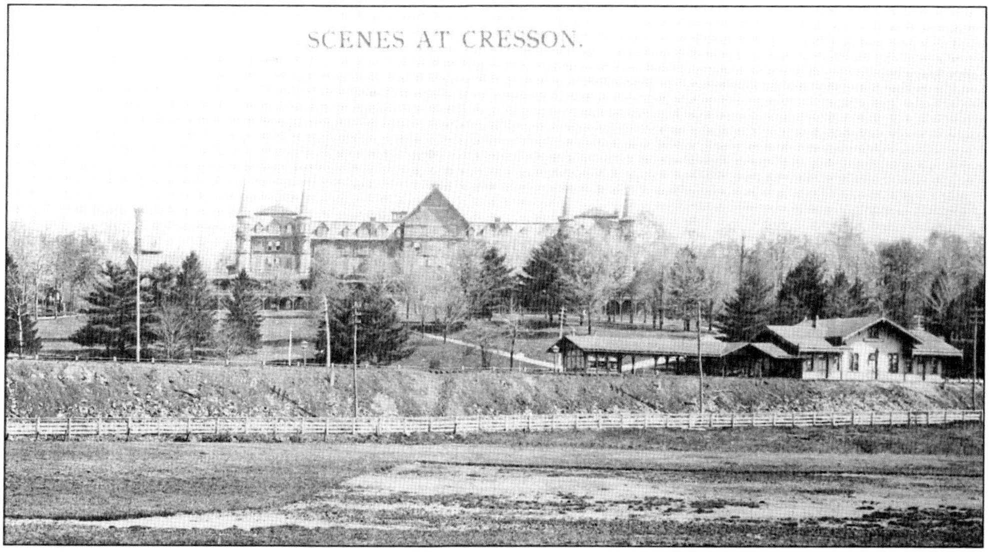

The Pennsylvania Railroad Station (right) at the foot of the Mountain House grounds. In 1854 the Pennsylvania Railroad bought 300 acres in Cresson to establish a health institute and recreational facility. Accessibility to the railroad was paramount to these early visitors!

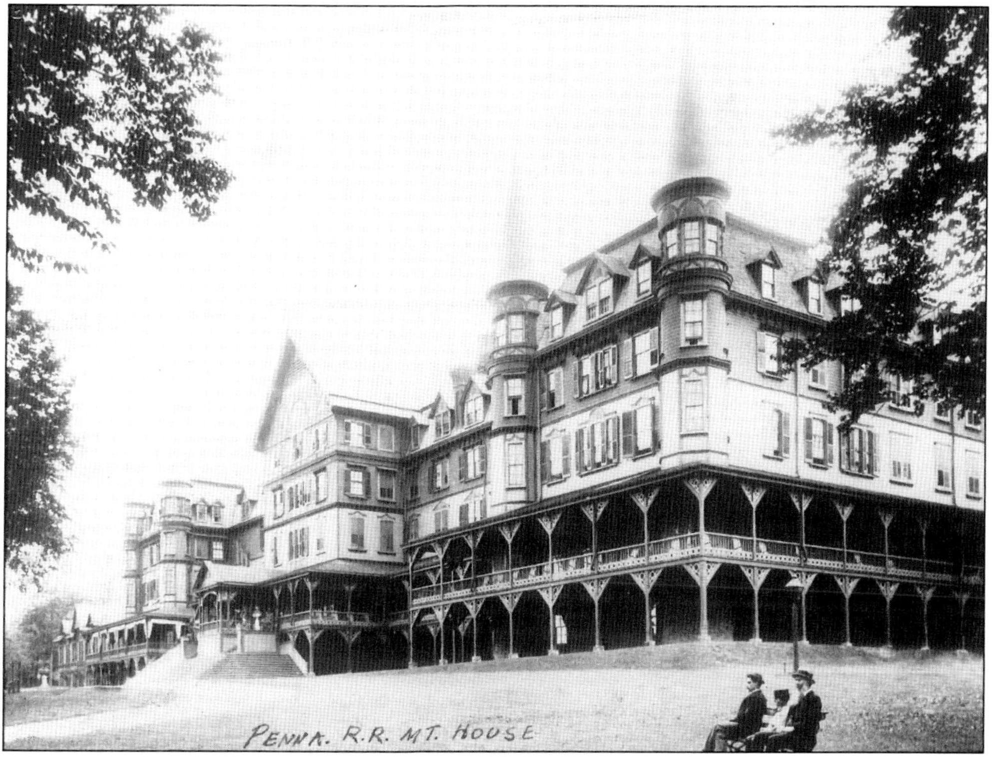

The Mountain House of 1880. The huge, striking, Queen Anne structure lured many notables to the area in the late 1800s. Organized in cooperation with the Pennsylvania Railroad, "Summer Excursion Rates" were offered. The railroad station stood east of the culvert and the Mountain House was situated just south of the station. The rise of seaside resorts marked the decline of mountain retreats.

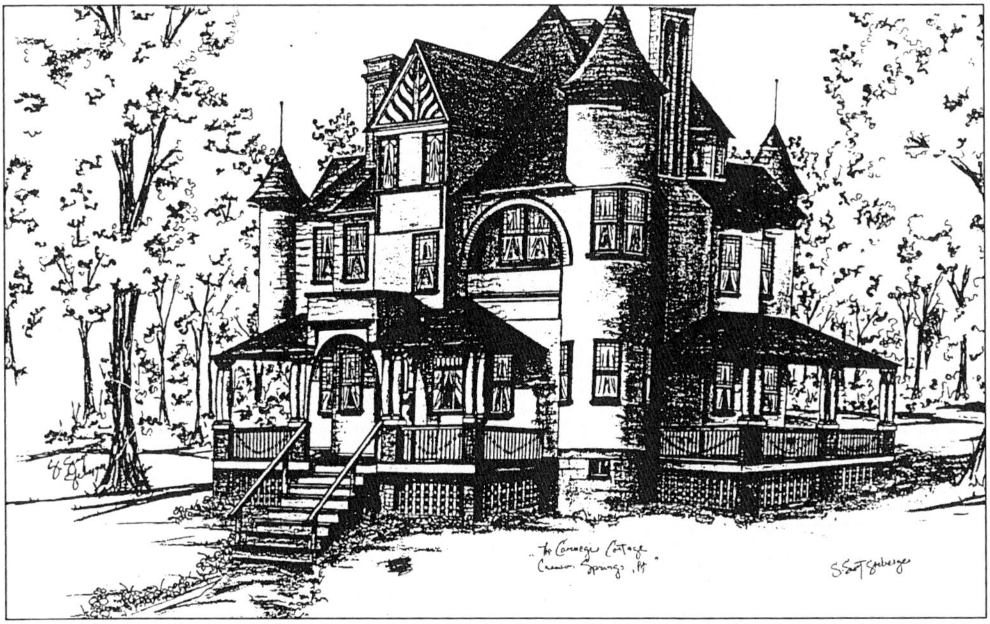

Andrew Carnegie's vacation house, known as Bramar (Scottish for "on the hill above the spring"). This is one of eight cottages remaining on the Mountain House grounds built by millionaires in the nineteenth century. Restoration is underway by the Cresson Area Historical Association, Inc.

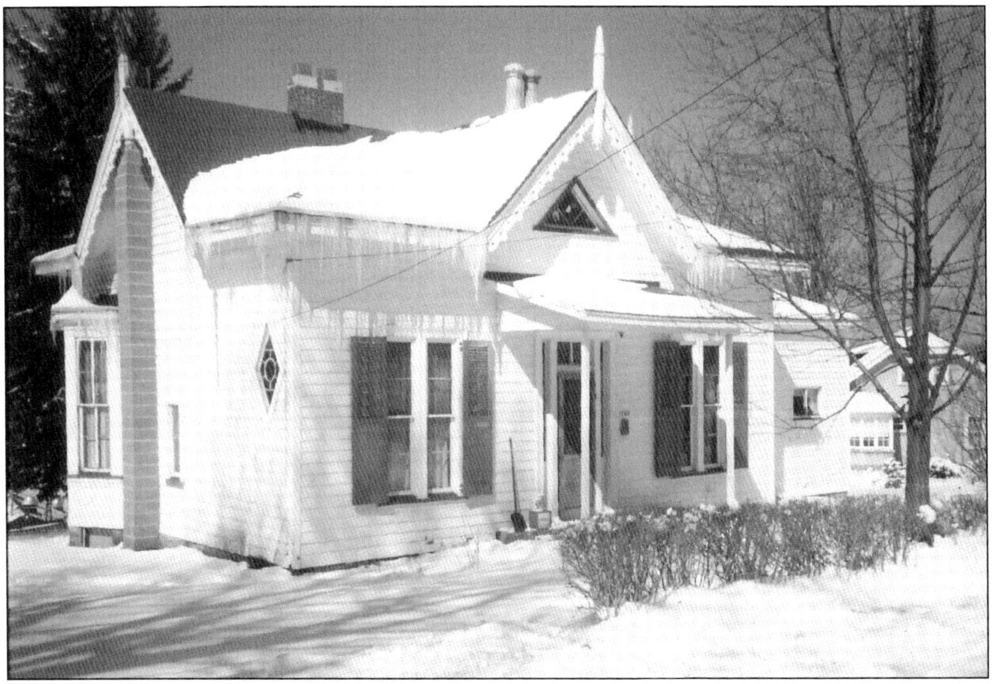

The Mullin Cottage, one of thirteen such dwellings that surrounded the Mountain House. Cottages provided seclusion and privacy in a quiet atmosphere. George Mullin, the hotel manager and caretaker of 500 acres of land, built this cottage in 1862. Today it survives as the home of the Mountain Top Art Gallery and remains a charming replica of a century ago.

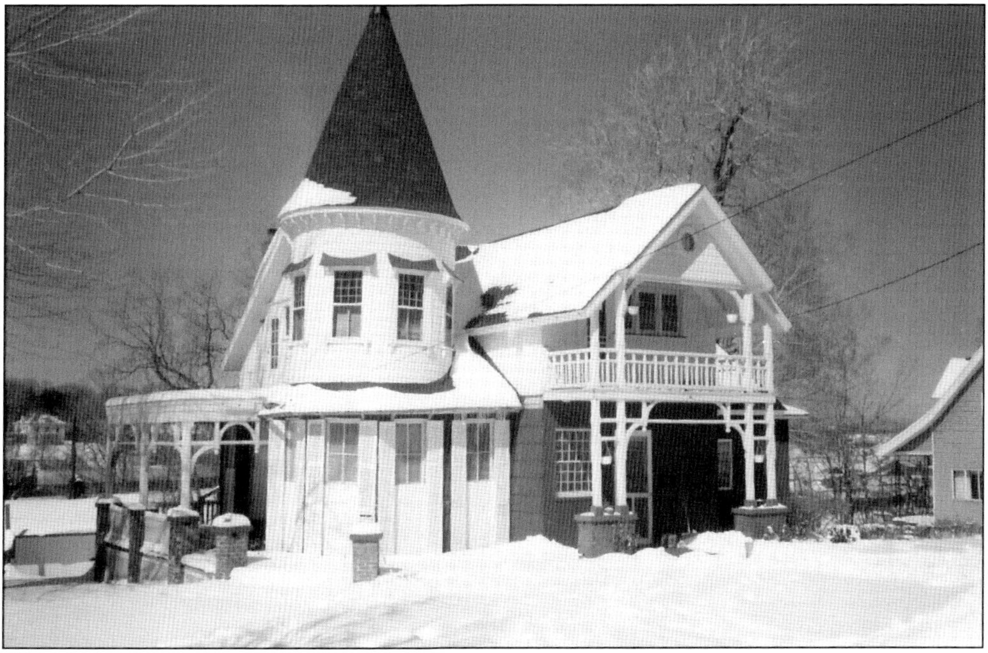

A chateau-like edifice, built by the Cresson Springs Co. in 1862. In 1916, when the Mountain House was demolished, a conical tower from that building was preserved on this structure, which still graces the landscape as a private residence.

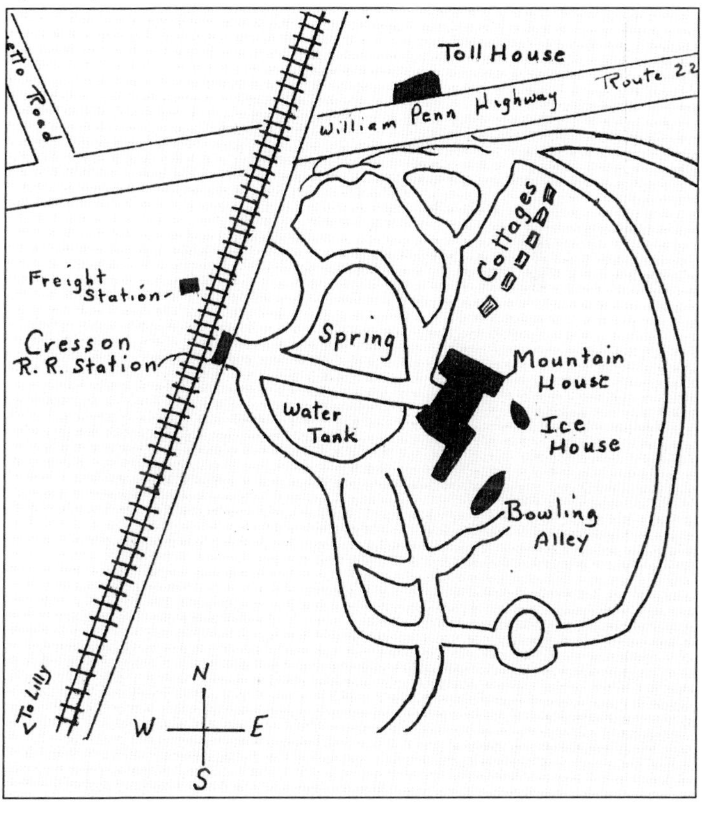

A map of the Mountain House grounds about 1890, when the resort was in its heyday. Part of the boardwalk is under restoration and eight cottages still remain. The railroad station faced the Mountain House southeast of the culvert.

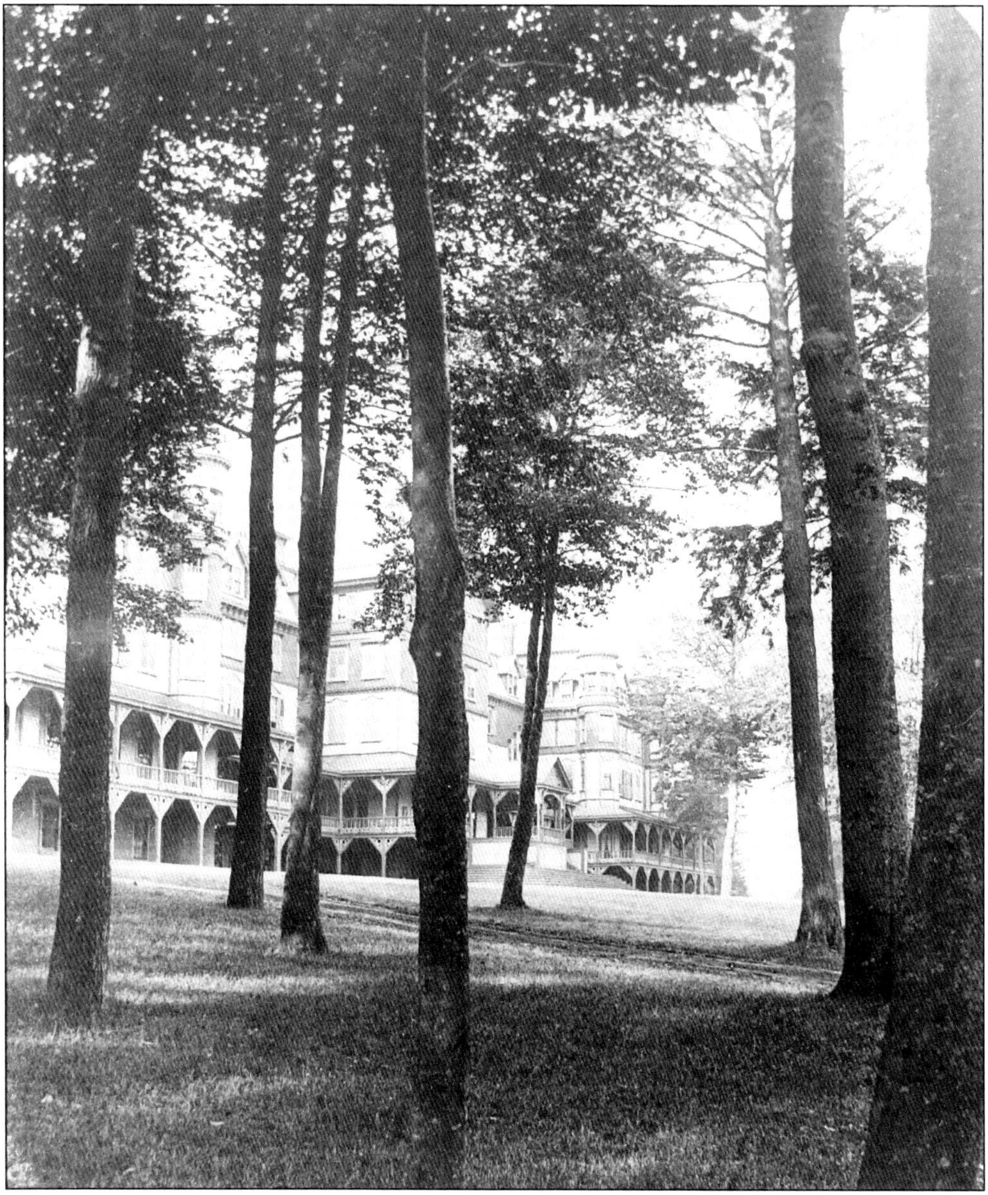

The Mountain House. The huge mansion, which accommodated nine hundred guests, presented a picturesque scene on the Cresson landscape until the turn of the century, when seaside resorts held greater attraction. The Mountain House was closed in 1897, stood idle for many years, and was demolished in 1916. The finale of this renowned attraction gave rise to many lodgings, inns, and hotels, which sprang up around Cresson at the turn of the century.

Four

Yesteryear around Town

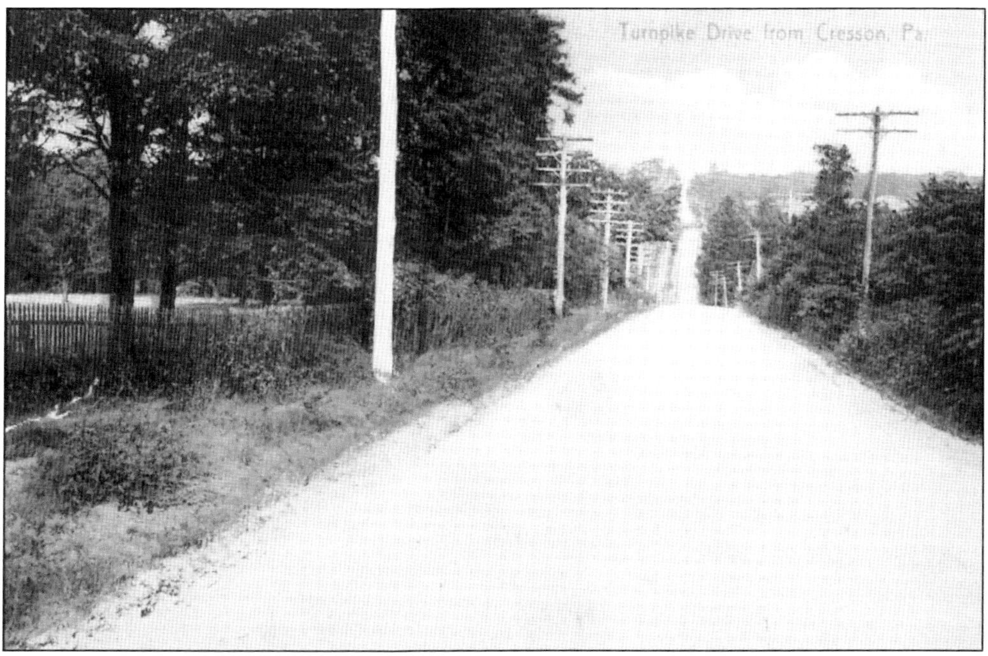

The Pike in 1910, looking west toward Cresson from the Summit. Ignatius Adams, a Revolutionary war veteran, was the earliest known settler at the summit. Elk, boar, and panthers roamed the dense forests. Native Americans had tramped out an east-west trail over the mountain which was to become the old Galbreath Road (sometimes called Frankstown Road), and later the Huntingdon, Cambria, Indiana Turnpike, linking Philadelphia and Pittsburgh. Often referred to as the Cresson Mountain it is now Route 22!

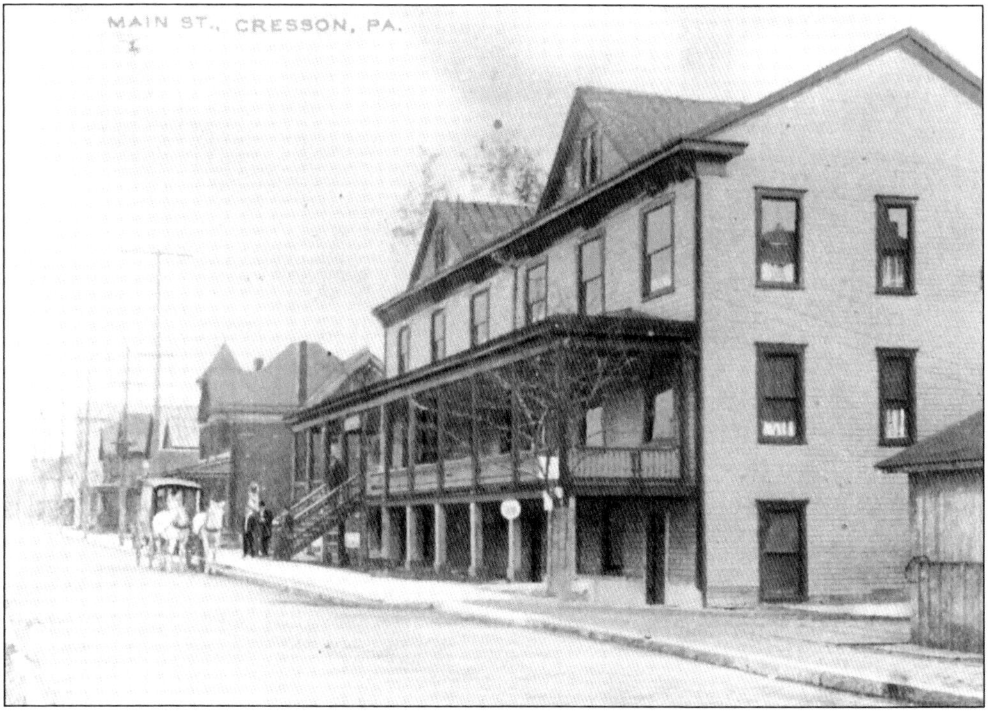

The Commercial Hotel on Front Street across from the railroad. In 1866 William Callan, contractor & builder, erected the Callan House, which later became the Commercial Hotel. He was proprietor until his death in 1874. It is now Station Inn.

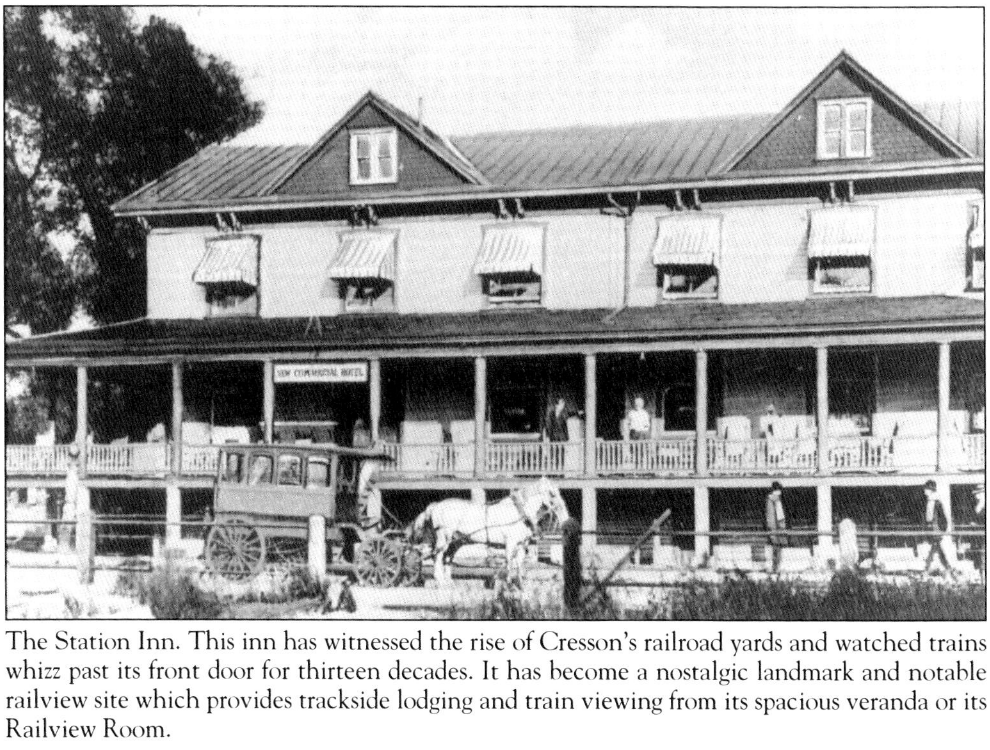

The Station Inn. This inn has witnessed the rise of Cresson's railroad yards and watched trains whizz past its front door for thirteen decades. It has become a nostalgic landmark and notable railview site which provides trackside lodging and train viewing from its spacious veranda or its Railview Room.

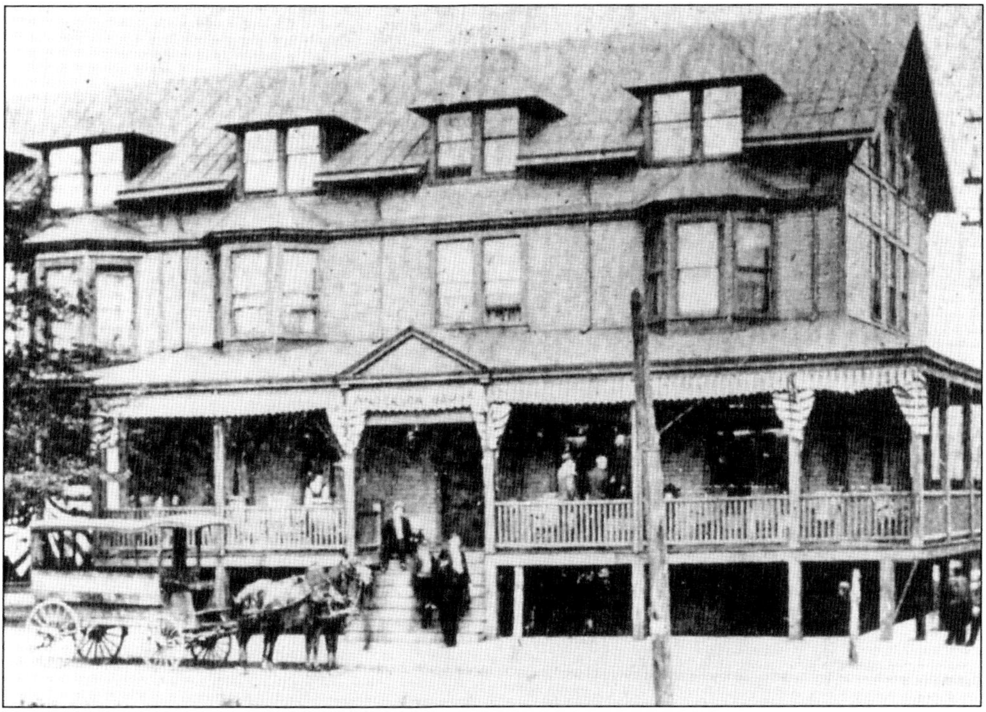

The Anderson House in 1900, on the northeast corner of Front Street and Ashcroft Avenue. Lodgings, inns, and hotels were prevalent in Cresson during and after the Mountain House era.

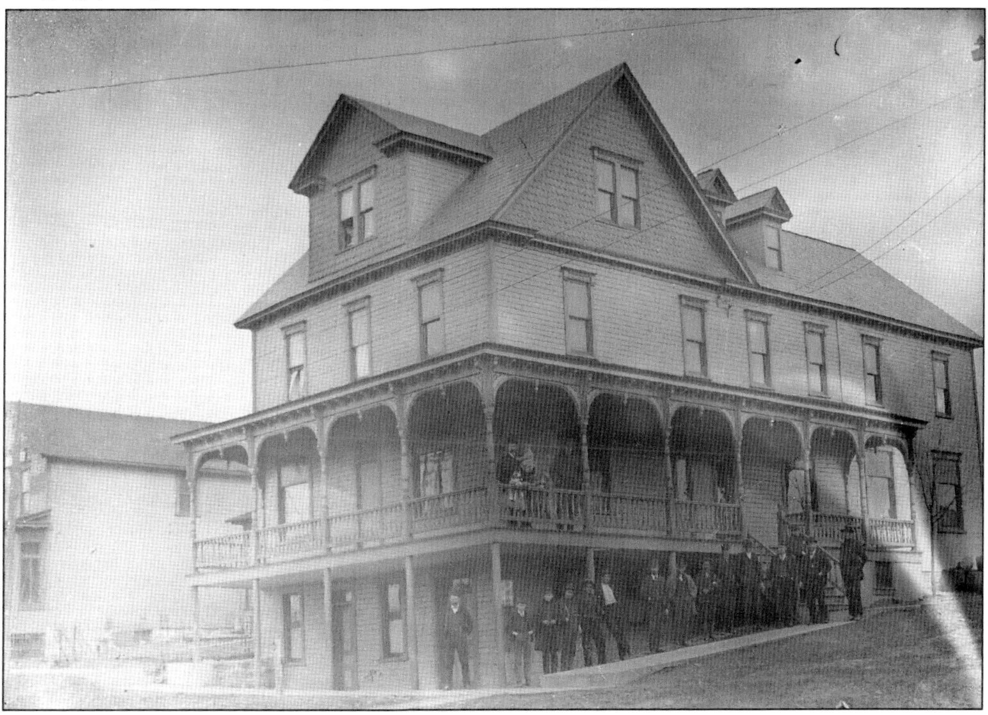

The old Central Hotel on the northeast corner of Powell Avenue and Front Street. This landmark is still partially in operation.

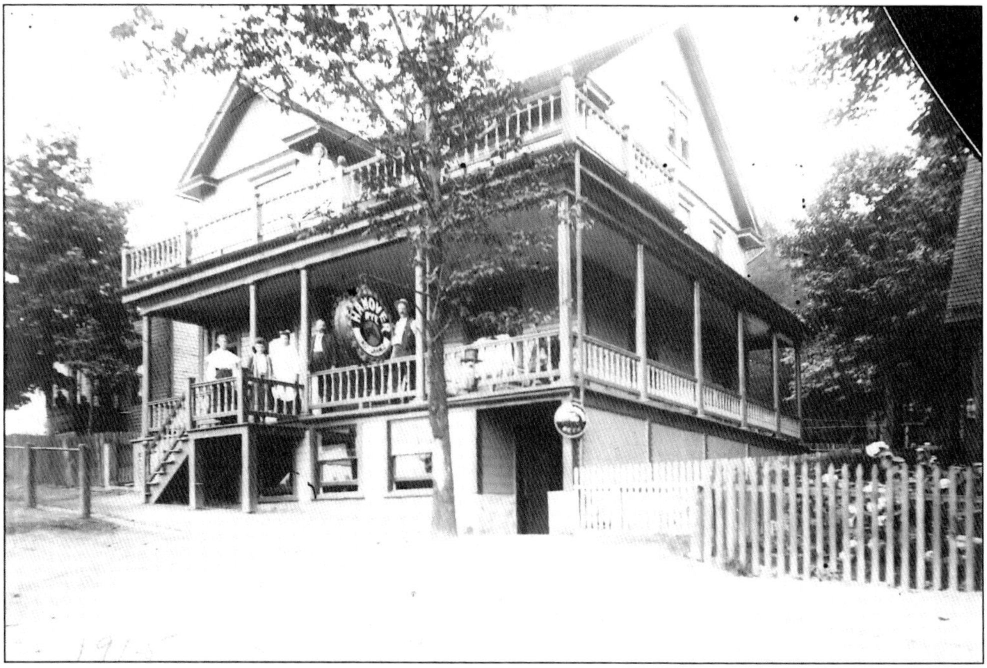

The Cottage Inn Hotel about 1910, located at the north end of Second Street opposite Hines Feed Mill. The building is now a private residence.

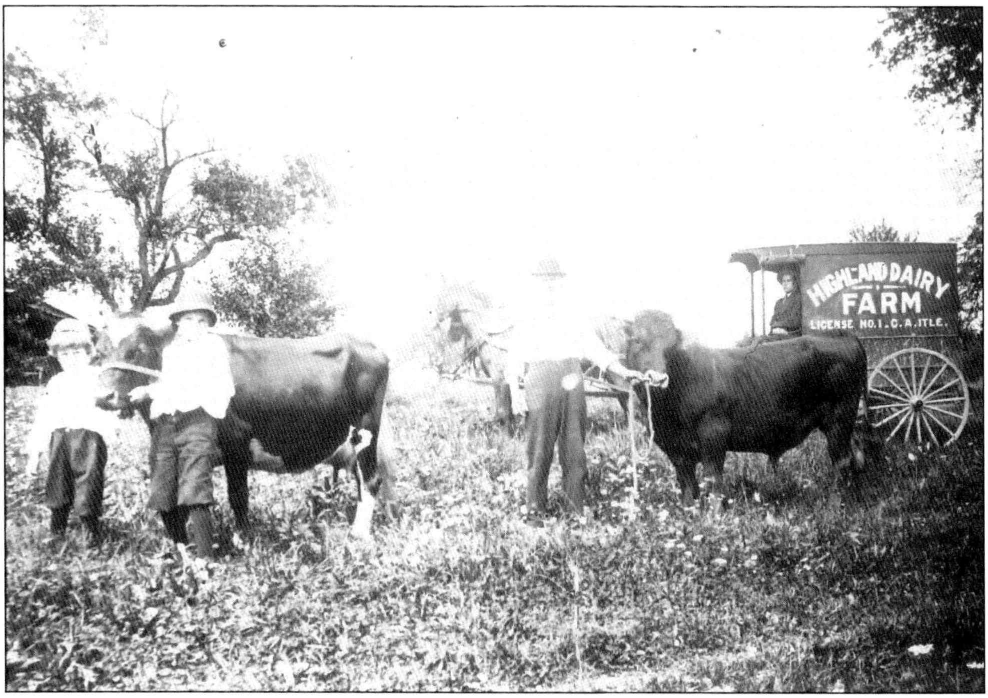

Fred Wills on the delivery wagon of the Highland Dairy farm. Charles A. Itle established the Highland Dairy Farm in 1914 with one horse and wagon. In 1933 a truck replaced the horse and the name Vale Wood replaced Highland. With his two sons, Gerald and Francis, he initiated a tradition of fine quality products that continues to this day.

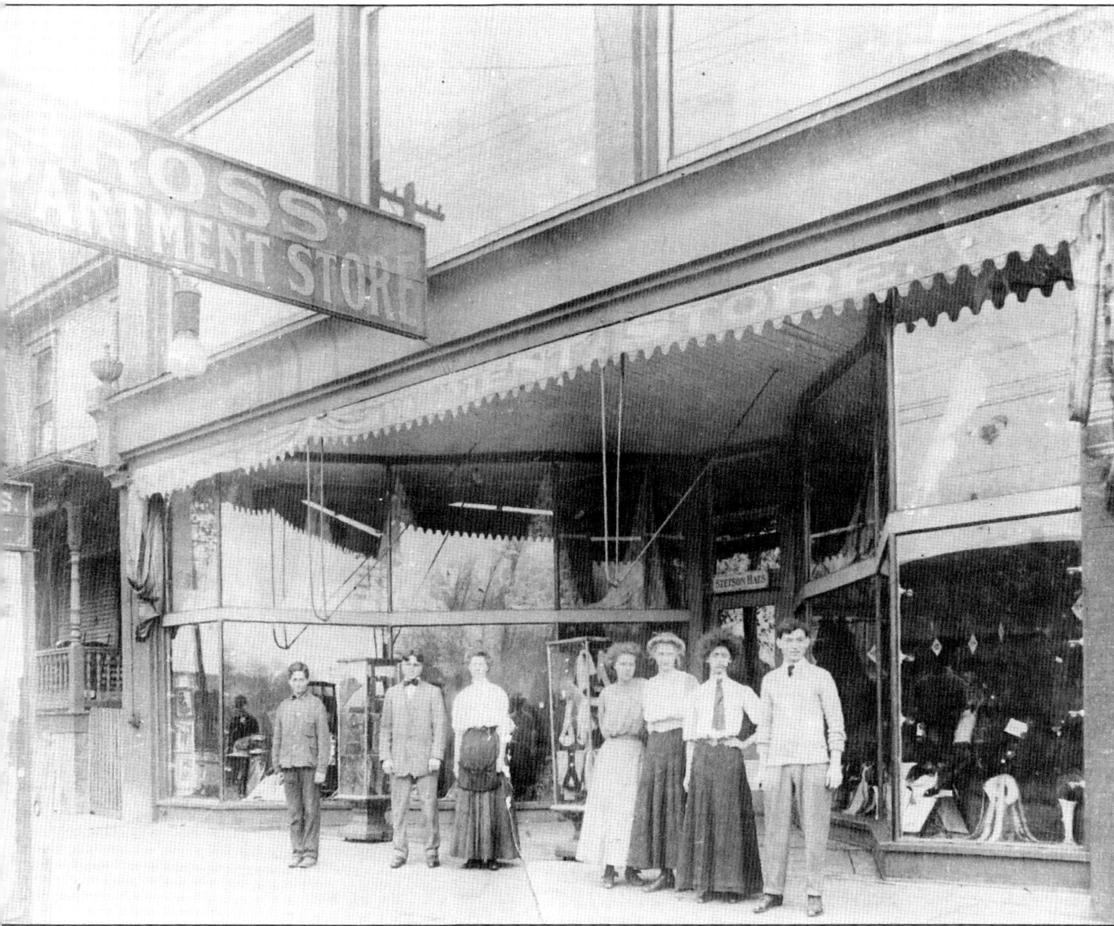

The Gross Department Store, established by Barney Gross on the northeast corner of Front Street and Keystone Avenue in November 1905. A native of Hungary, Gross was born in 1875 and immigrated fourteen years later. He married Anna Hendler of Altoona. His daughter Ella, a graduate of Mount Aloysius, took over the women's department of the store, and his son Jacob became assistant manager. Daughters Dorothy, Sarah, and Molly periodically visited New York for the latest fashions in coats, dresses, shoes, and hats. The site later became Latterners Produce and Grocery Store.

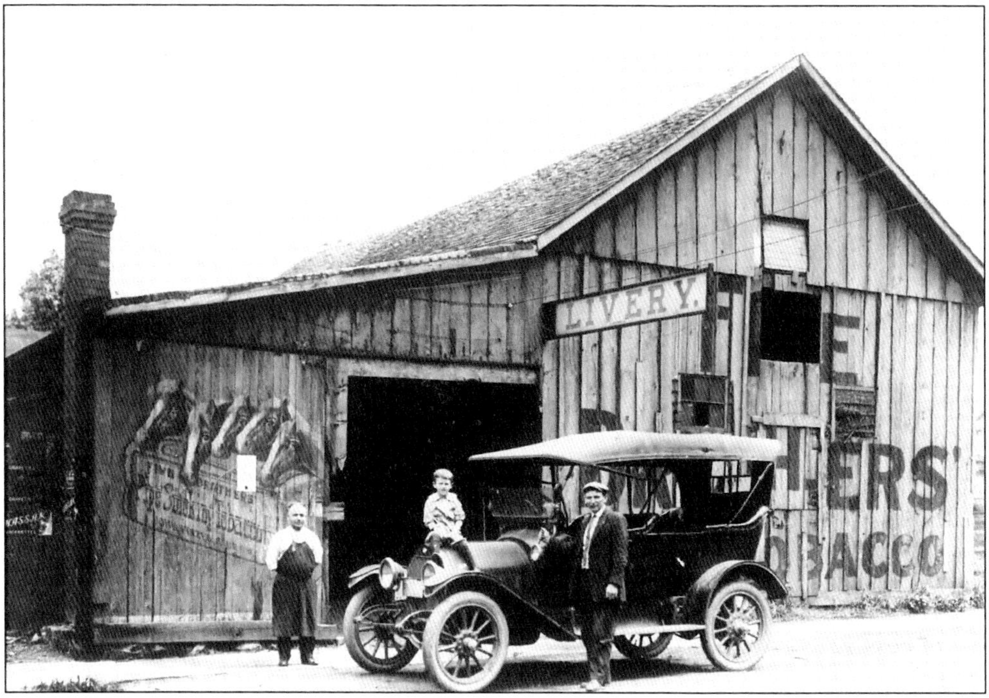

The Schettig Livery Stable on Ashcroft Avenue and Second Street. Harold Schettig is on the hood of the Oldsmobile with his father, Albert Schettig (right), and shoemaker Dominic Carbott.

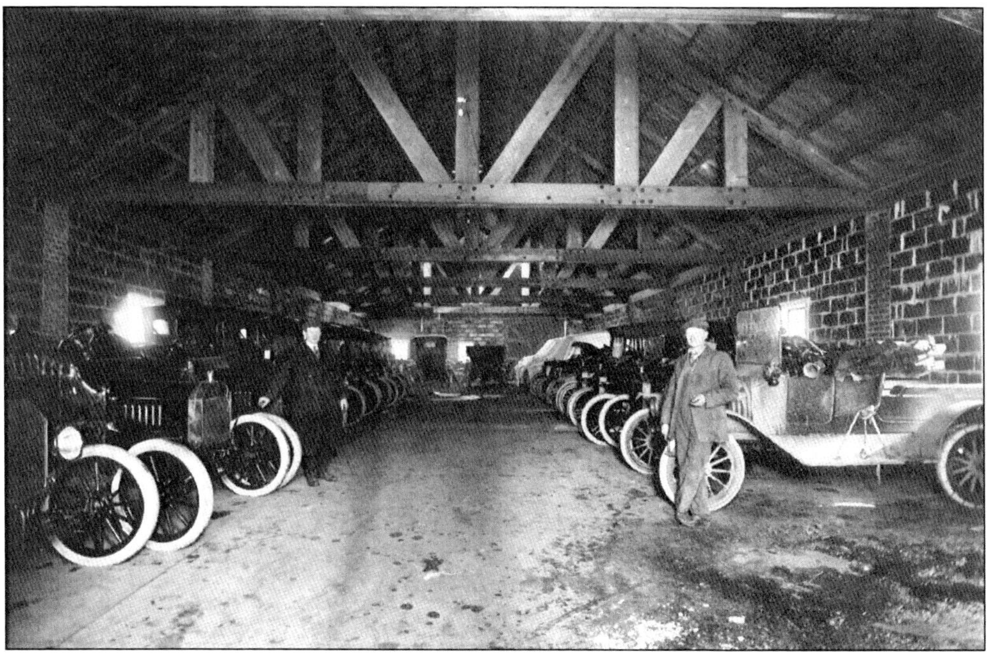

Schettig Garage. Once a livery stable, the building lent itself to a new, innovative concept in 1915 when Model-T Fords were assembled here.

The Schettig Garage and family in 1936. Sheldon is holding the dog with Robert! In the back row are Lester, Gene Sellers, and Albert C. Schettig (founder of the business and grandfather of the boys). Albert once worked as a chauffeur at the Mountain House.

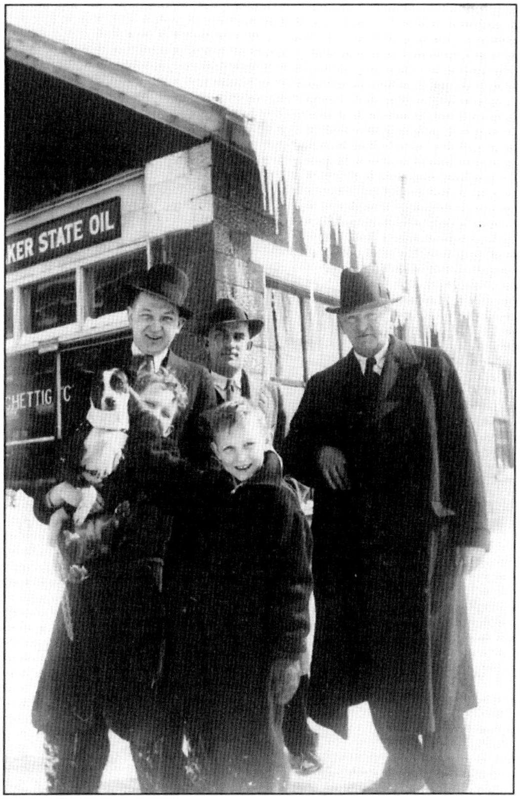

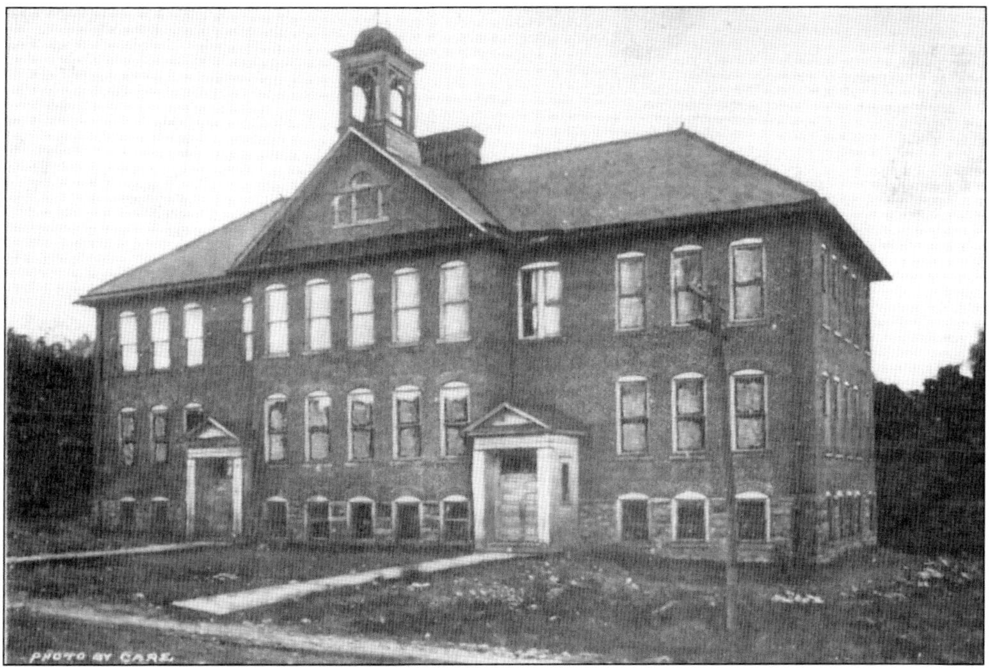

The Cresson Public School, originally built in 1903 with John McGann as principal. An addition was added in 1912 for an expanding population. Part of its retaining wall still graces the northeast corner of Keystone Avenue and 4th Street.

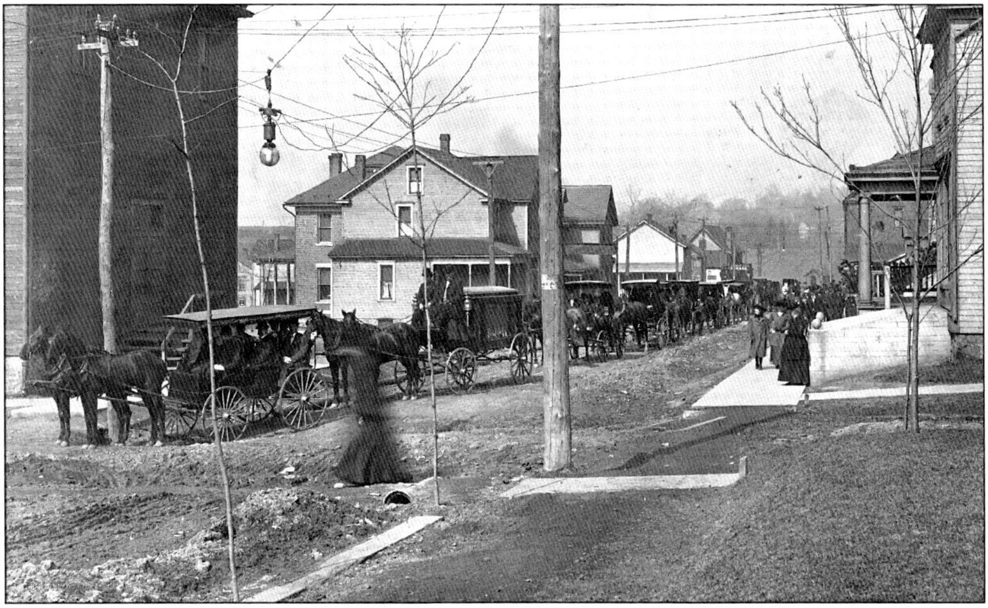

The funeral of Ellen Bruce Buck in March 1910. The horse and buggy funeral procession wends its way north along Powell Avenue, providing a nostalgic remembrance of a bygone era. The Opera House is on the left. This was the site of an old stone quarry and would eventually be replaced by the St. Francis Xavier School.

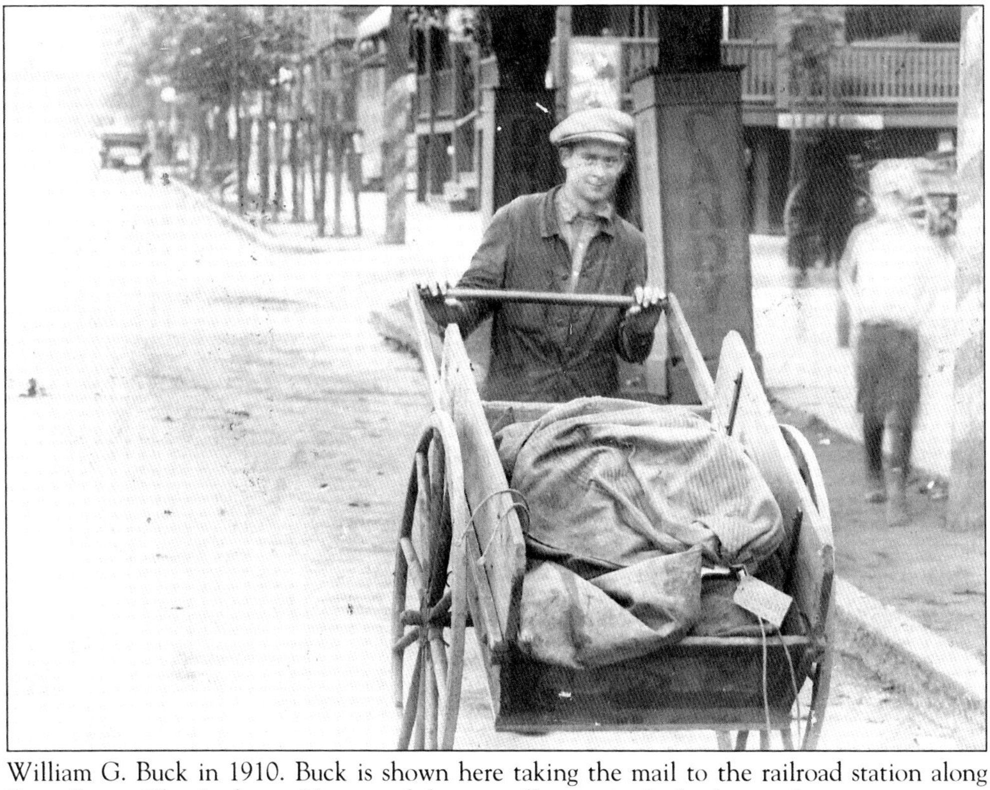

William G. Buck in 1910. Buck is shown here taking the mail to the railroad station along Front Street. The Anderson House and the post office are in the background.

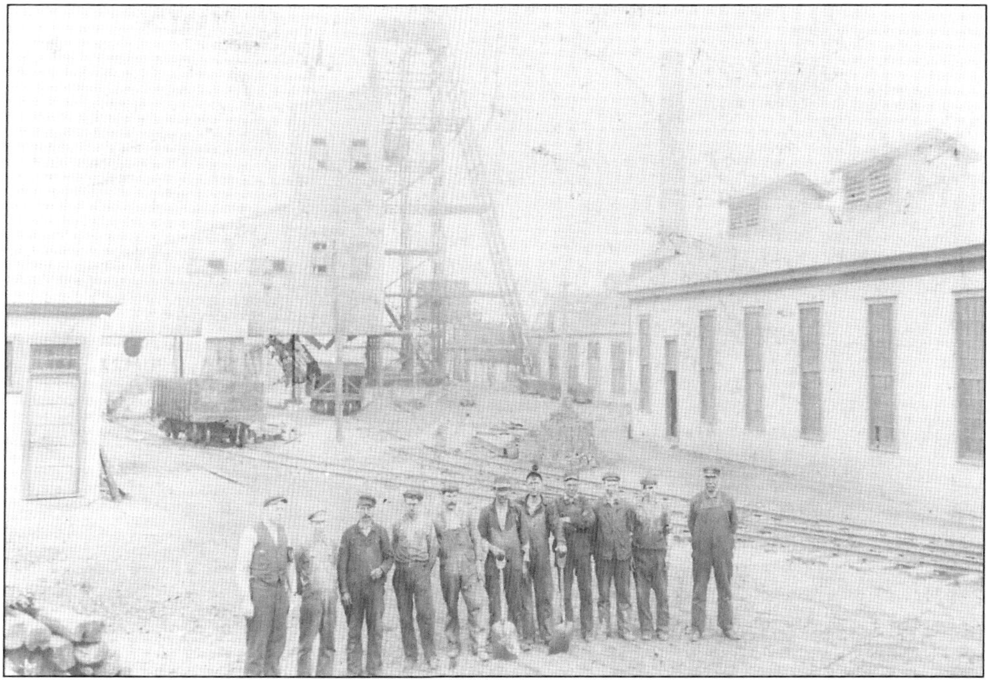

Cresson Shaft #9 and coal tipple, c. 1920, established in 1915 by the Webster Coal and Coke Co. The miners, from left to right, are Tom Abernathy, Bill Kingsley, Joe Sloan, Tom Dobbie, Max Miller, Ellis Keith, Casper Beiswinger, Edward Cully, John Cully, Mike Chervenak, and Gene Glass.

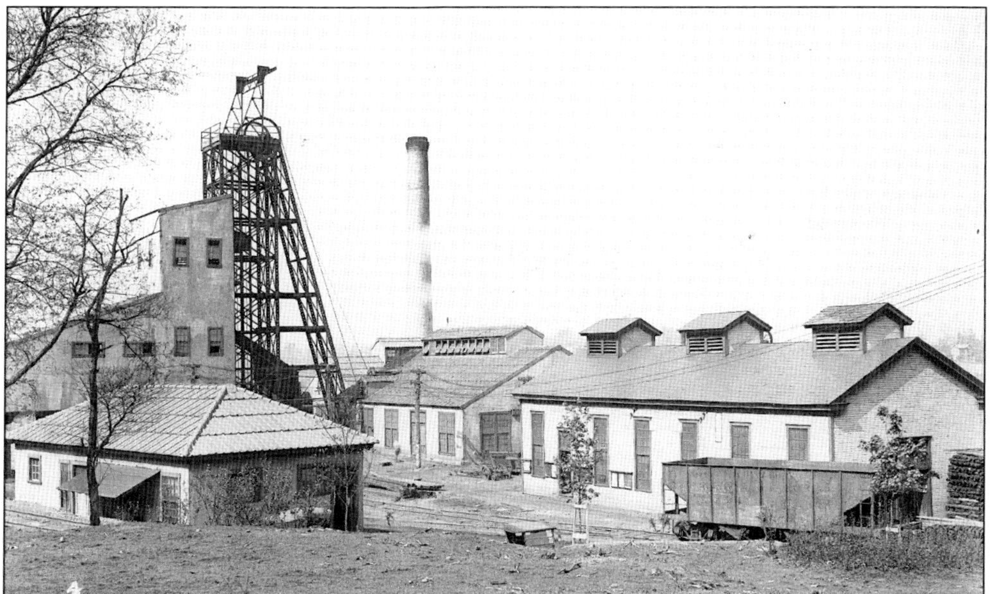

Cresson Shaft, c. 1938, situated north of the village between Gallitzin Road and the railroad. John Ashcroft and John Powell were its founding engineers. Picks and shovels were the order of the day. The shaft remained in operation until 1949. Bitumuous coal is abundant in the Alleghenies.

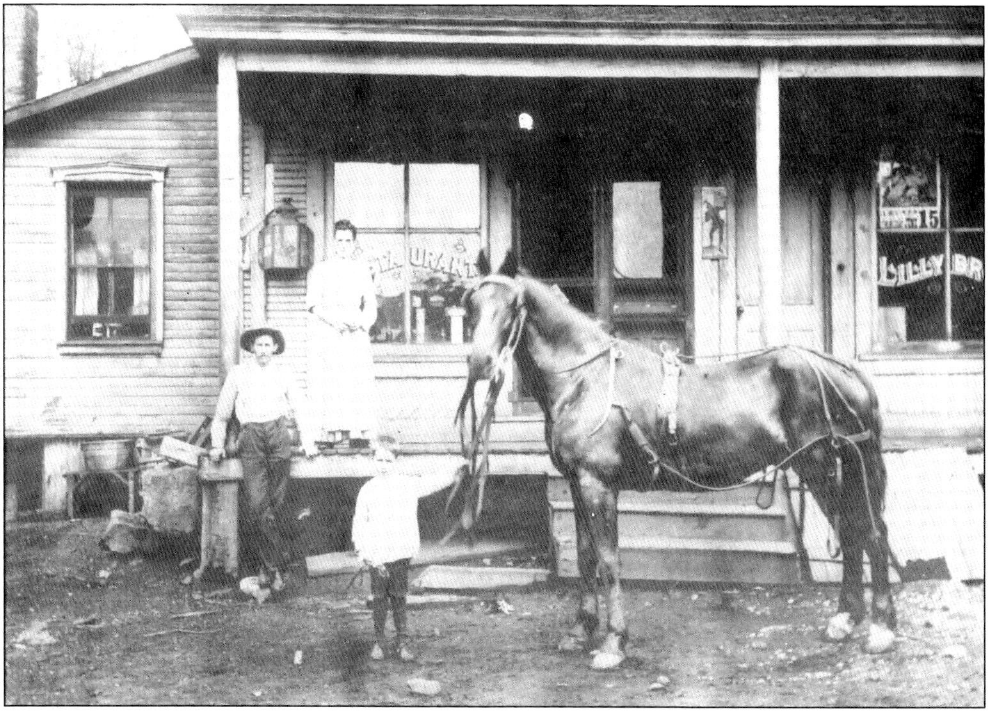

The Lilly Brothers Meat Market and Restaurant, located on the west side of Second Street north of Keystone Avenue.

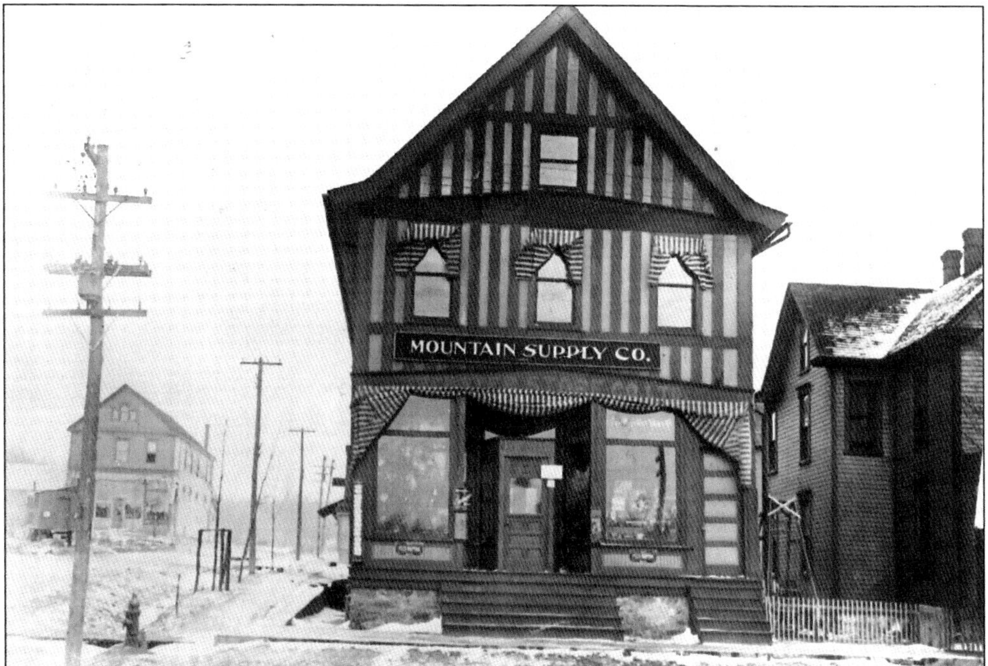

Mountain Supply, known as Mercantile Supply until W.P. Harris took it over. This was a company general store for the railroad, located on the northeast corner of Front Street and Powell Avenue. It later became the Webster Coal Co. Store.

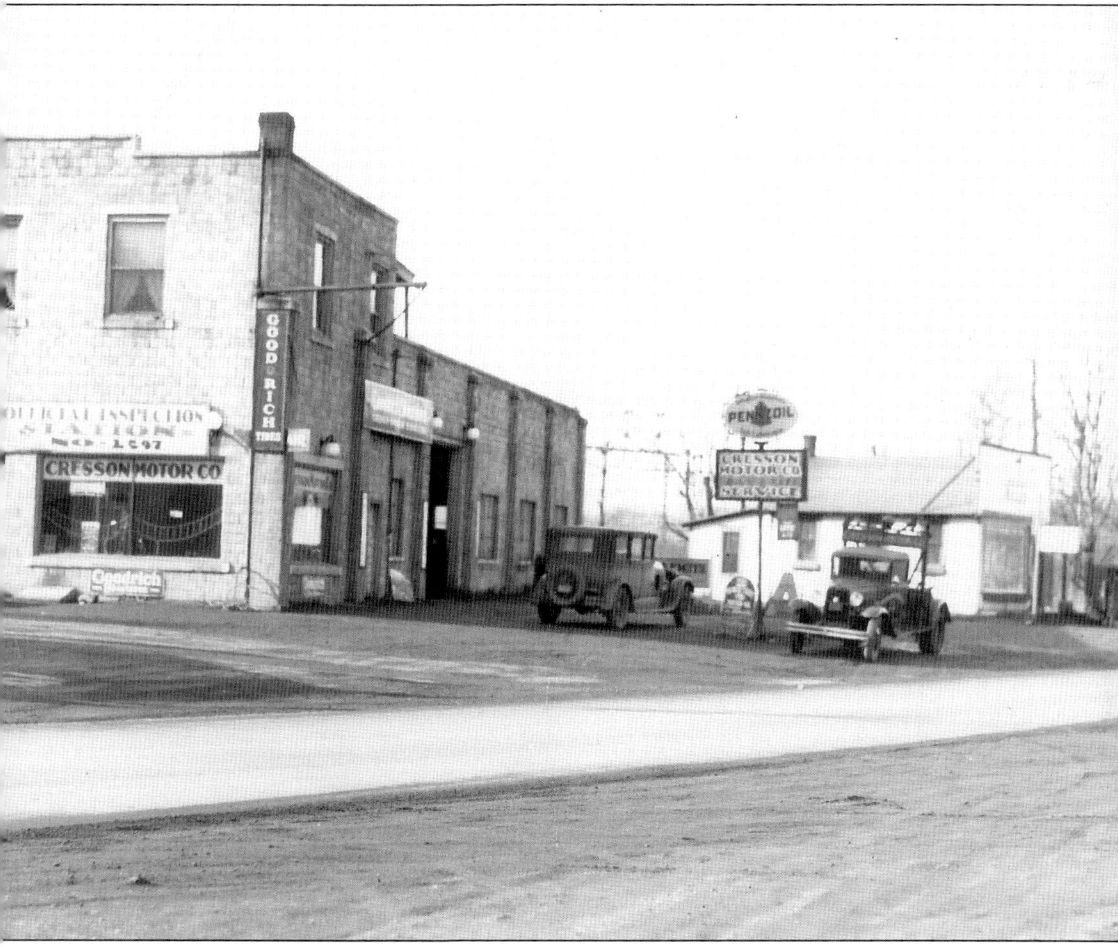

Looking west in 1934 at the intersection of Routes 22 and 53. Cresson Motors (on the southwest corner) and Beavers' Lunch Room have been replaced by Sheetz. Cresson is conveniently located near the steel, coal, lumber, and industrial areas of the state. Cresson Motors, a mechanical repair shop and state inspection center originally located on south Front Street (present Tupperware), was created by George and Jim Sheraw, who owned the first Ford dealership in town. They split up before World War II and Jim moved the business into the establishment built by Bill Bannon (where Sheetz is now located).

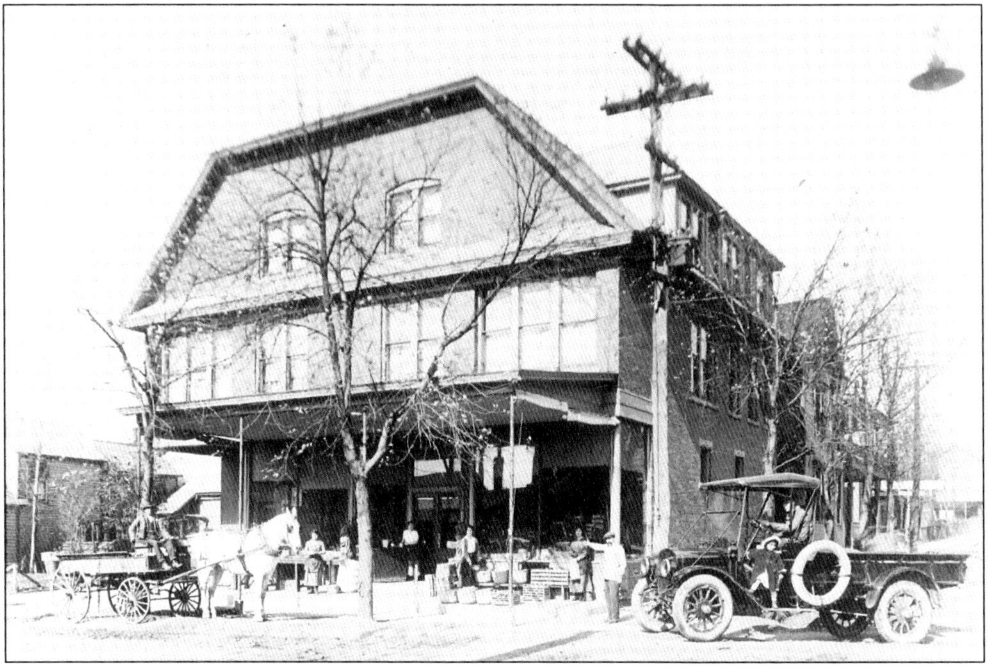

Runzo Store on the northwest corner of Second Street and Keystone Avenue in 1915. Steve Runzo is standing on the corner, Joe Runzo is driving the truck, and Rose Runzo is on the running board, with customers in the background.

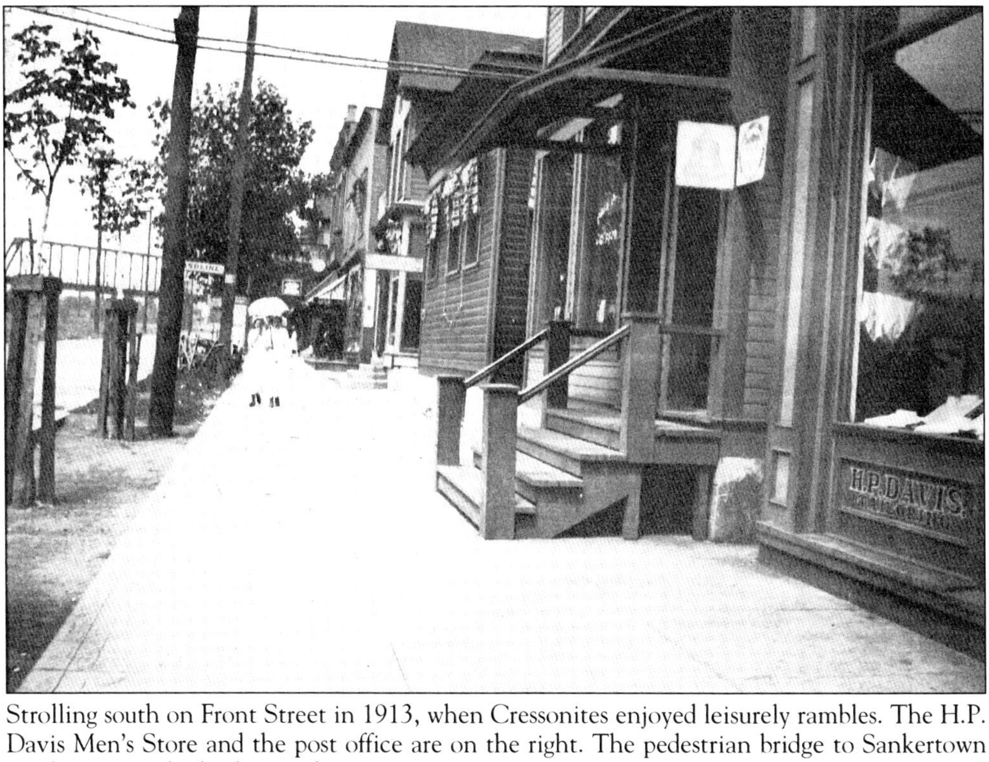

Strolling south on Front Street in 1913, when Cressonites enjoyed leisurely rambles. The H.P. Davis Men's Store and the post office are on the right. The pedestrian bridge to Sankertown can be seen in the background.

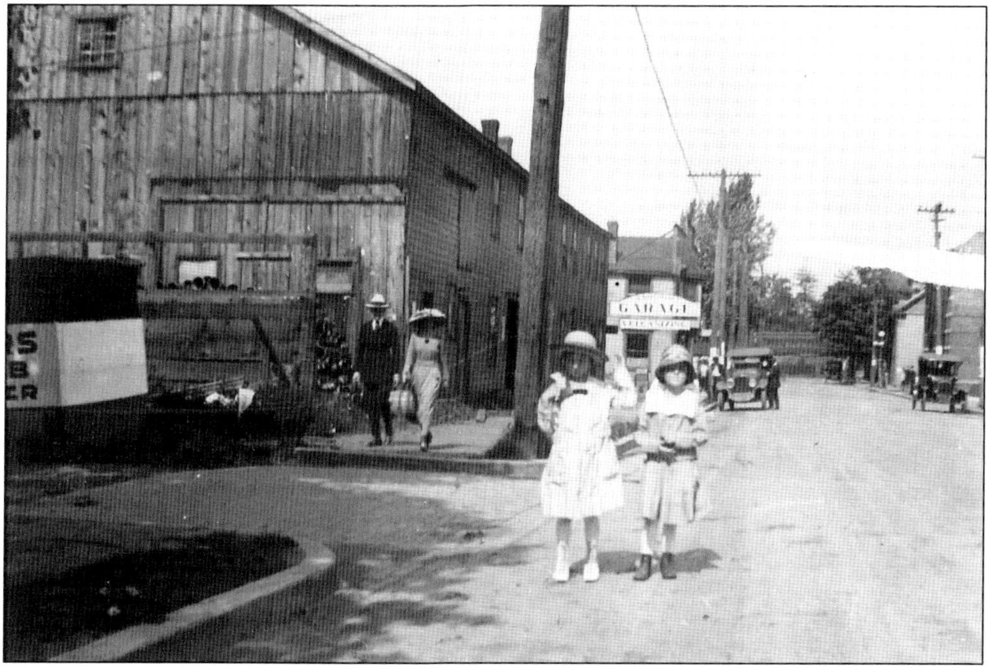

The Diamond Livery Stable on the southwest corner of Second Street and Ashcroft Avenue, looking toward the railroad. William Ashley and his wife pose here with nieces Jean and Phyllis Hertzog.

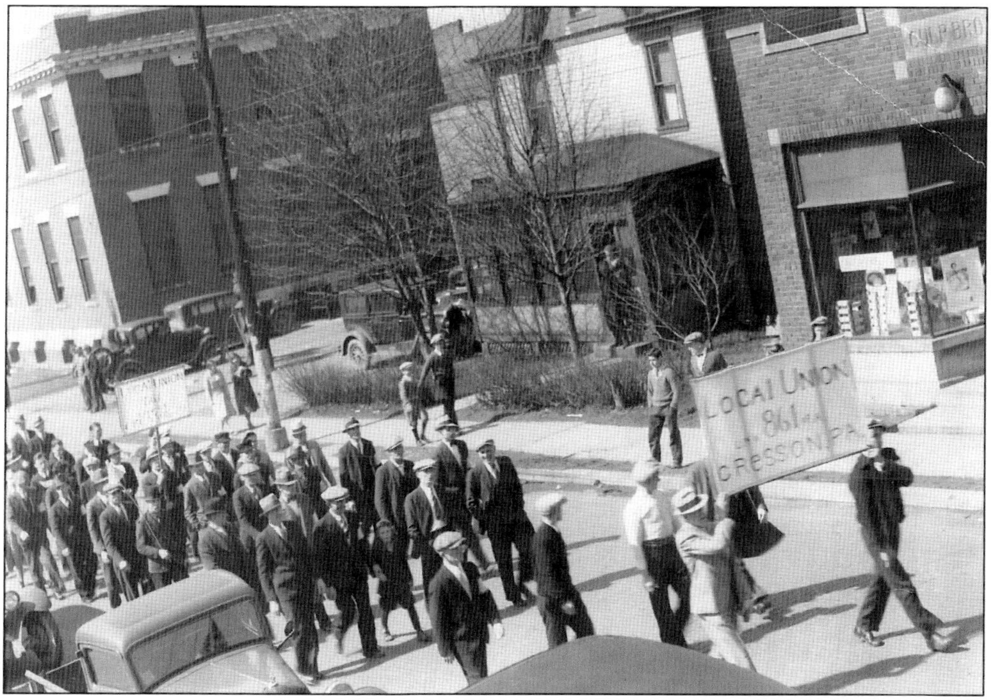

United Mine Workers, Local Union 861, in a parade on Second Street in 1931. The Coal and Coke building is on the left. The "Culp Bros Building" on the right was a meat market established by Martin and Albert Culp after World War I. It is now Servinsky Jewelers.

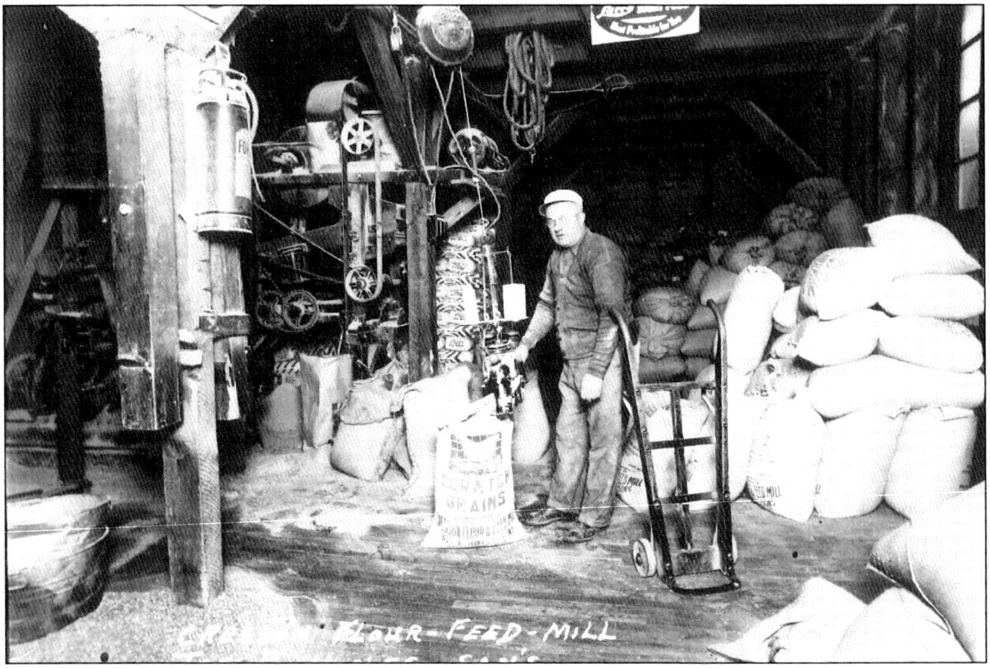

The flour and feed mill established by Joseph Hines on north Second Street prior to World War I. The fourth generation is now extending the family tradition.

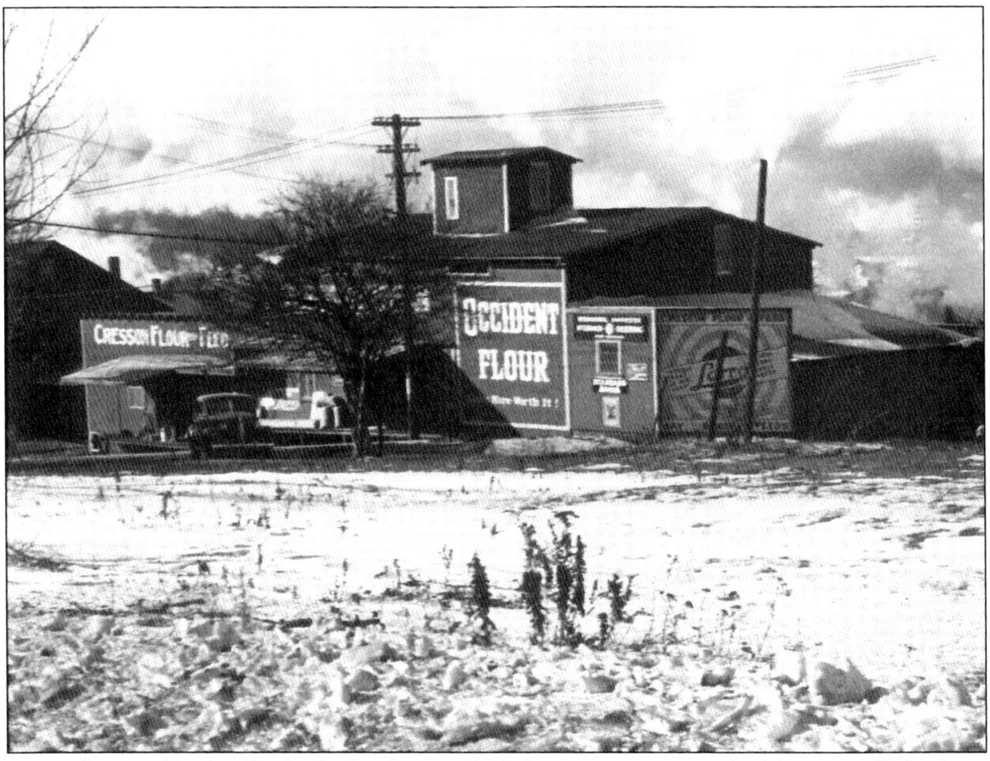

Hines' flour and feed mill. The feed mill expanded when an ammunition building in Hollidaysburg was transported to Cresson, after World War I, and reconstructed as an addition.

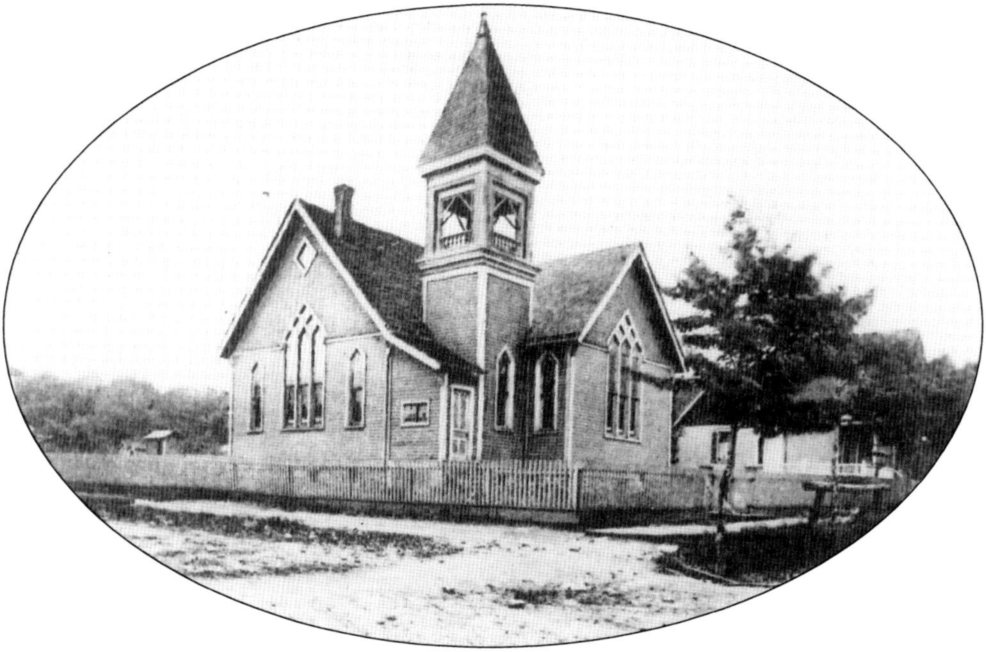

The Keystone Presbyterian Church, founded in 1847 at the Summit. During the Mountain House era, the congregation relocated to a small, round building (which later became the Circle Gas Station), where it stayed until 1894, when it moved to its present location on the northwest corner of Keystone Avenue and Third Street.

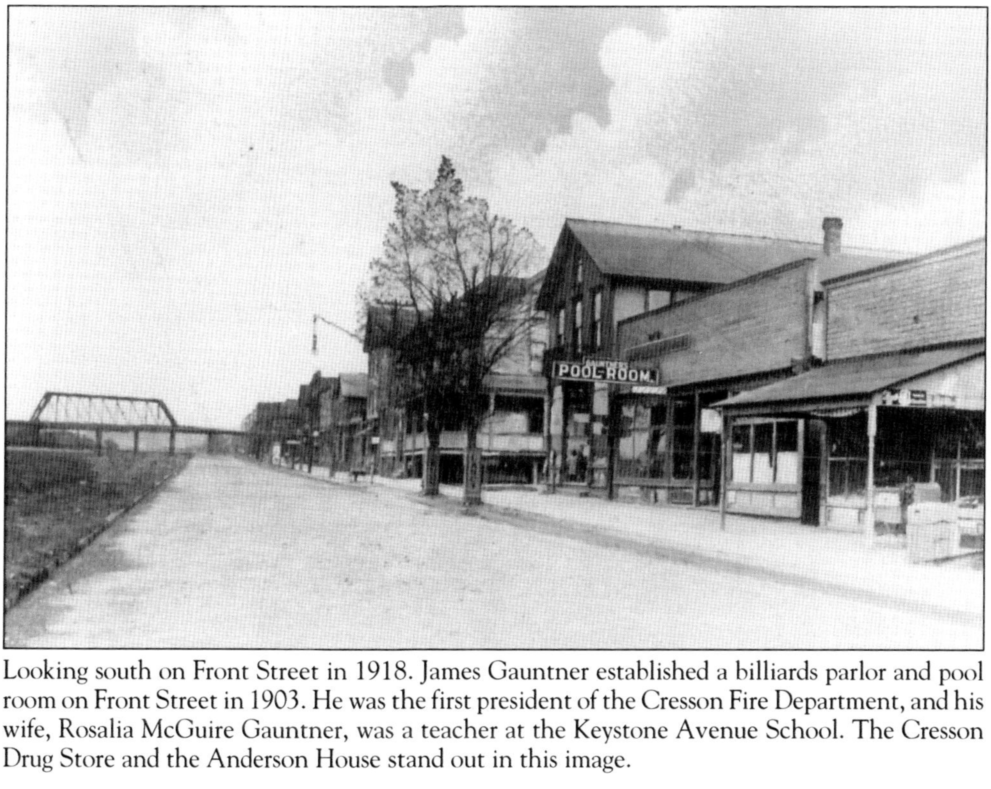

Looking south on Front Street in 1918. James Gauntner established a billiards parlor and pool room on Front Street in 1903. He was the first president of the Cresson Fire Department, and his wife, Rosalia McGuire Gauntner, was a teacher at the Keystone Avenue School. The Cresson Drug Store and the Anderson House stand out in this image.

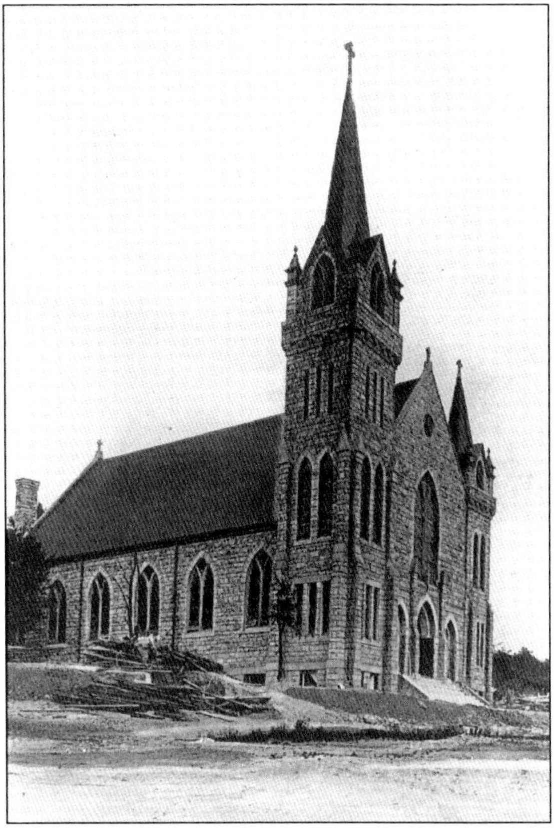

The St. Francis Xavier Church, established on Powell Avenue on the site of a stone quarry. Its stately steeple has become a landmark.

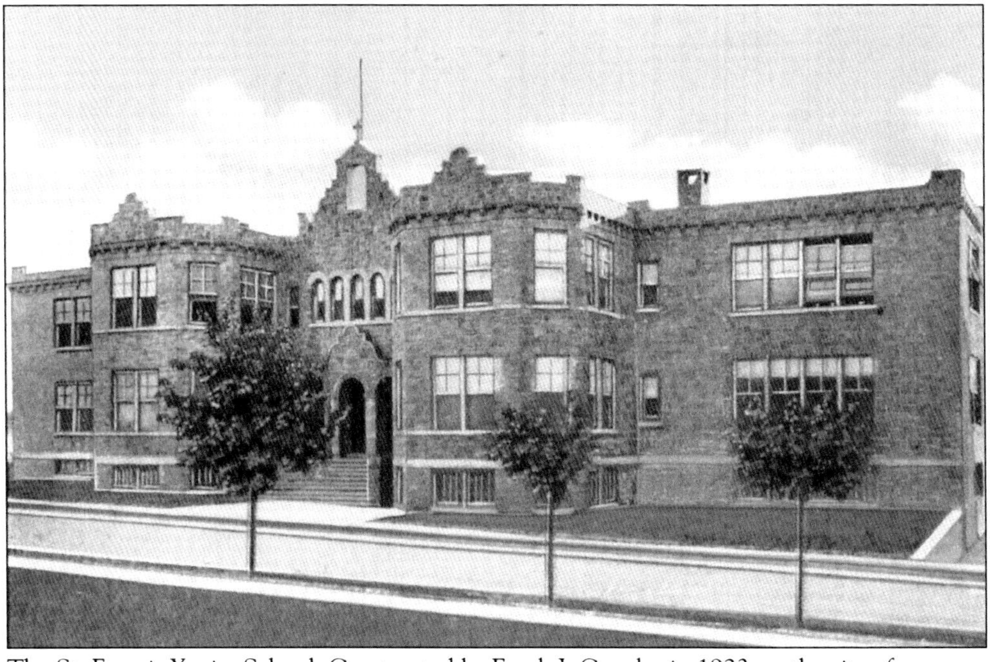

The St. Francis Xavier School. Constructed by Frank J. Cupples in 1923 on the site of an opera house (and previous to that, a stone quarry), this school was long staffed by the Sisters of Mercy.

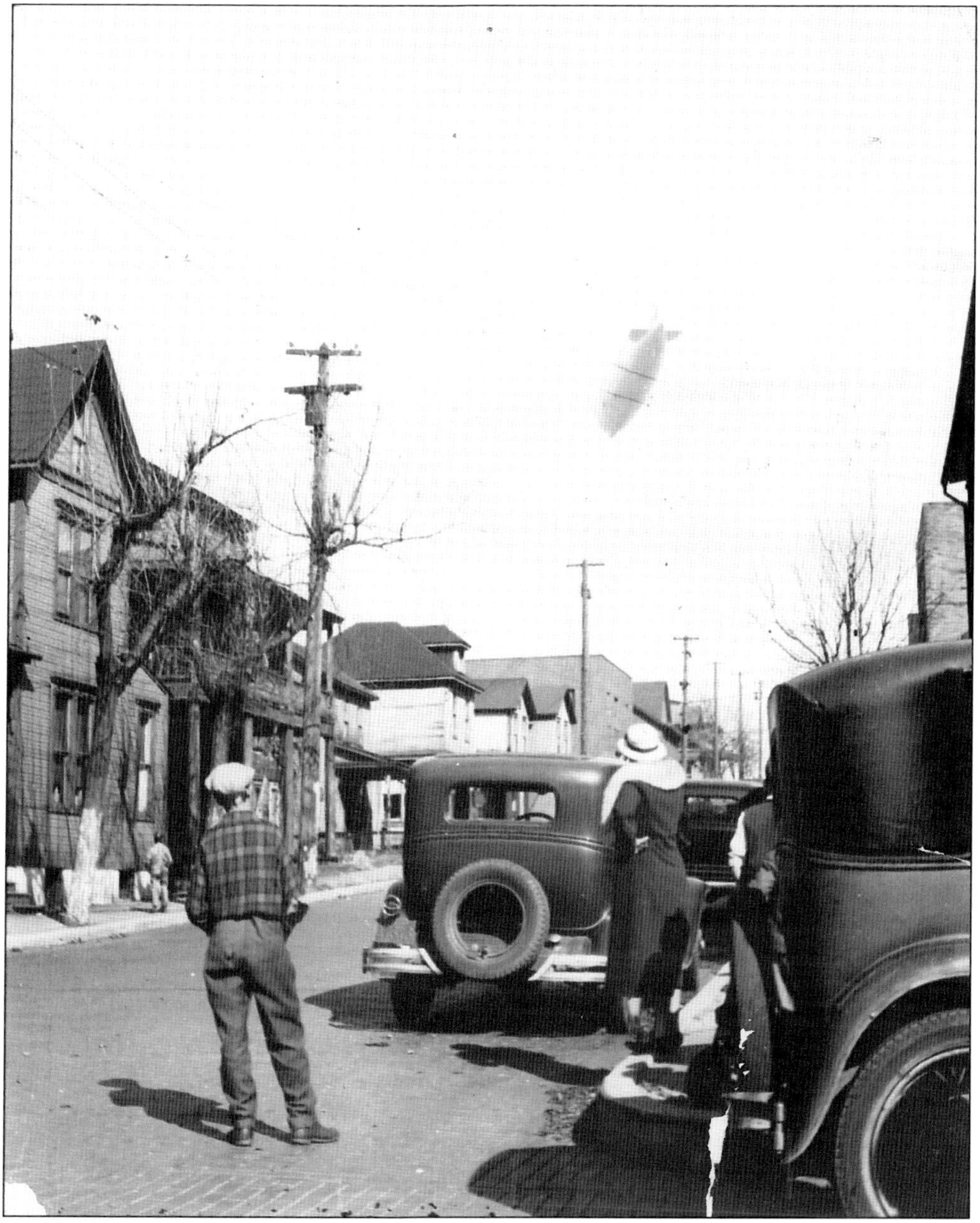

The German dirigible (Graf Zeppelin airship) #LZ127 over Cresson on August 5, 1929 en route to Lakehurst, N.J. Built in Germany, the 172-foot-long airship held townsfolk captive as it sailed gracefully overhead. It completed a dramatic world flight, financed by William Randolph Hearst, in twenty-one days; the sensation and enthusiasm generated by this could have led to transoceanic airship travel, but the stock market crash intervened two months later. This photograph was taken by William Moore, manager of the local A&P, while local carpenter Scott Riddler looked on.

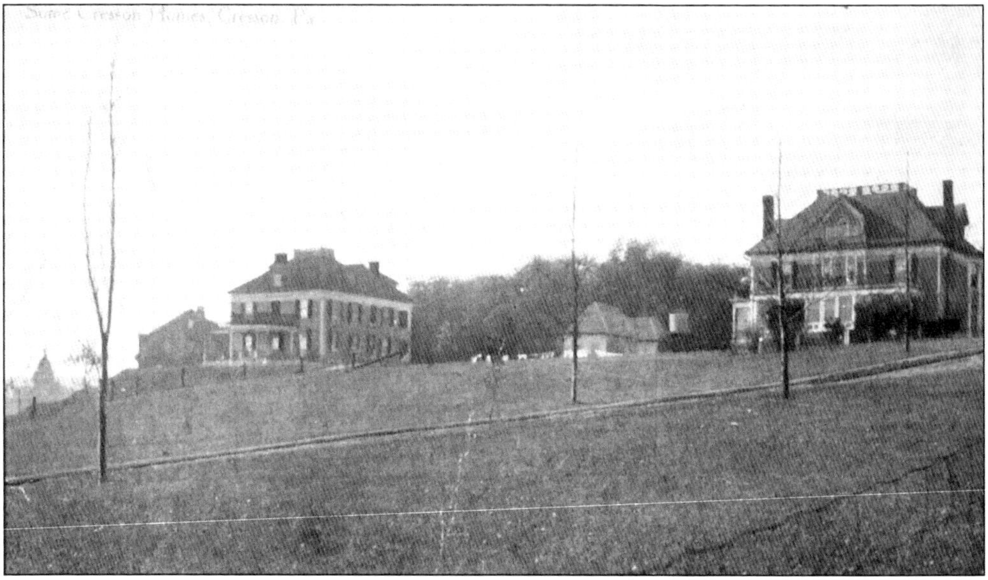

Webster Hill, where railroad personnel settled. The 1899 mansion house (left) housed the superintendent of the railroad; an almost exact duplicate, built in 1906—complete with widow's walk—is now the Convent of The Sisters of The Sacred Heart. The trees along Arch Street were planted by Mrs. Mary K. Thaw. Note the tower of Mount Aloysius Academy on the left.

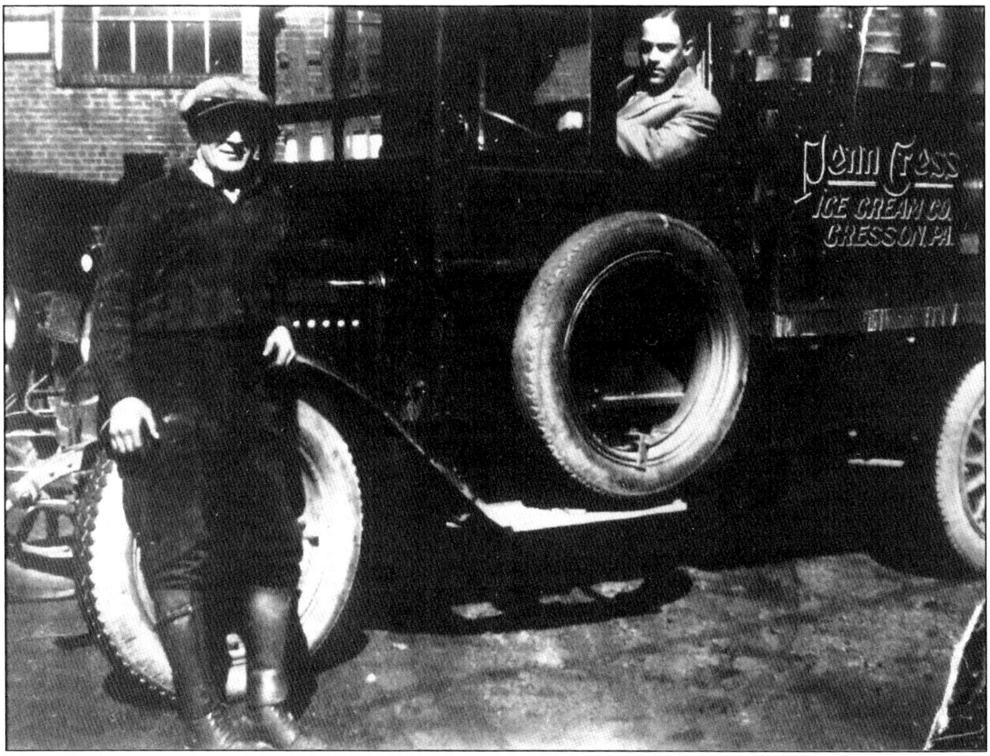

Roy Trexler beside his Penn Cress truck, used to deliver ice cream. Trexler established the Penn Cress Ice Cream Factory on west Park Avenue after World War I. The driver is Marty Howe.

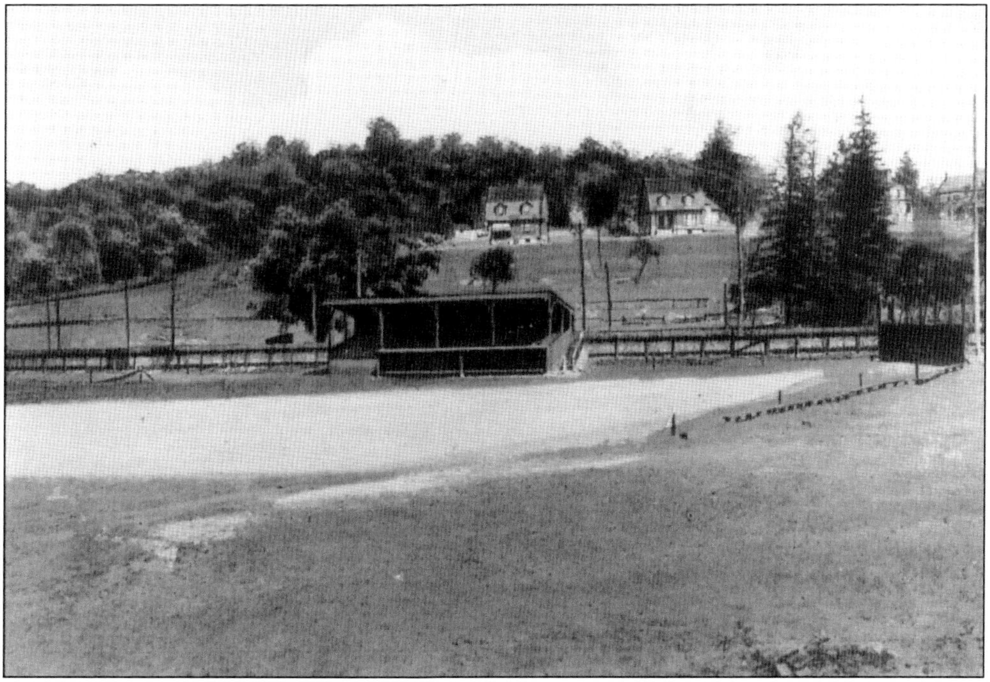

The athletic field on William Penn Highway across from the present McDonald's. Webster Hill is in the background. The red brick house on the extreme right is now the Convent of The Sisters of The Sacred Heart.

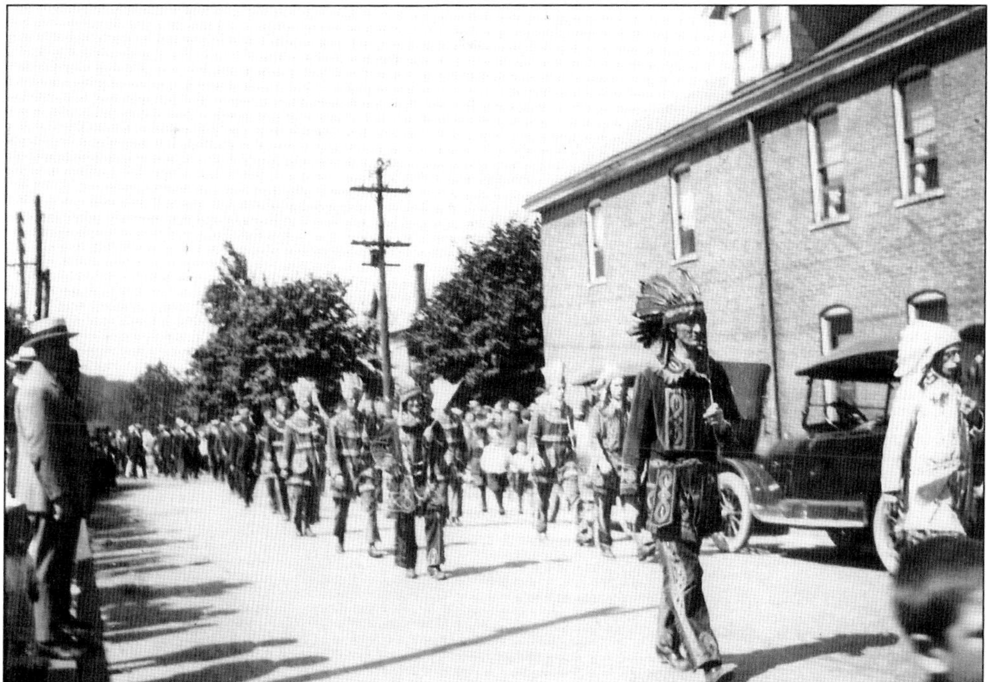

Red Men's Lodge members at the intersection of Third Street and Keystone Avenue in 1913. The Cashier Building on the right is now Kennedy Holl Funeral Home.

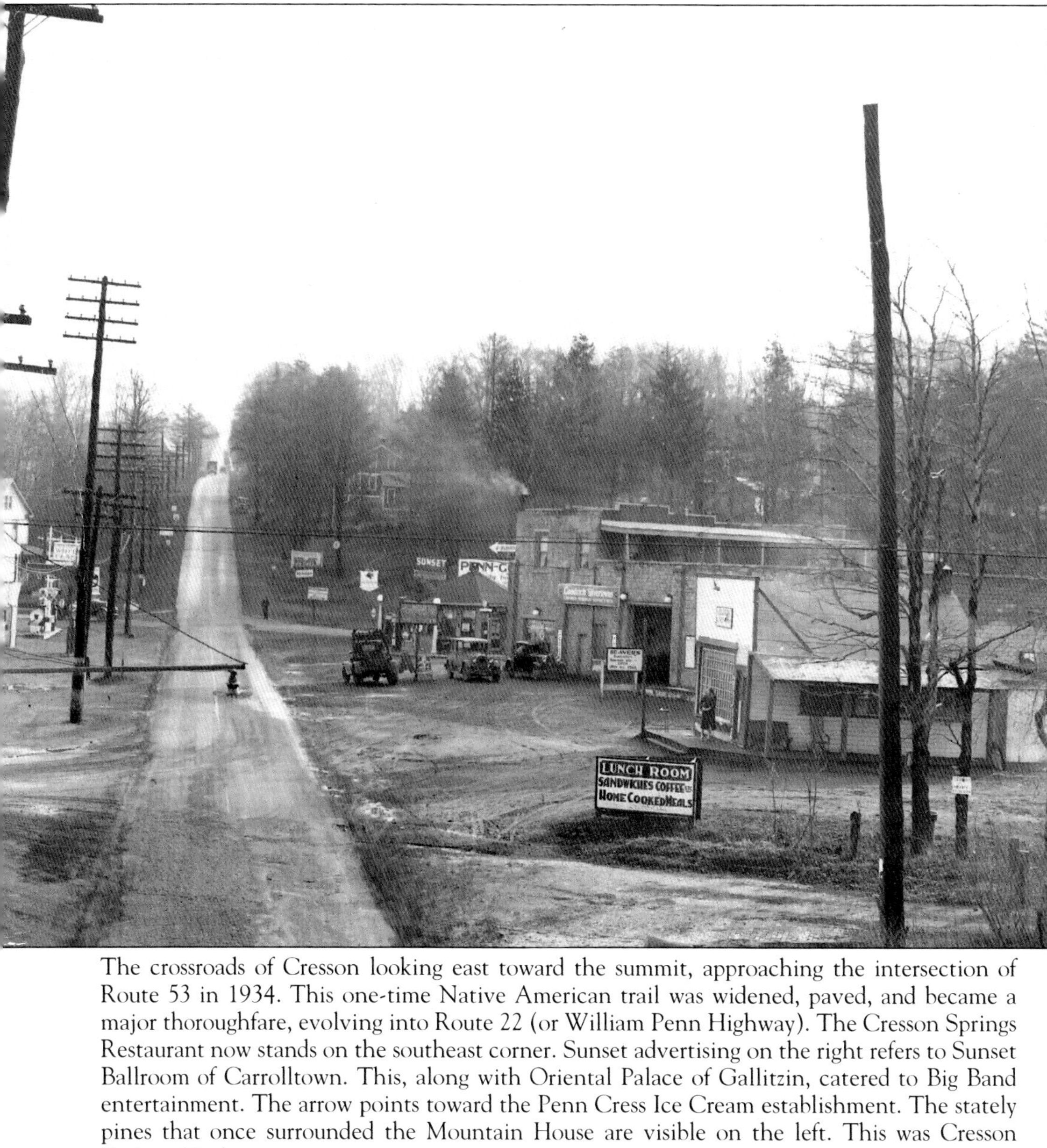

The crossroads of Cresson looking east toward the summit, approaching the intersection of Route 53 in 1934. This one-time Native American trail was widened, paved, and became a major thoroughfare, evolving into Route 22 (or William Penn Highway). The Cresson Springs Restaurant now stands on the southeast corner. Sunset advertising on the right refers to Sunset Ballroom of Carrolltown. This, along with Oriental Palace of Gallitzin, catered to Big Band entertainment. The arrow points toward the Penn Cress Ice Cream establishment. The stately pines that once surrounded the Mountain House are visible on the left. This was Cresson Springs Circle.

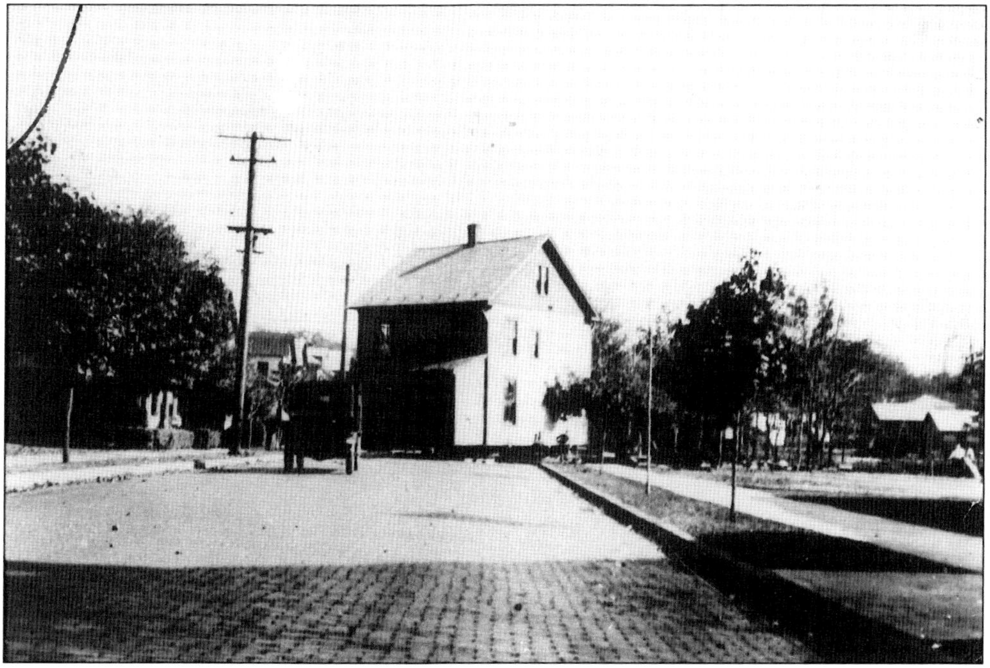

The S. Cooney House in the 1930s. This house was moved from Fifth Street west on Keystone Avenue, and it became Larry Shonto's home before being replaced by the Maplewood Apartments parking lot.

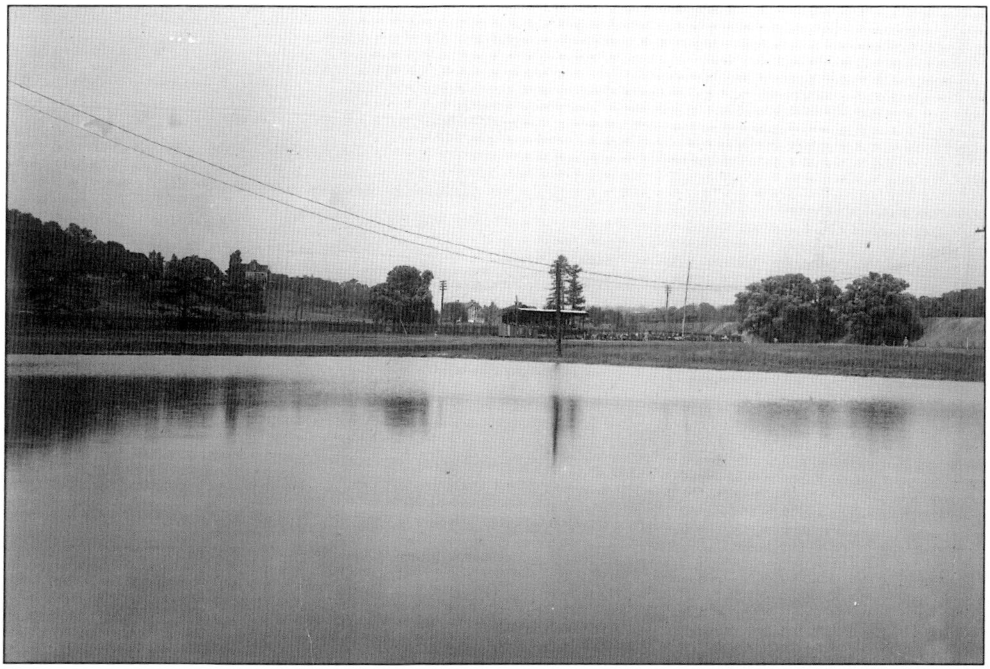

The Ice Dam looking north across Route 22, the athletic field, and the railroad toward Webster Hill. The dam, always shallow, provided ice skating in winter. Blocks of ice were available here for home use. A flag was hung from an Anderson House window when ice was thick enough for skating.

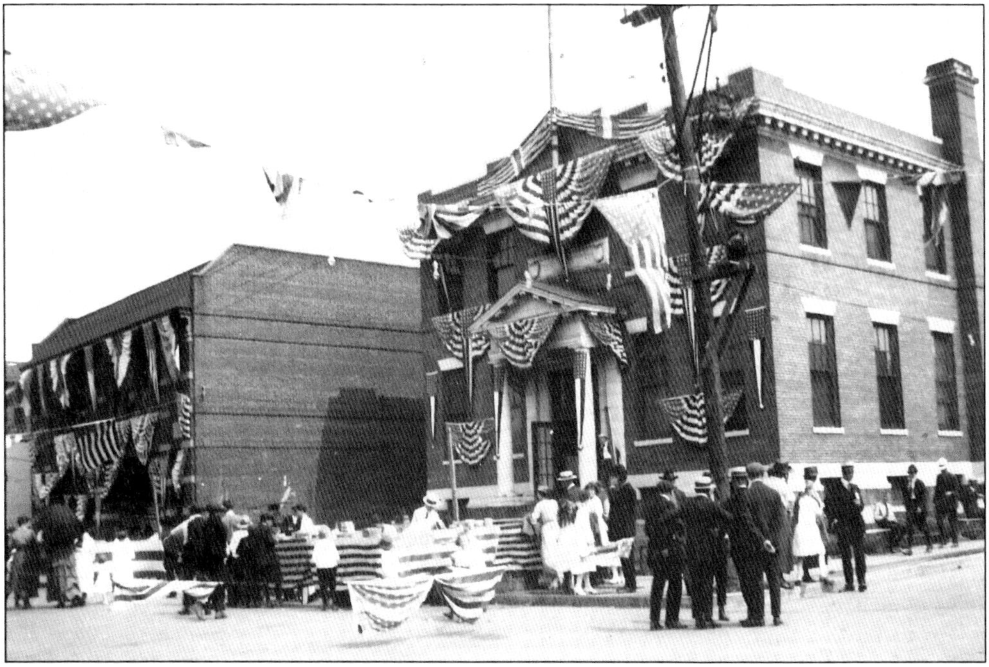

A block party celebration on the Fourth of July on Ashcroft Avenue following a parade. The Coal and Coke building lends itself to the festivities.

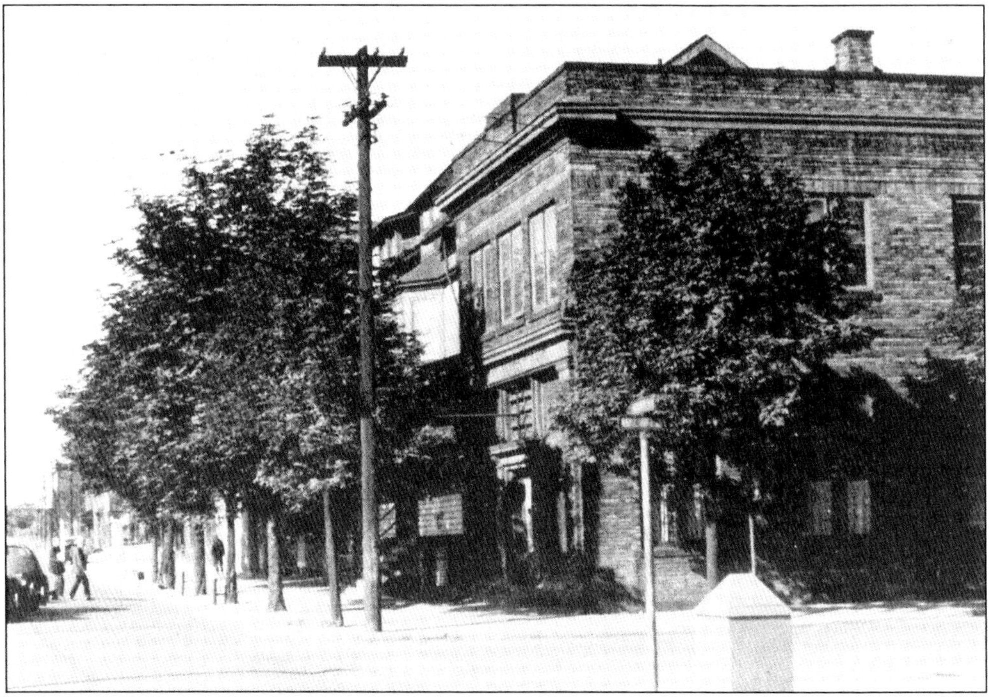

The Farmer's Bank and the Anderson House on the northeast corner of Ashcroft Avenue and Front Street looking north. James Gailey has just parked his 1939 Ford and Robert Connacher his 1937 Studebaker.

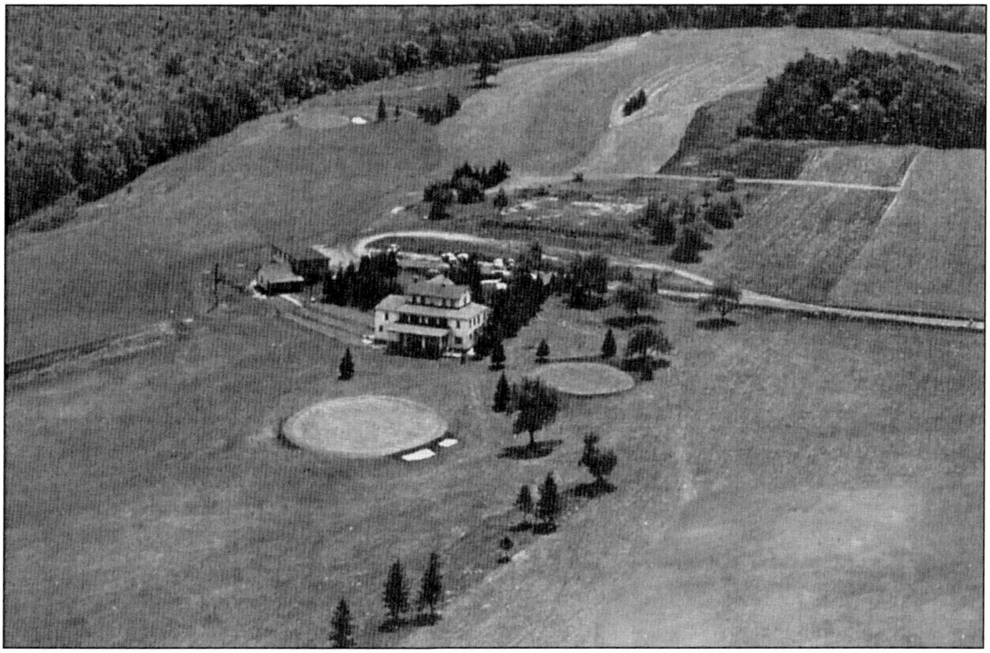

The picturesque Cresson Country Club. This club was established in 1923 with a 9-hole golf course on Country Club Road. In 1968 Edward Ault designed an 18-hole golf course on these rolling hills and fairways. The clubhouse was part of Boland's home, and the surrounding land part of his estate.

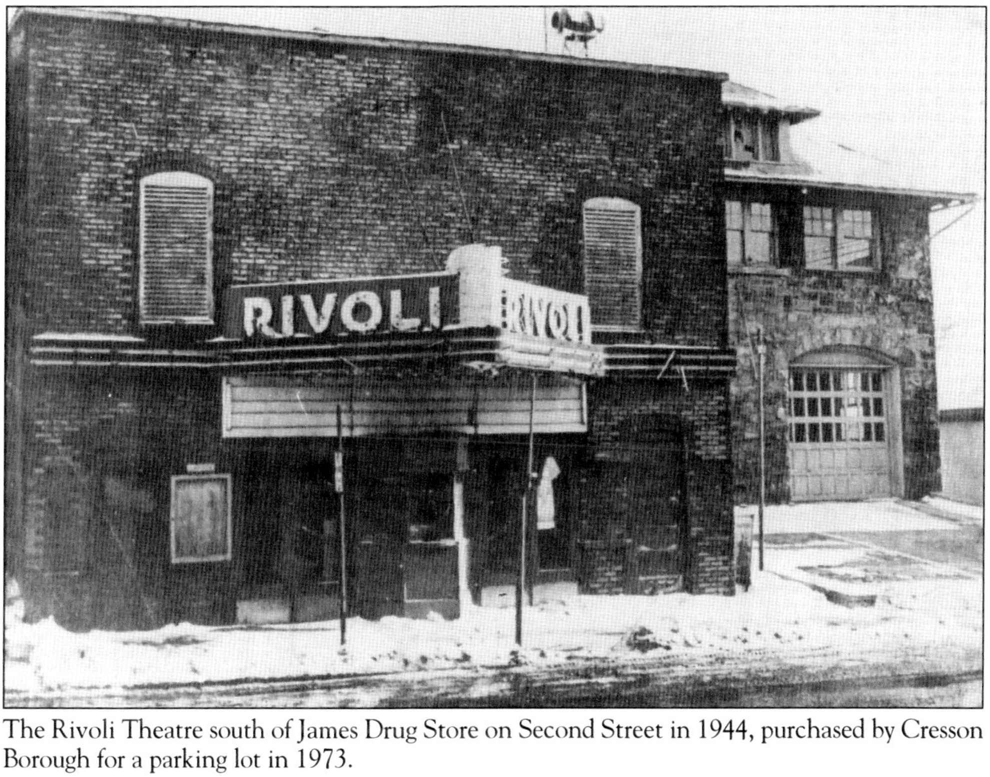

The Rivoli Theatre south of James Drug Store on Second Street in 1944, purchased by Cresson Borough for a parking lot in 1973.

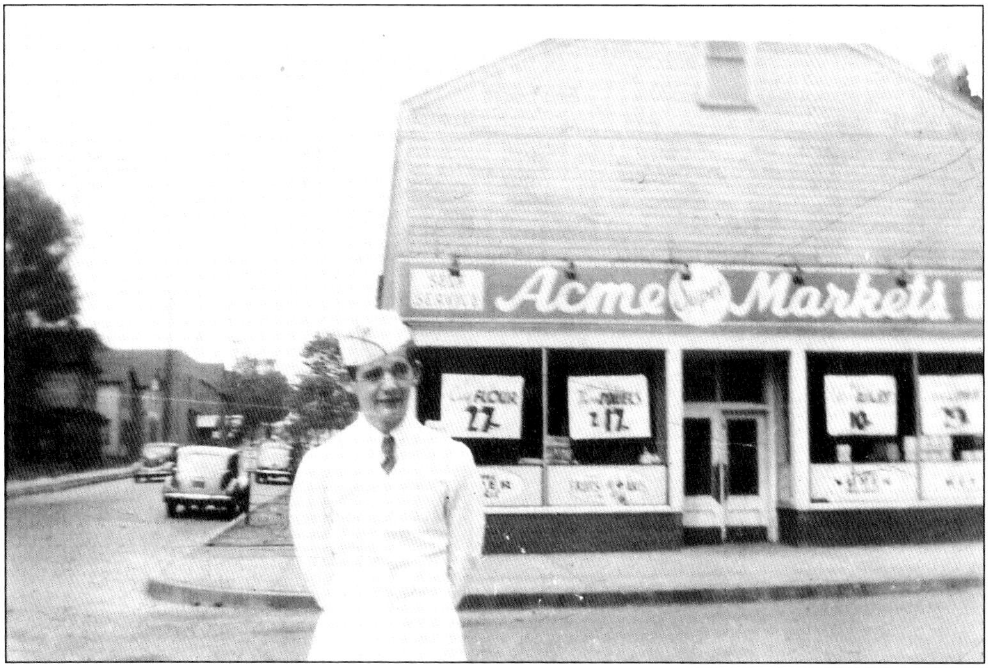

Acme Market with clerk Bill Parrish, established on the northeast corner of Second Street and Powell Avenue in 1940. A new innovation of that era was the self-service concept in supermarkets, complete with shopping carts.

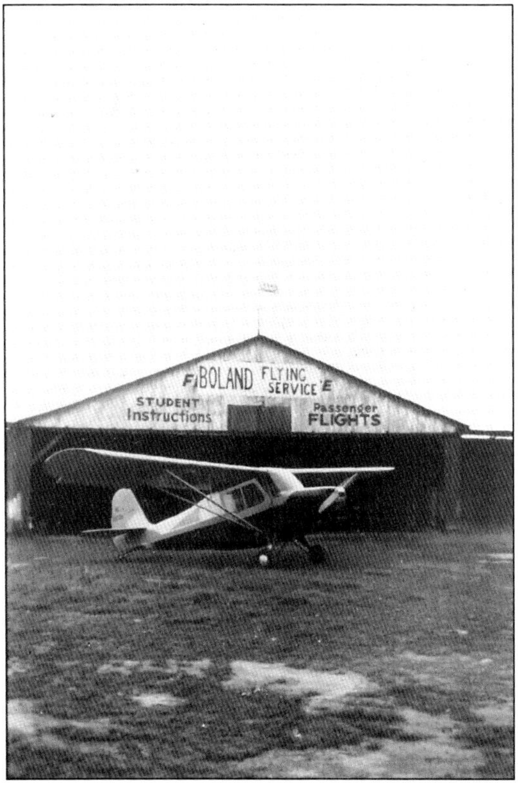

Boland's Flying Field. This business was established along Country Club Road by Harold J. Boland in 1944 on a portion of his father's farm. The name was later changed to Cresson Airport. It gained prominence in 1944 when private aviation was entering an era of expansion. Harold's son Robert was a flying instructor! Another son, Jay, became the aircraft mechanic, and son Clifton kept the family tradition alive as a pilot.

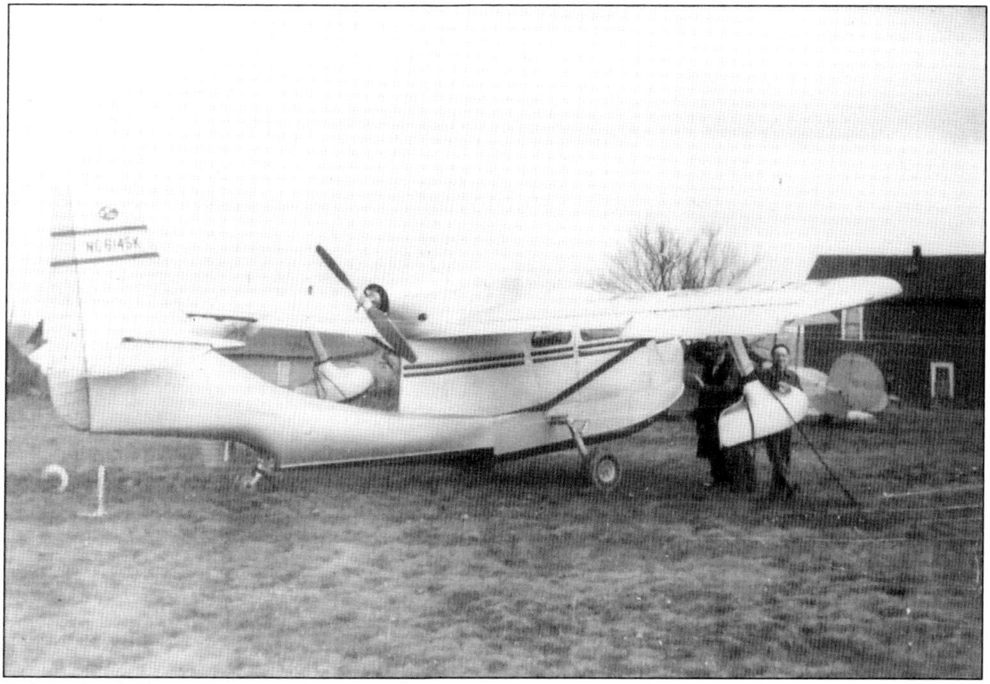

Bob Boland (far right) with a visitor beside his aircraft, before soaring into the heavens on an instructional flight. Boland first soloed in 1938 at Duncansville. Airports were always sites of interest and recreation for the Boland family.

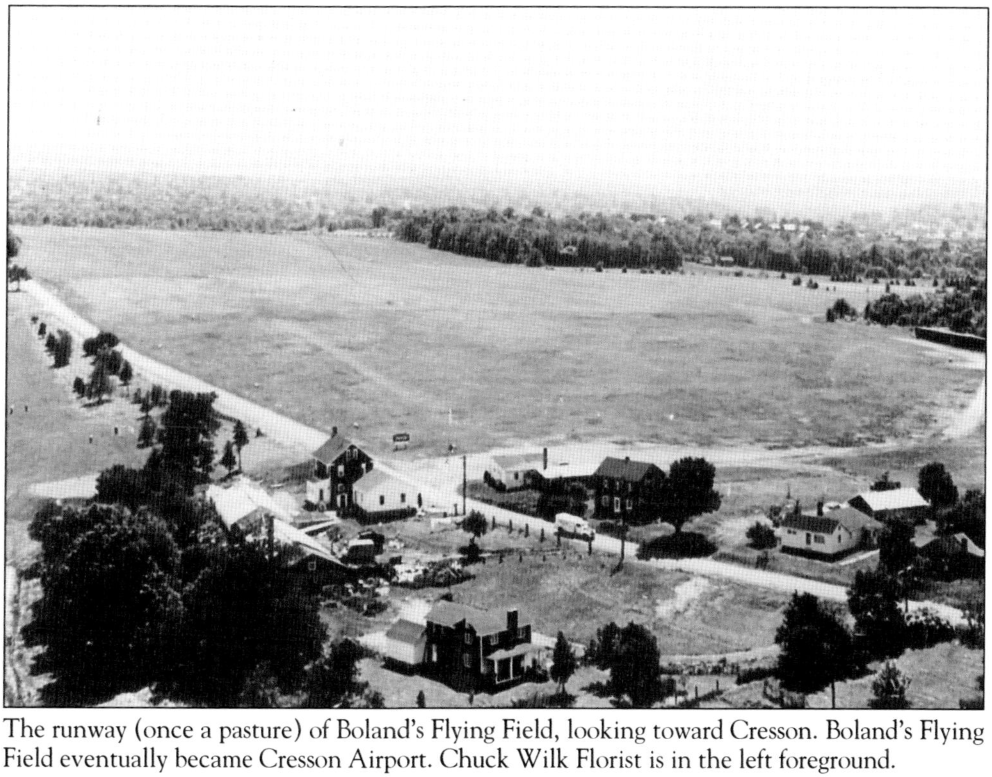

The runway (once a pasture) of Boland's Flying Field, looking toward Cresson. Boland's Flying Field eventually became Cresson Airport. Chuck Wilk Florist is in the left foreground.

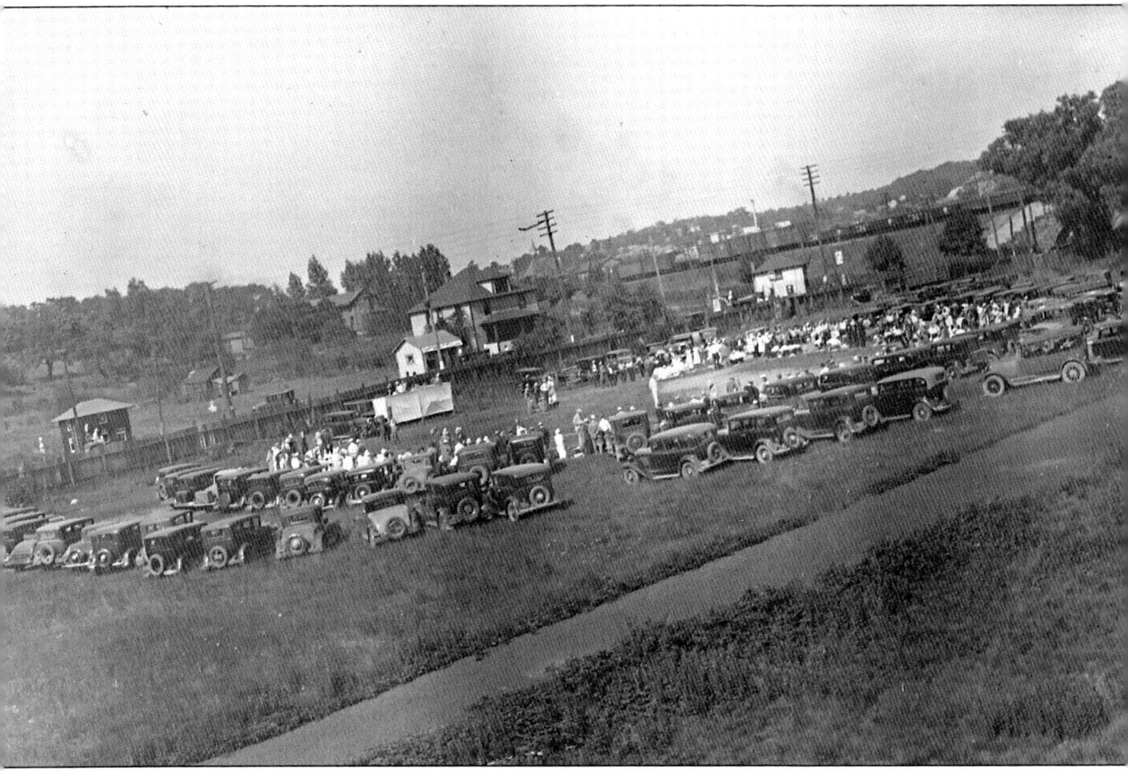

A good turnout at the Pennsylvania Railroad Athletic Field for an United Mine Workers First Aid meeting in 1933. Located on the south side of Route 22, west of the railroad, the field provided a gathering place for townsfolk and recreation for youngsters.

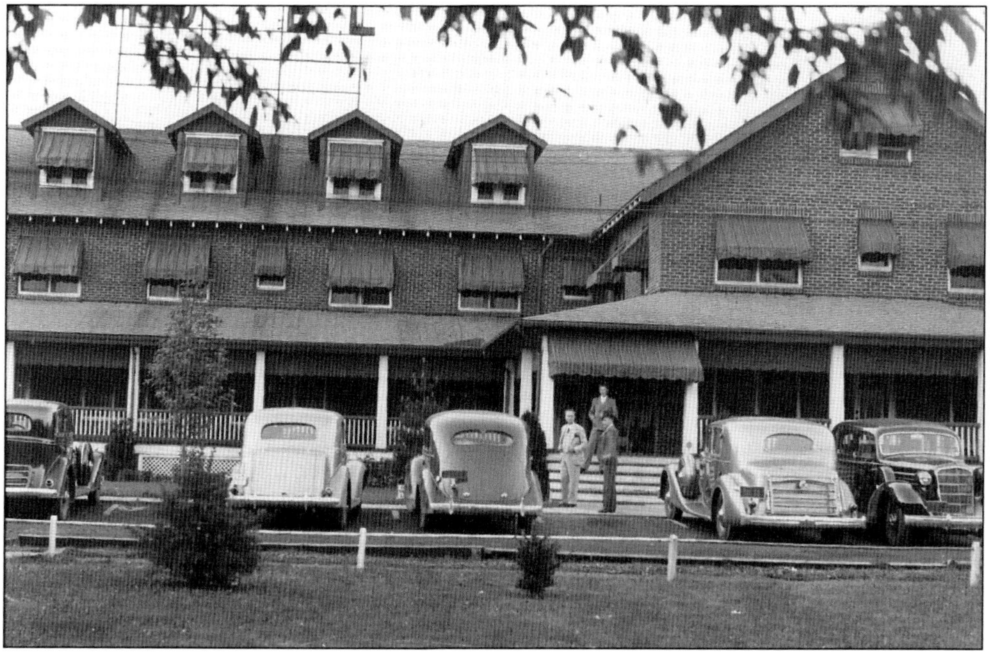

The Lee Hoffman Hotel on Laurel Avenue and Second Street, near present-day Sheehan's Car Wash. The hotel was a prominent landmark that afforded ample accommodation when the pure mountain air of Cresson was still considered a beneficial natural resource.

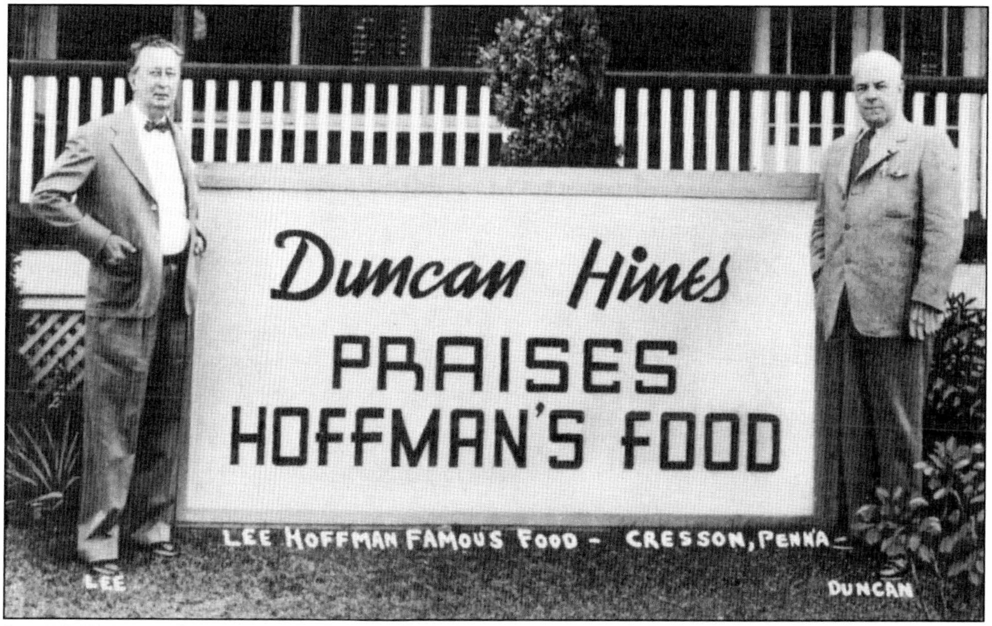

Lee Hoffman and Duncan Hines. Hoffman was recognized and recommended by Hines for the excellent food served at the hotel in 1949. Hines had explored eateries across the nation and listed them in his directory *Adventures of Good Eating*. Dubbed "A Dinner Detective," his name is synonymous with Duncan Hines Cake mixes.

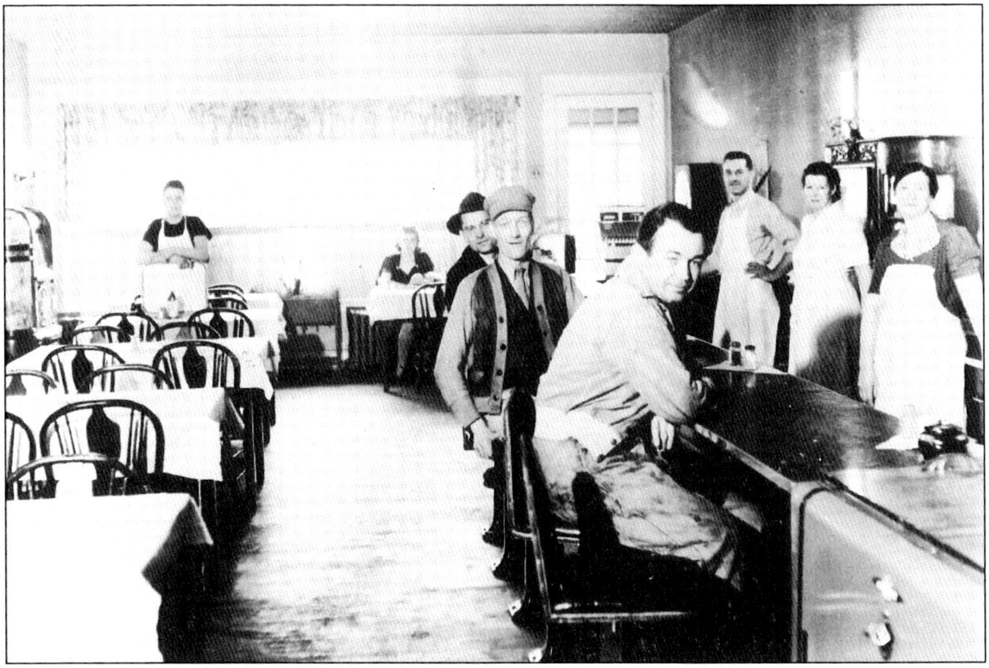

Hoffman's Tea Room in 1943! Behind the counter are G. Myers (left), Helen Crilly Myers (center), and Ethel Crilly. To the far left is Ralph Gardina and an unidentified customer. Two of the lads at the counter are Wilmer Calderwood and Walter Sloan.

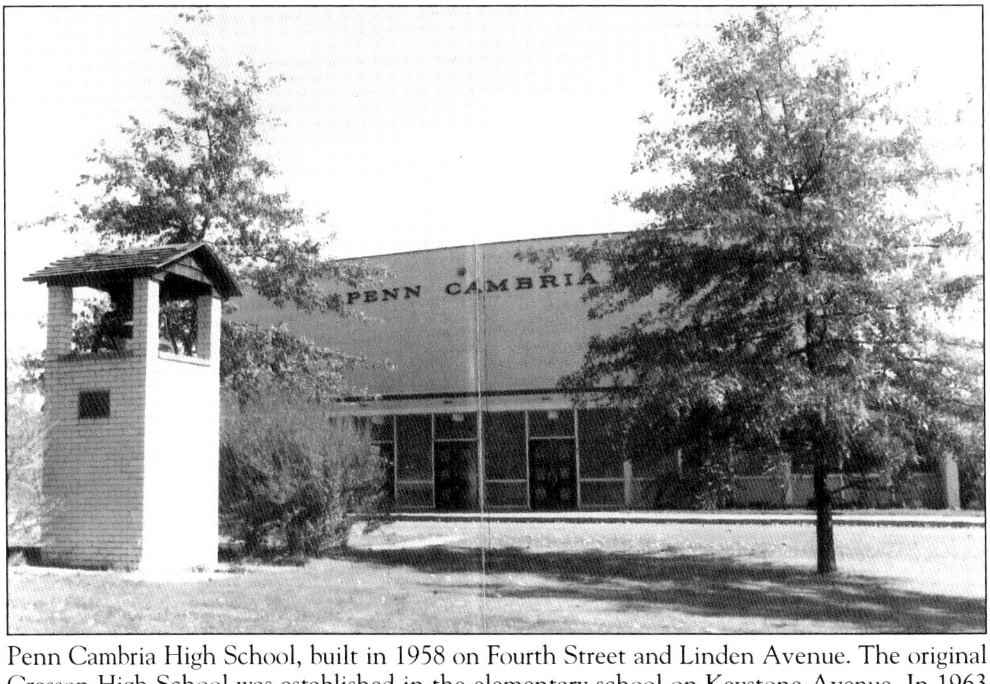

Penn Cambria High School, built in 1958 on Fourth Street and Linden Avenue. The original Cresson High School was established in the elementary school on Keystone Avenue. In 1963 the School District Reorganization Act mandated consolidation. The the new high school incorporates thirteen surrounding municipalities centralized in Cresson. The bell is a stirring reminder of school days on Keystone Avenue.

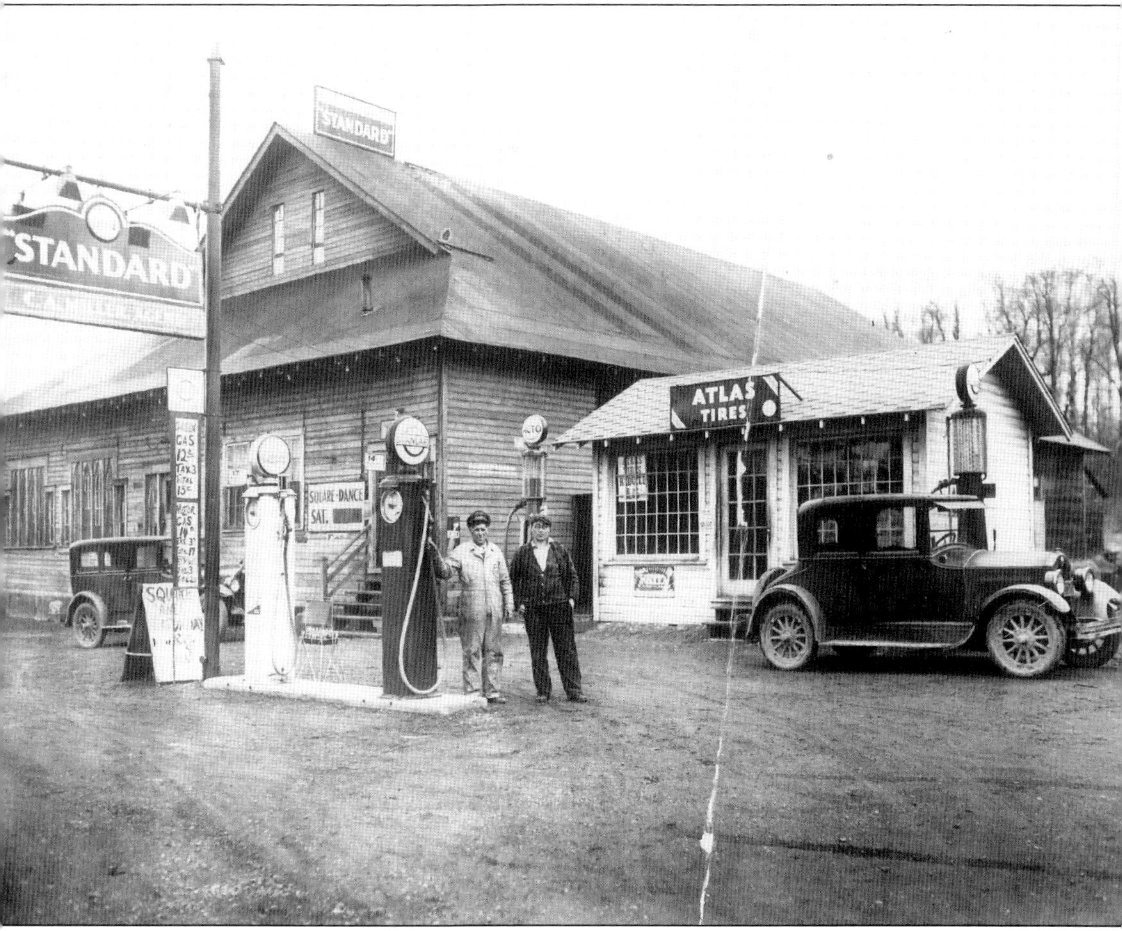

Penn Pavilion, a combination skating rink, dance hall, gymnasium, restaurant, and gas station, c. 1929. Many Cresson High School basketball games were played here. Owned and operated by Charles Miller along Route 22, "The Penn" was a popular entertainment center between 1929 and 1952. Charles stands between the pump and his brother Sylvester. Charles' Dodge is on the left and Sylvester's Buick on the right. The building has been transformed into Dunny's Pizza. Note the price of gas!

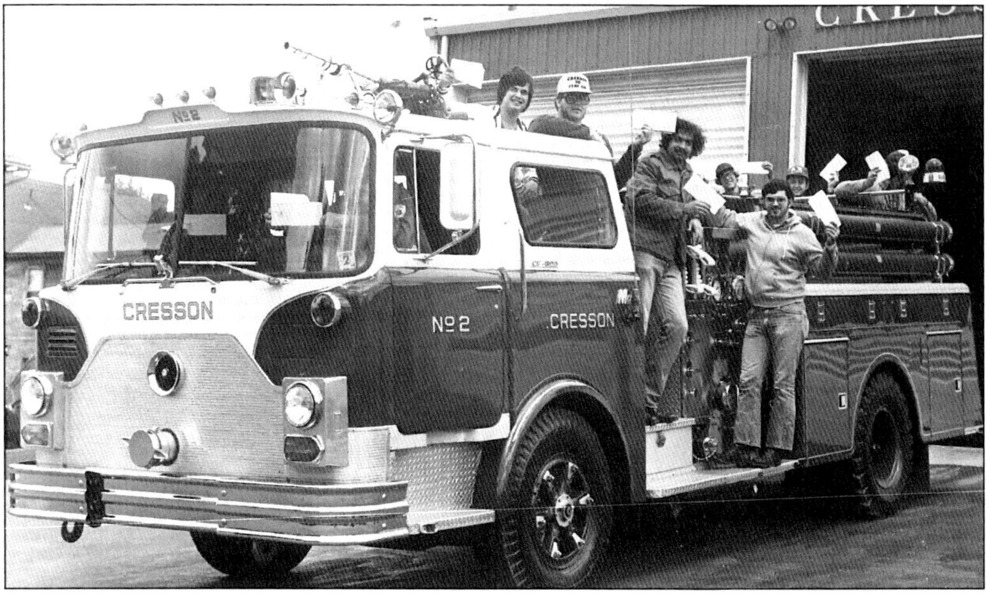

The Cresson Volunteer Fire Department, organized in 1908 with few men and very primitive equipment. On a fund drive in 1979 are Robert Hogue (driver), ? Regan, Barry McGuire, Thomas Laino, D.J. Reffner, Jim Glenn (on the running board), and Joseph A. Adams (a future president and fire chief).

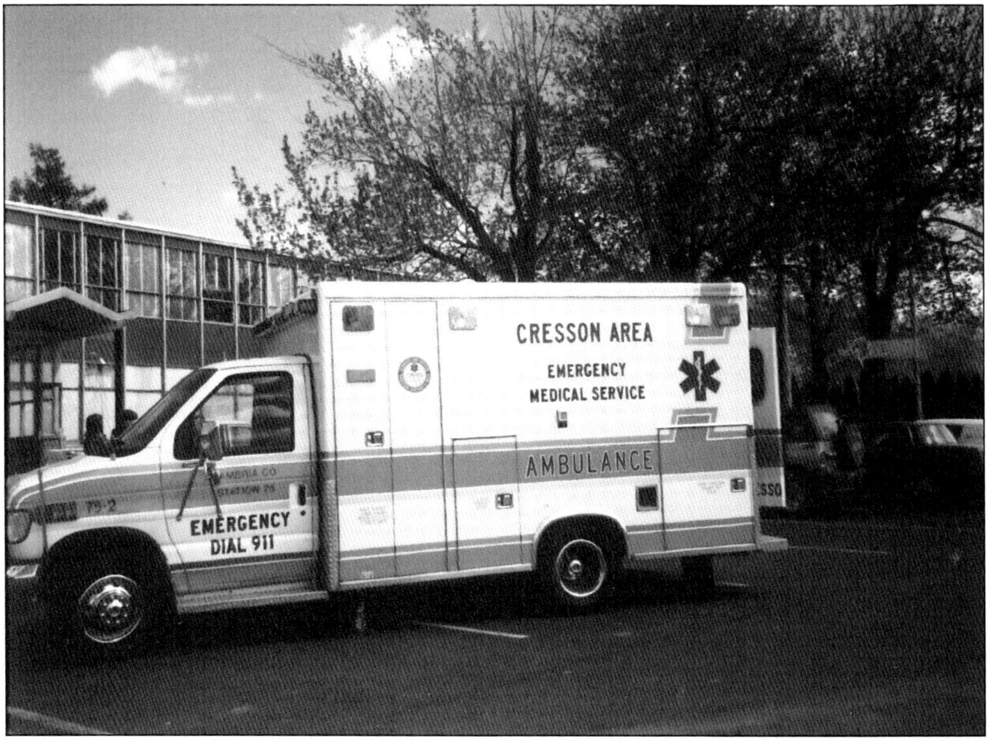

The Cresson Ambulance Service. The service, which has expanded with the times, has a team of volunteer medical technicians and paramedics who bring the emergency room to the patient. The up-to-date, well-equipped emergency vehicles are housed on Laurel Avenue.

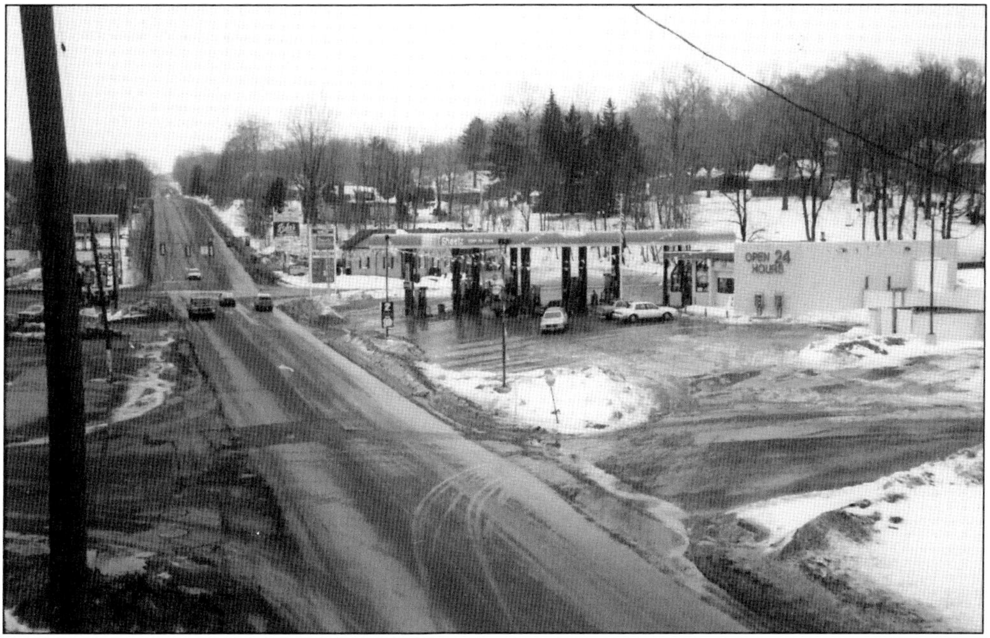

Looking east toward the summit in the 1990s. Mountain House cottages are visible on the right hillside and Sheetz has added a new look. Founded in 1952 in Altoona, Sheetz convenience stores have evolved into a chain which exemplifies excellence in product quality and management effectiveness. Gas pumps were added in 1973. This unique family business employs four thousand people in nearly two hundred stores. In 1995 Sheetz was inducted into the Convenience Industry Hall of Fame.

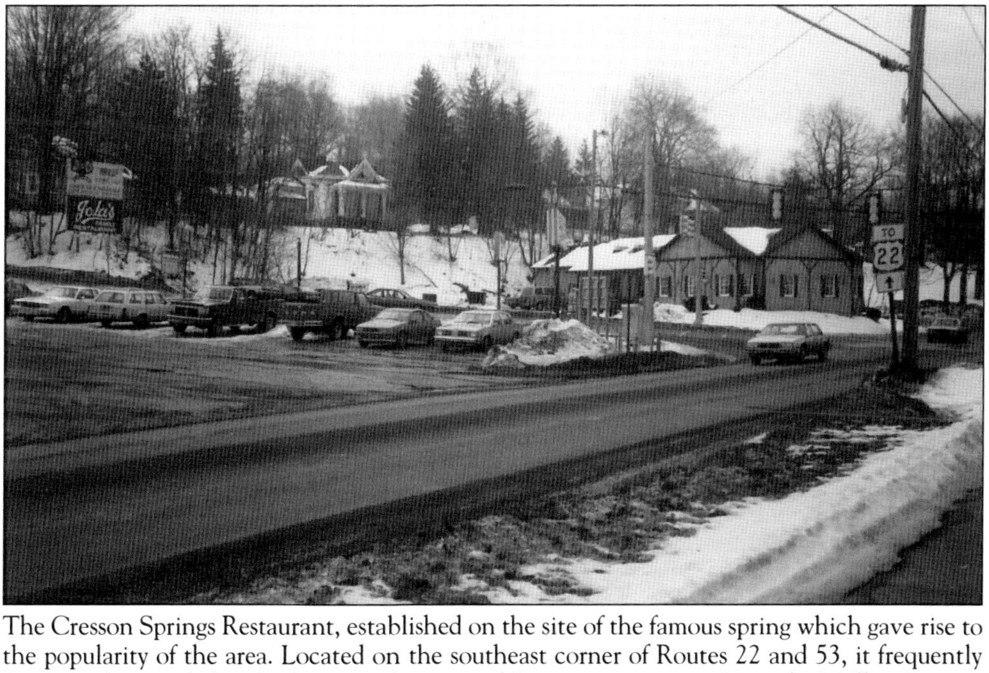

The Cresson Springs Restaurant, established on the site of the famous spring which gave rise to the popularity of the area. Located on the southeast corner of Routes 22 and 53, it frequently features, along with fine foods, a nostalgic tour of Cresson in its prime. Note the Mullen Cottage on the hills to the left.

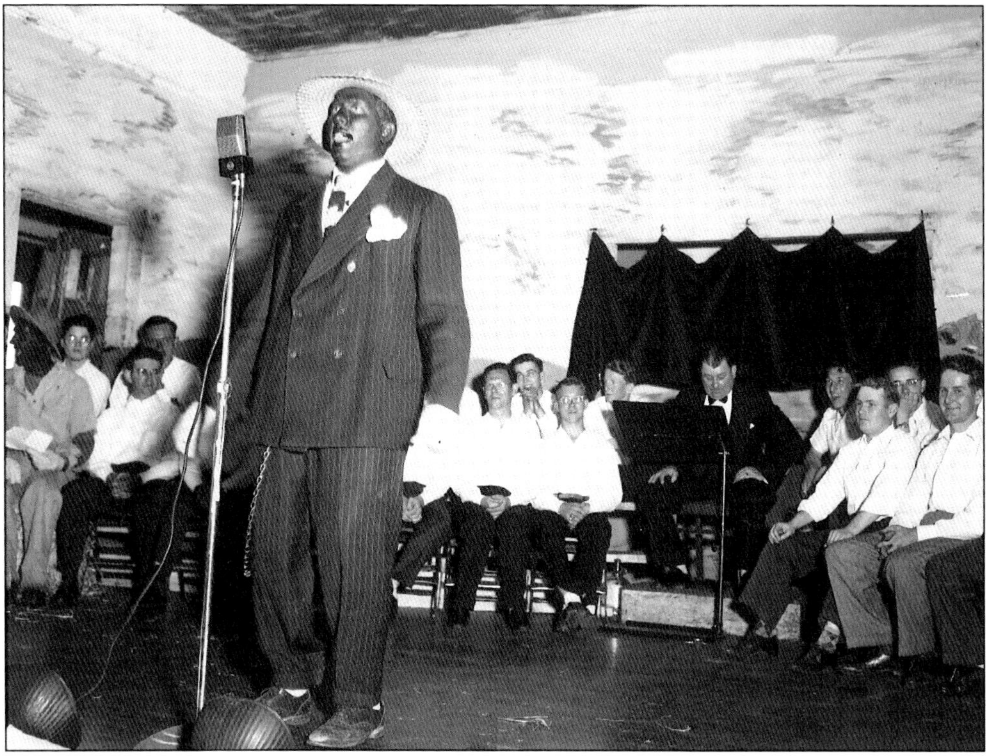

Larry Shonto and Herman Mower, in a minstrel directed by John Criste at the local high school in the late 1940s. In those pre-television days, minstrels provided entertainment that everyone could enjoy.

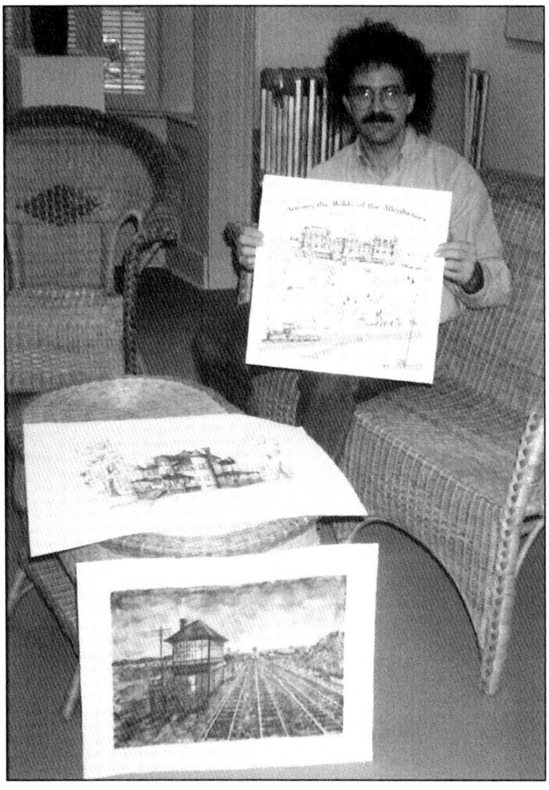

Scott Steberger, director of the Mountain Top Art Gallery. Steberger, a native of Lilly, graduated from Penn State University with a BA in Fine Arts. He has been the recipient of numerous awards and exhibitions. The gallery exhibits works of artists in the southern Allegheny region. Among Scott's local works are the MO Tower, Bramar, and *Among the Wilds of The Alleghenies*.

Dr. Claude Kirby, a veteran of World War II. Kirby, who came to Cresson in 1934, was Staff Surgeon of the 13th Air Force Service Command. In the Asiatic Pacific he became a lieutenant colonel with five battle stars during three years of jungle service. He then resumed general medical practice on Second Street until his retirement in 1986, completing fifty-two years of service to the people of Cresson. He died on September 11, 1996.

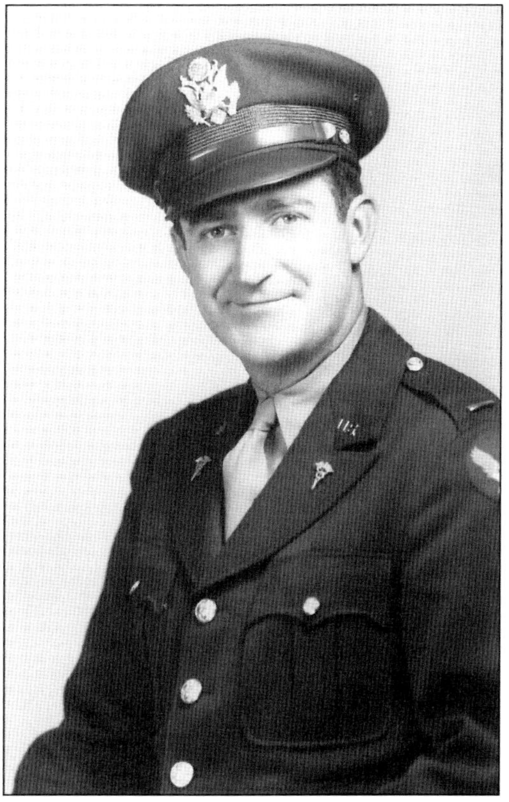

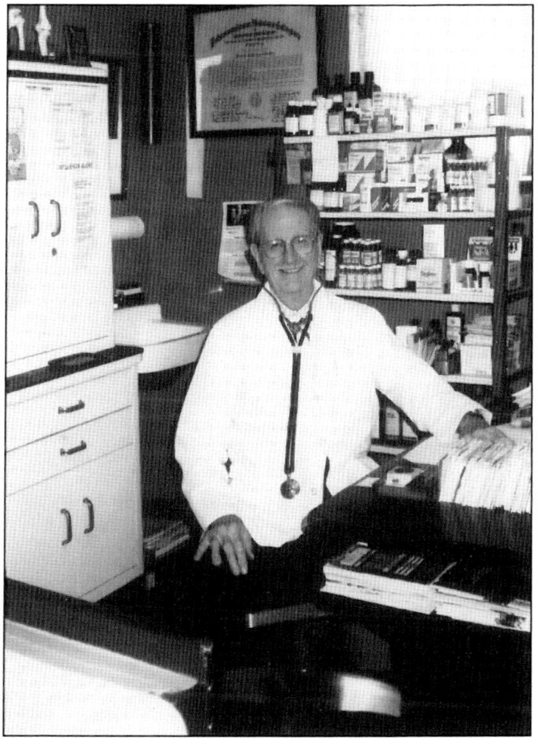

Dr. Joseph Cassidy. Cassidy established his medical practice during World War II while awaiting a call into military service. He had previously applied for a commission into the Army but the call never came. He has served the Cresson area for over a half century, and in 1985 he was among the first laymen of the Diocese of Altoona-Johnstown to become a Permanent Deacon at the St. Francis Xavier Church.

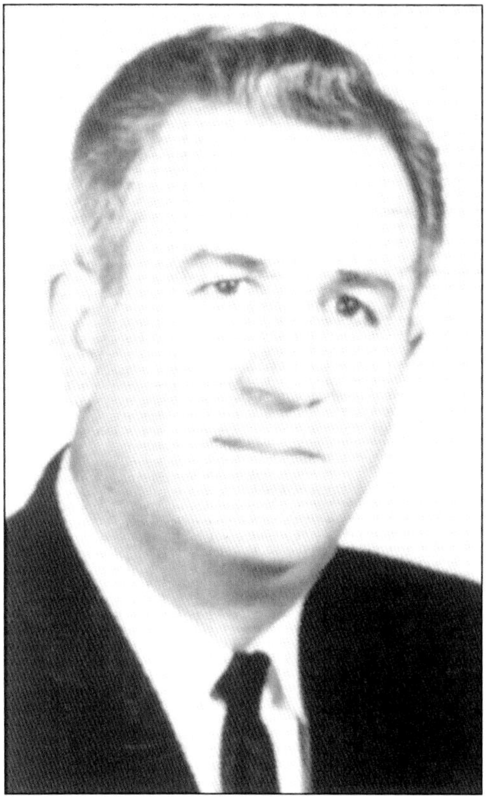

Joseph Roberts. Roberts was a railroad patrolman when he was appointed chief county detective, then deputy sheriff, and then treasurer. In 1959 he was elected commissioner, a position he held for three decades. He was elected three times to the Democratic National Convention and holds an Honorary Doctor of Law Degree from St. Francis College.

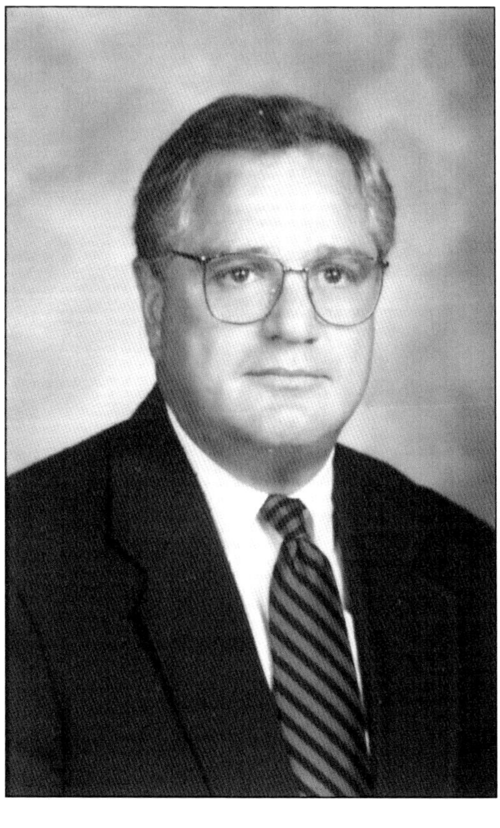

Jay Roberts, a graduate of St. Francis College. Roberts ranked first in his class at the Municipal Police Academy in Indiana (IUP). He worked on the railroad as a welder, served as the mayor of Sankertown Borough, and then became detective of Cambria County in 1977. In 1986 he was elected sheriff of Cambria County.

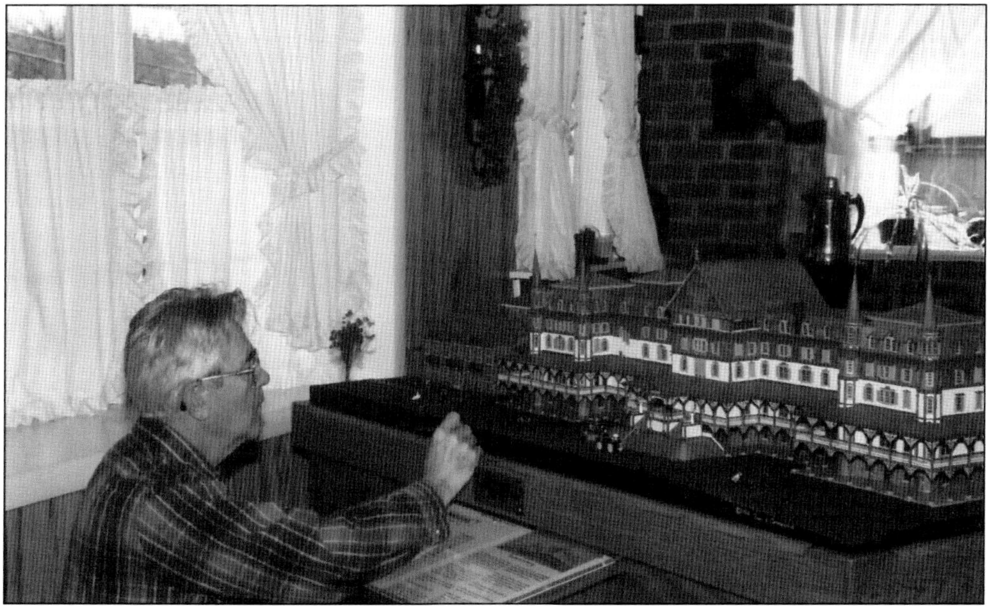

Fred Connacher. Connacher was long associated with the Pennsylvania Coal and Coke Co, Aircraft Drafting, and mining machinery. He studied art on Saturdays at Mount Aloysius, an experience that served him in the military. He later scaled models of the #9 Colliery Shaft, the Allegheny Portage Railroad Museum, and, in 1990, he completed an authentic reproduction of the Mountain House.

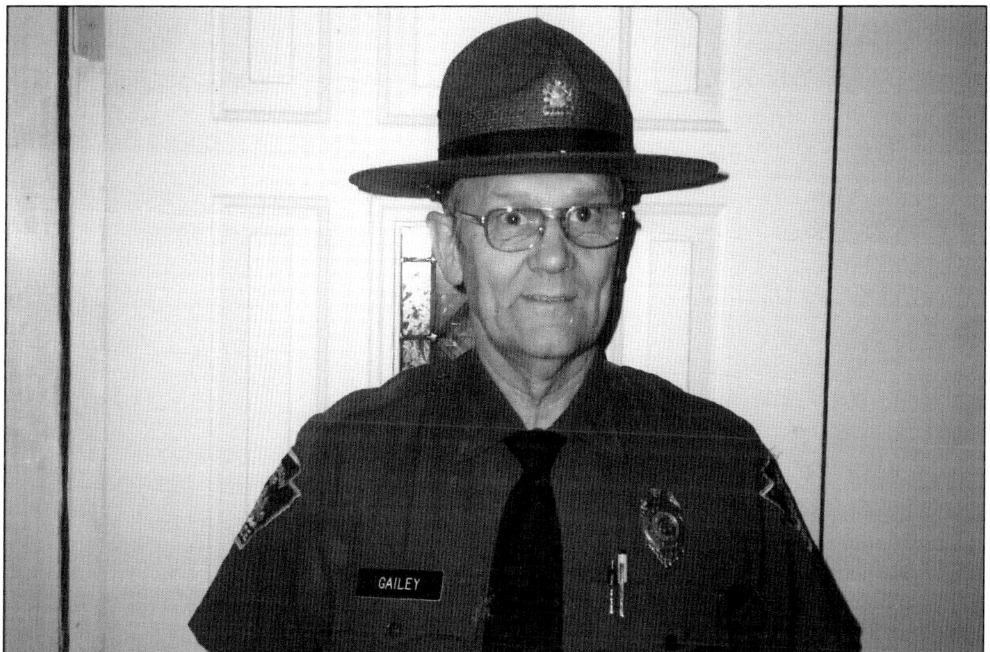

Cliff Gailey, a Cresson native. Gailey served the township as chief of police for twenty-six years. He married Lois O'Donnell and the couple have seven children. They have collected an elegant display of Cresson memorabilia and have converted their basement into a gallery of history.

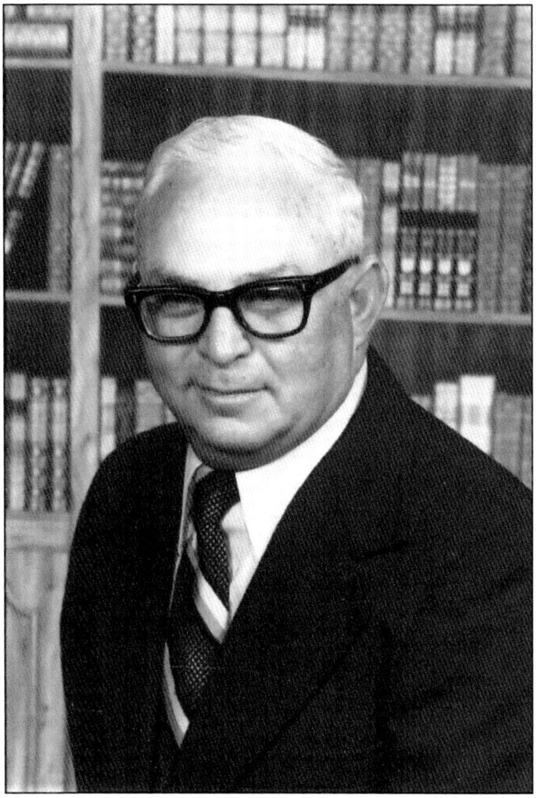

Clarence Eger, a native of the area. A Cresson Township supervisor for nearly a half century, Eger began in the coal mines. He was instrumental in the establishment of a new township building, paved roads, updated water lines, and a new pump station, among many other improvements in the township.

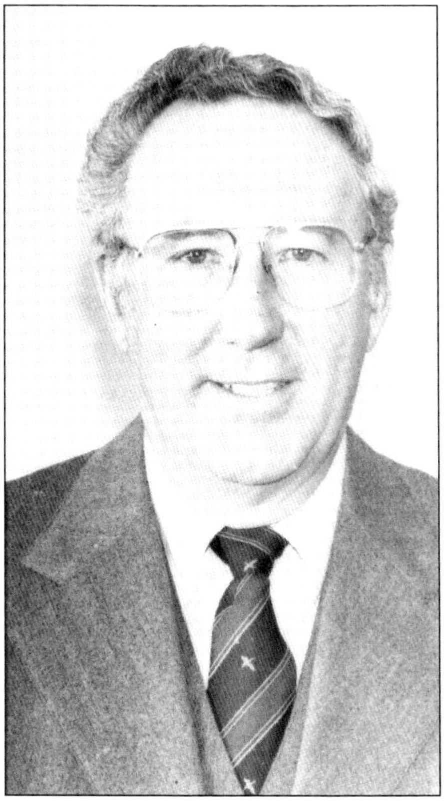

H. Connell Lang, the son of George Lang. The elder Lang bought Stout Insurance in 1910, and H. Connell took over the business in 1956, following his discharge from the Navy. In 1937 the Cambria County Federal Savings and Loan Association was established at the same site, where it remained until 1981. Connell served on the board of trustees at the Mount and is on the president's board at St. Francis College, which he graduated from in 1953.

Five

Cresson Takes Its Place in History

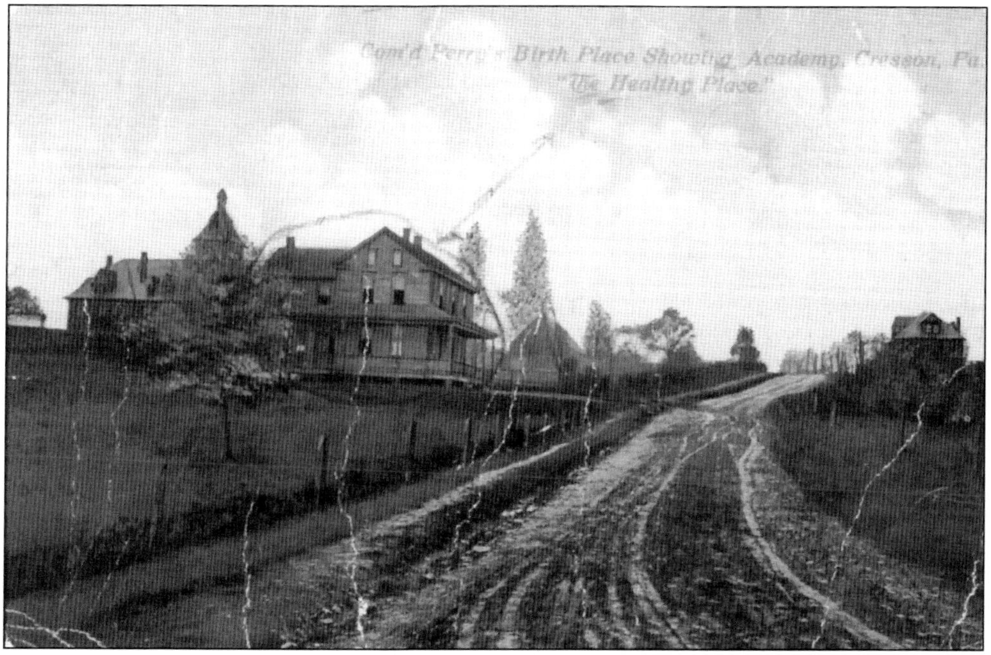

The birthplace of Admiral Robert E. Peary, *c.* 1916. Built before 1850, this house was located along the "The Pike" near the fork of two historical roads—the state turnpike (later called William Penn Highway, or Route 22), which linked Philadelphia and Pittsburgh, and Loretto Plank Road. Mount Aloysius Academy is in the left background, and the Mount Guest House is on the right. The Peary House was razed in 1983.

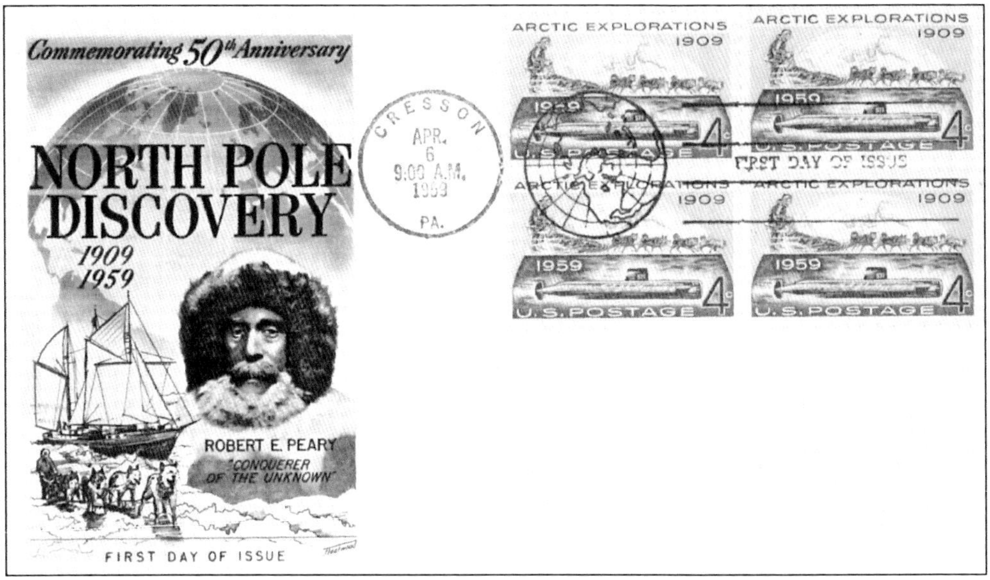

The Arctic Explorations postage stamp This stamp was released at Cresson on April 6, 1959, commemorating the 50th anniversary of the discovery of the North Pole. Peary's parents, Charles and Mary Wiley Peary, migrated from Maine and joined relatives in the shook business (the manufacture of barrel heads and staves). Robert Peary was born on May 6, 1856.

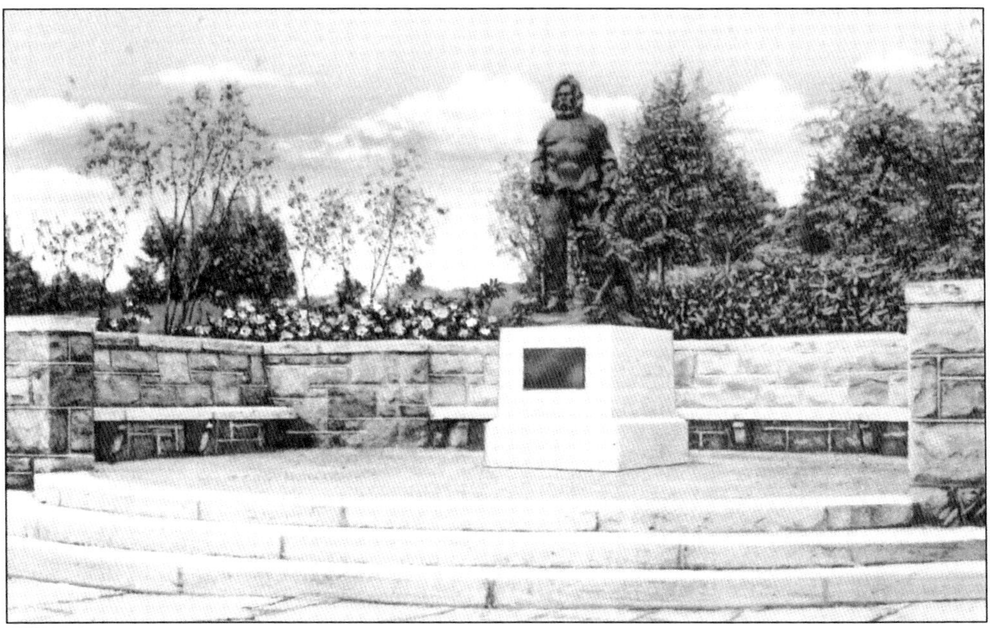

Admiral Robert E. Peary. Peary conquered the unknown when he discovered the North Pole on April 6, 1909. This monument of Peary with his Eskimo sled dog was dedicated in 1937 near his birthplace. Peary's daughter Marie—or "Snowbaby" as she was sometimes called, because she was born in Greenland and her white skin fascinated the Eskimos—unveiled the statue of her famous father.

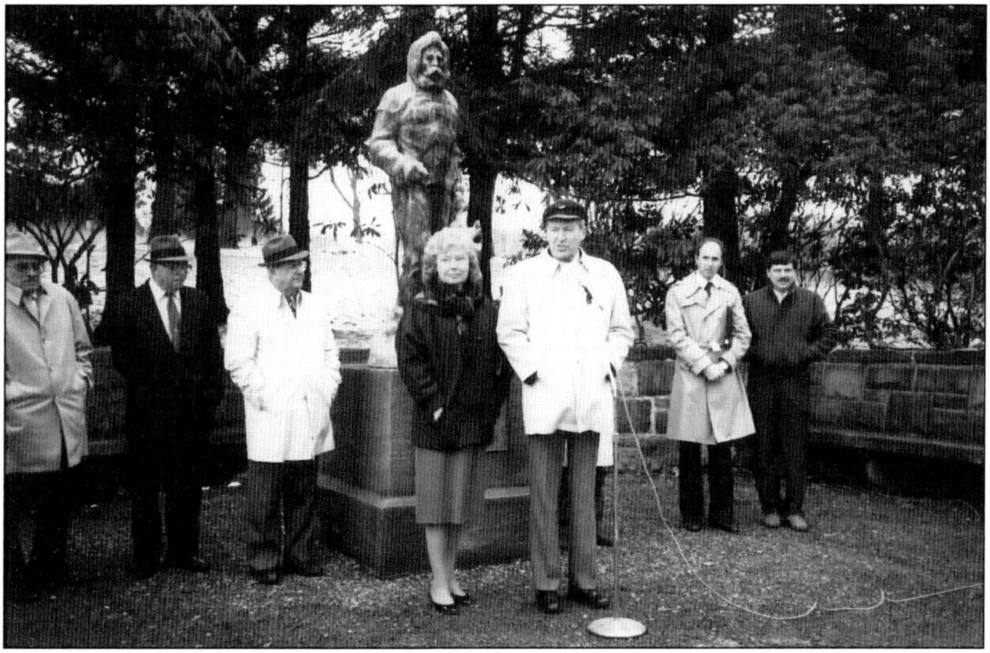
Peary's grandson, Commander Edward Peary Stafford. Stafford visited Cresson with his wife Charlene in April 1989, on the 80th anniversary of his celebrated grandfather's achievement. Shown here are Chairman Norman Weiland, Supervisor Clarence Eger, Commissioner Joseph Roberts, Commander and Mrs. Edward Peary Stafford, Michael McGuire (a Charter member of the Cresson Area Historical Association Inc.) and President Charles Miller.

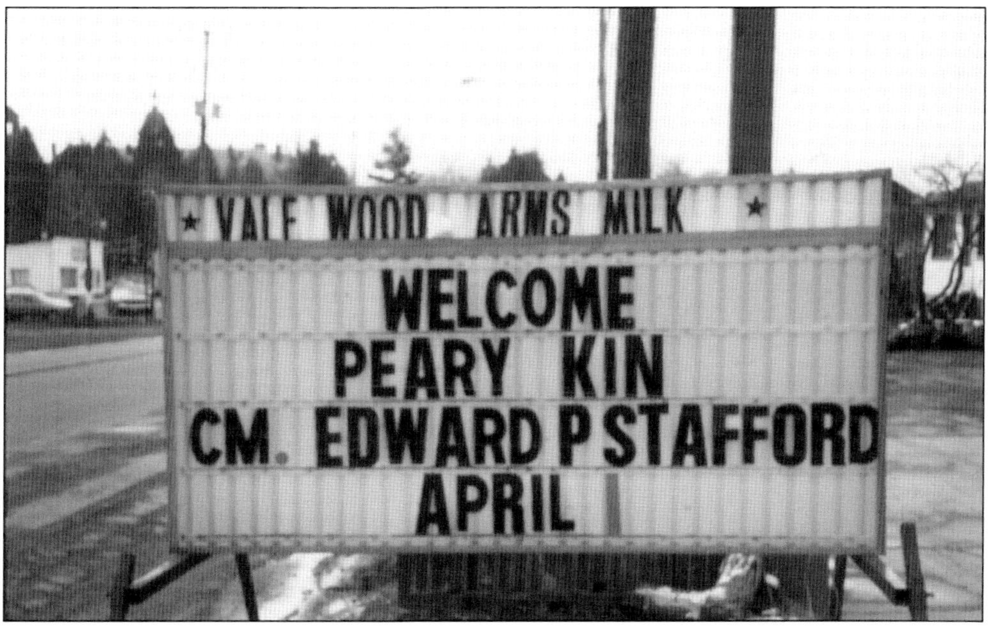

Miller's service station, near the site of the historic monument. On April 1, 1989—the 80th anniversary of Peary's historic discovery—a welcome awaited Commander Edward Stafford and his wife.

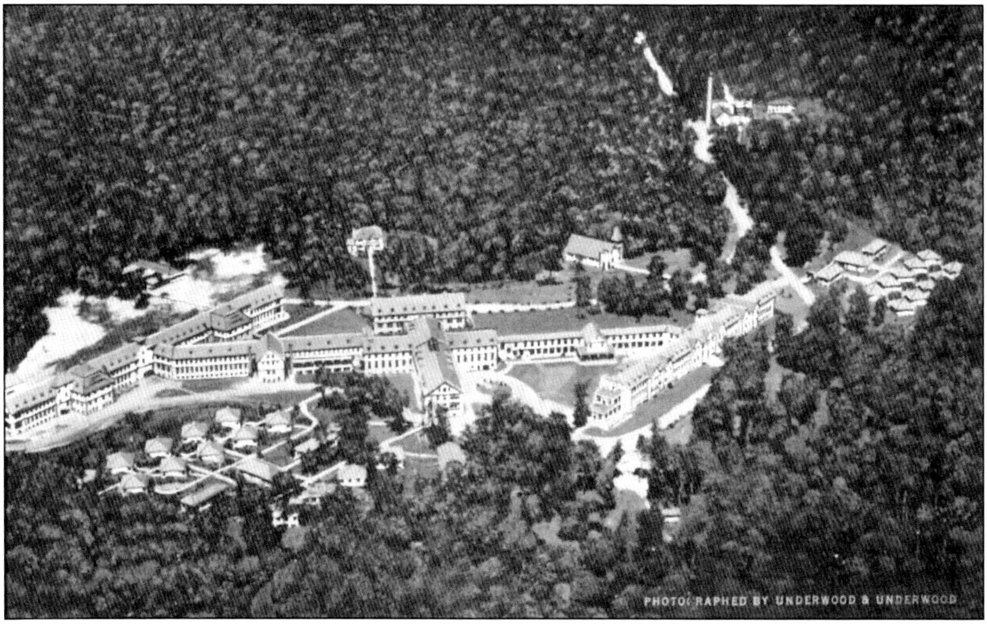

The Pennsylvania State Sanitarium, established at Cresson Summit on 500 acres of land donated by Andrew Carnegie. Opened in January 1913 for the care of tubercular patients, it served for over half a century. The first buildings erected were the administration building, the dining hall, and the east wing, which were all connected through corridors. This institution is presently a large correctional facility.

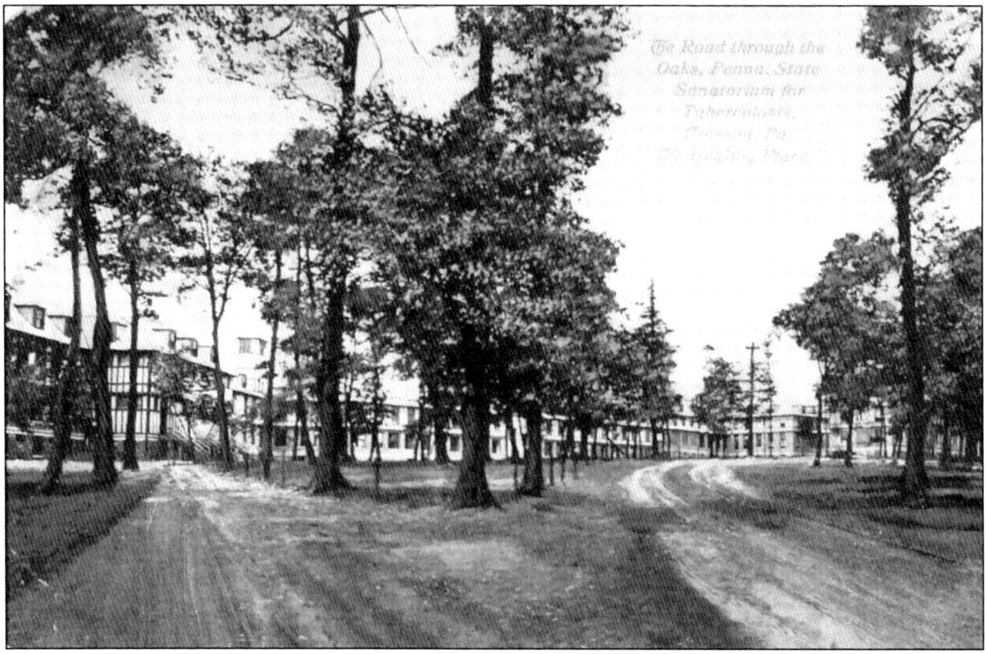

The "San." High up on the crest of the mountains, 2,500 feet above sea level, in the heart of the Alleghenies, the San afforded patients an opportunity to spend time in "The Healthy Place." Its picturesque setting was believed to be an asset to recovery.

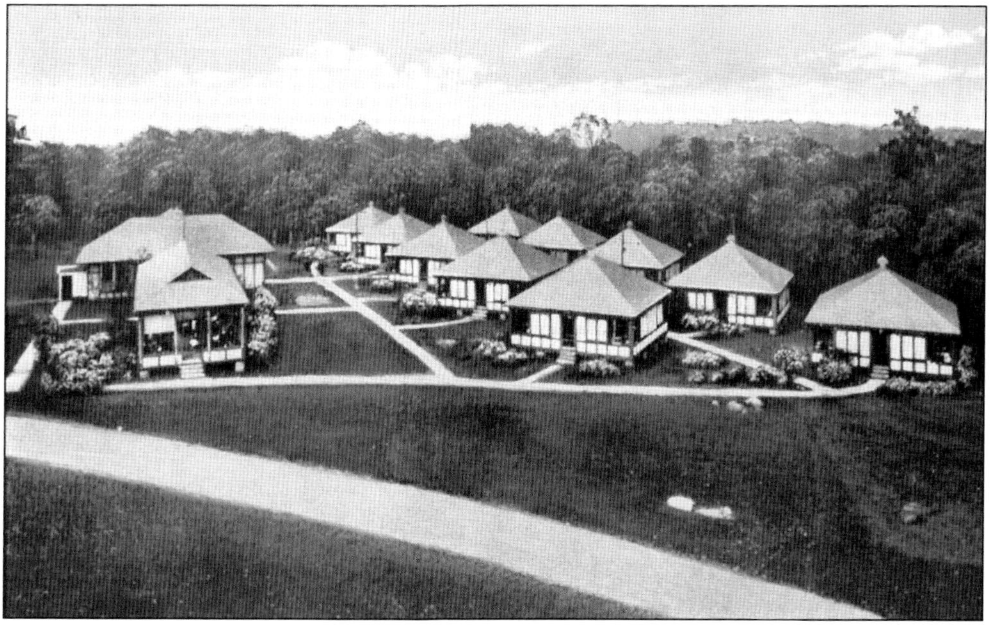

Housing at the San. Twenty cottages and four open pavilions were offered here. The smaller group dwellings, used year-round, provided welcome accommodations to people with moderately advanced cases.

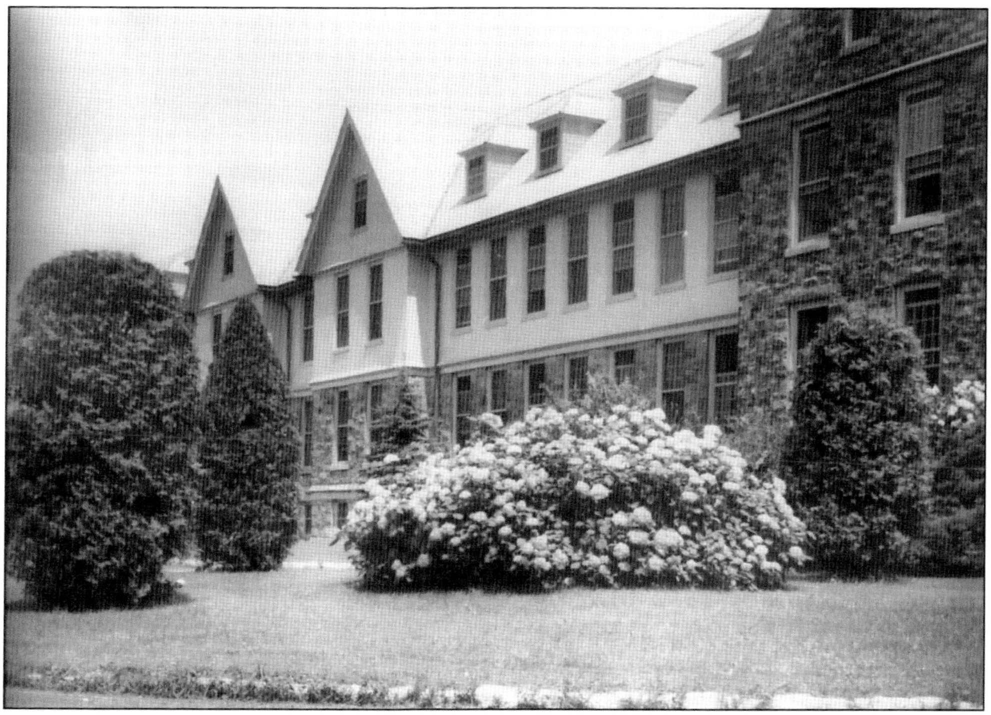

The administration building at the San. The facility had a patient capacity of 750, with 230 beds for children in need of hospital care. William G. Turnbull was first director.

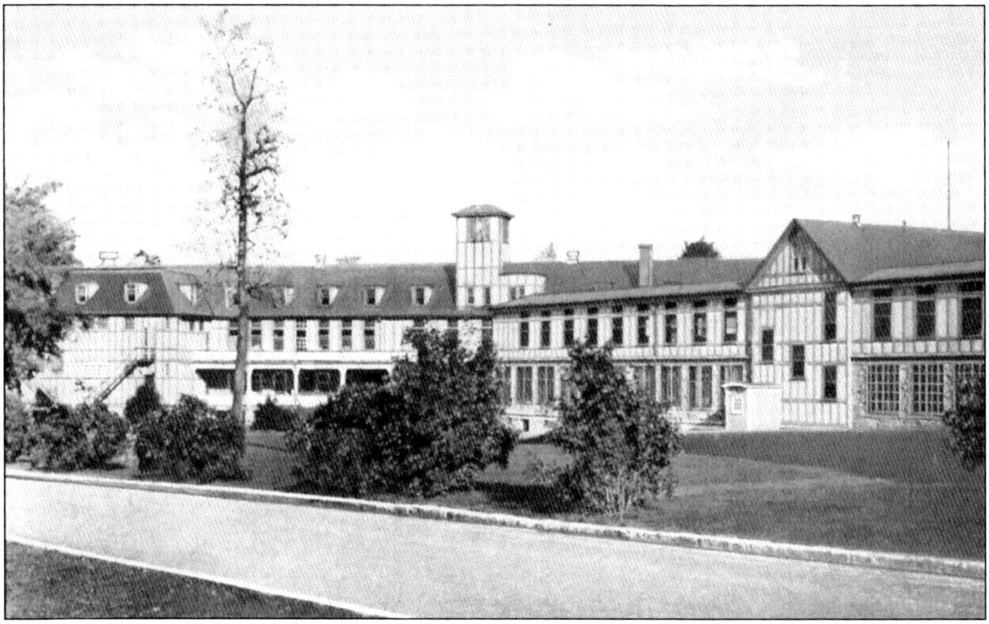

A rising patient population. The number of buildings kept pace with the increase in newcomers, who were retained in receiving wards for evaluation before placement. Sun porches and fresh mountain air were considered essential to combat this disease.

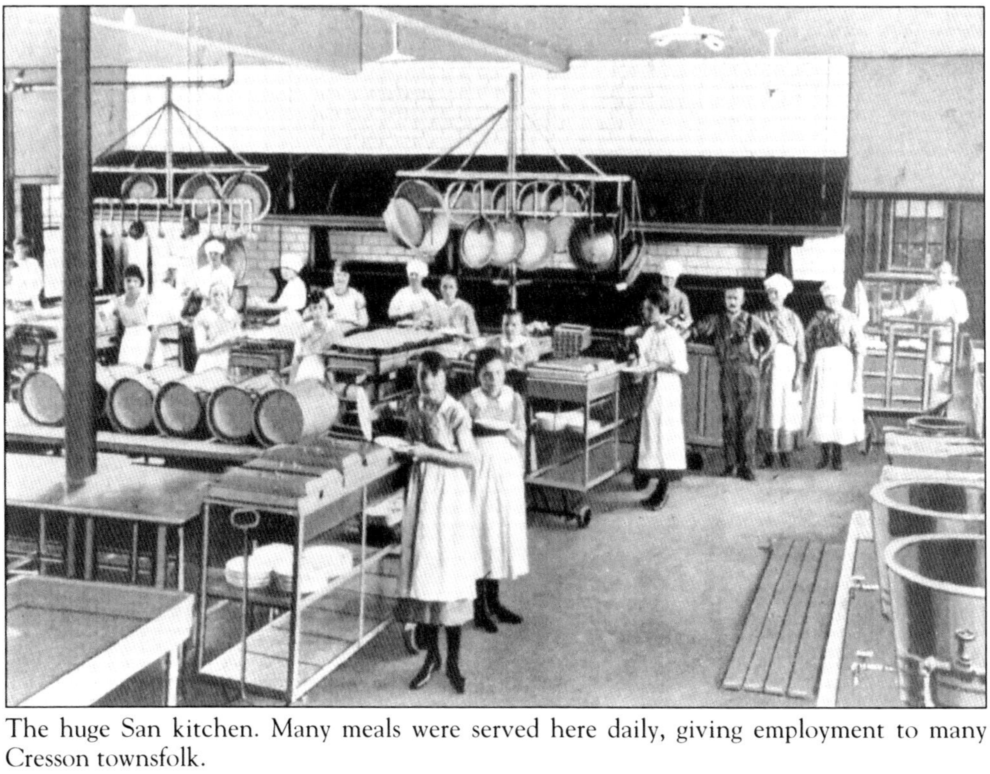

The huge San kitchen. Many meals were served here daily, giving employment to many Cresson townsfolk.

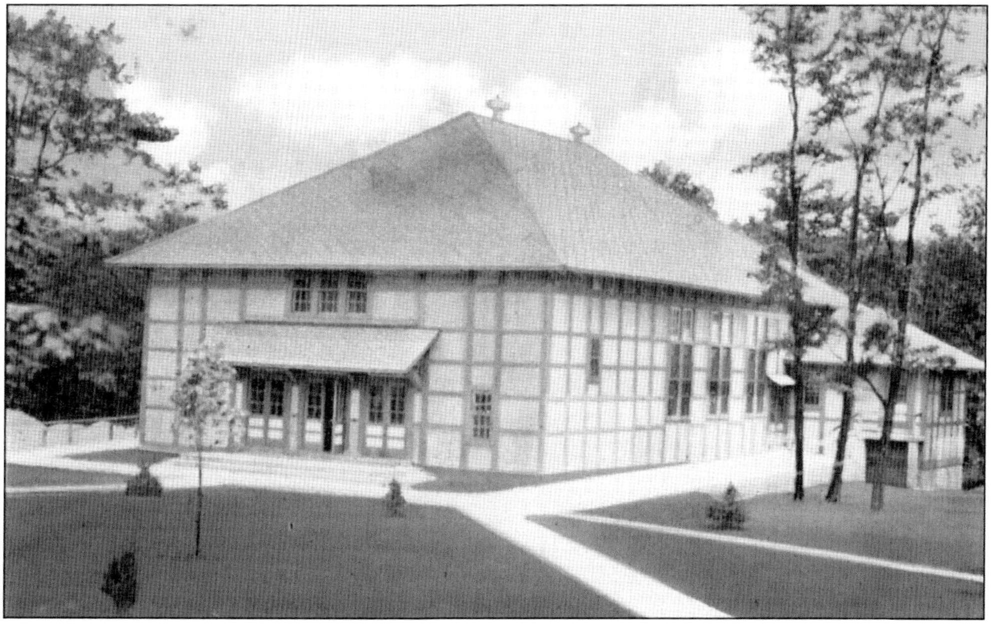

The Amusement Hall at the San. Films and plays for the entertainment of patients and staff were featured here.

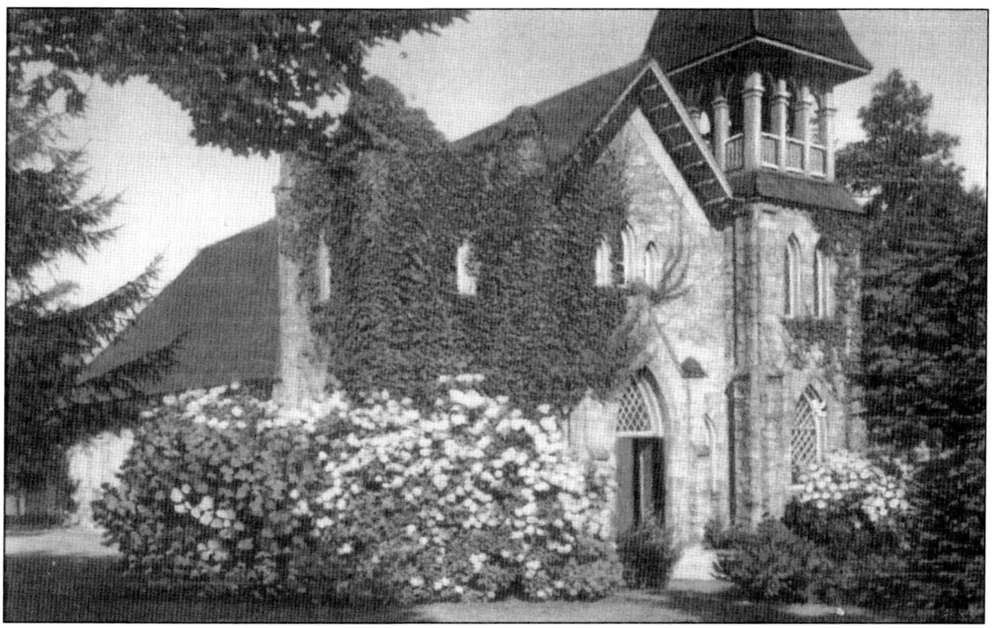

The interdenominational chapel, constructed at the eastern side of the San complex for the benefit of Jewish, Catholic, and Protestant faiths.

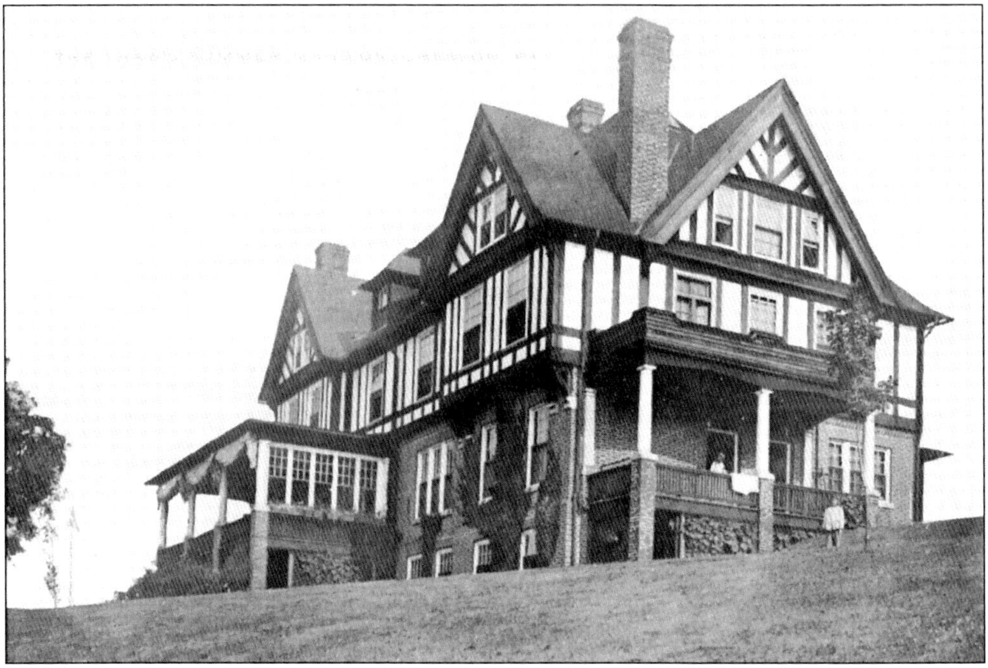

Elmhurst, built about 1900. William Thaw's twenty-room mansion was designed in English Tudor style by Stanford White, a noted New York architect. White's talents went into such structures as Madison Square Garden, where he was later shot by Thaw. The estate is located on a picturesque cliff west of Cresson and is now a private residence. Helen Keller visited Elmhurst in 1927.

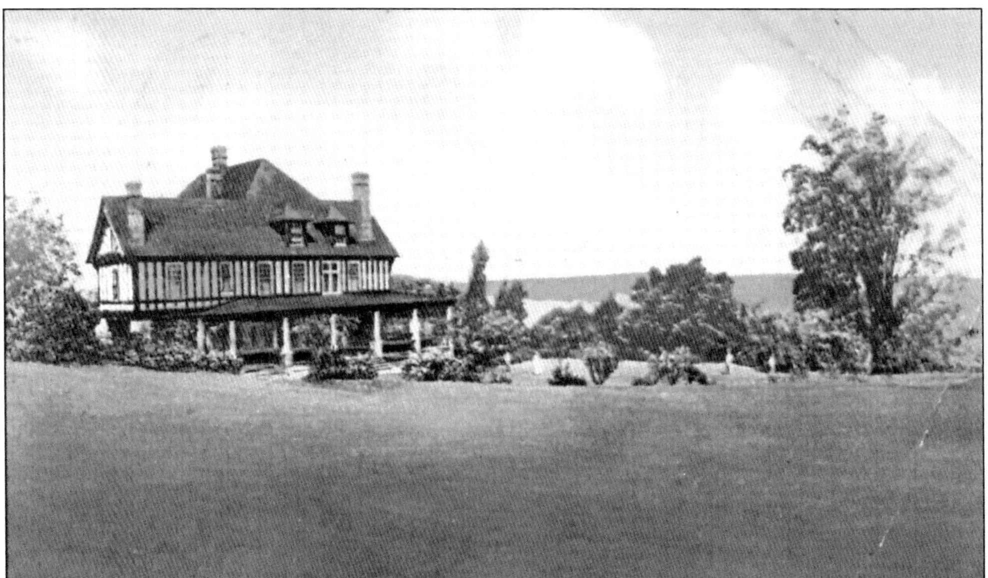

The Elmhurst estate. Multimillionaire William Thaw, a steel magnate of Pittsburgh, had this mansion established for his wife, Mary K., and son, Harry K. Thaw, who summered here amid secluded rolling hills and verdant woodlands.

Tent life on the Thaw estate. During the Depression, Mary Kay Thaw fed the poor, especially children, in tents on her property. The stately elm tree still graces Elmhurst. Mary, William's wife, was responsible for the many maple trees that lined Arch Street.

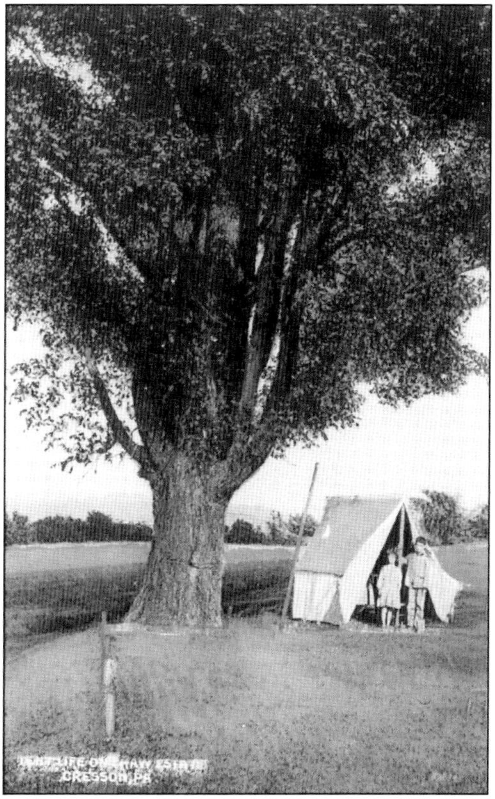

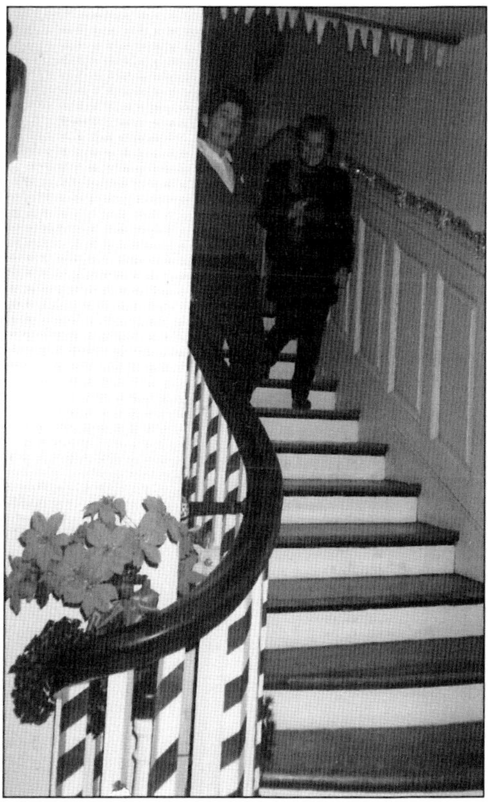

Linda Lewis and Jean Long on a Christmas tour of the palatial mansion. The spacious staircase is characteristic of the elegant interior at Elmhurst.

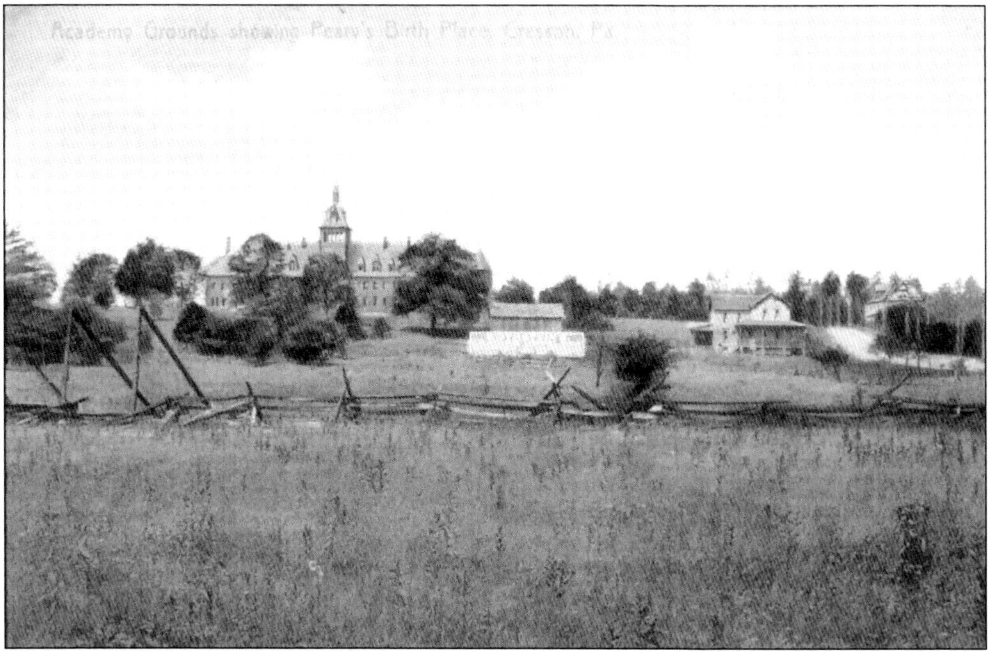

The academy, Peary's birthplace, and the Mount Guest House (which later became a faculty house). The sign on the garage advertises Rothstein's Jewelers, and Route 22 (or William Penn Highway) winds its dusty way westward.

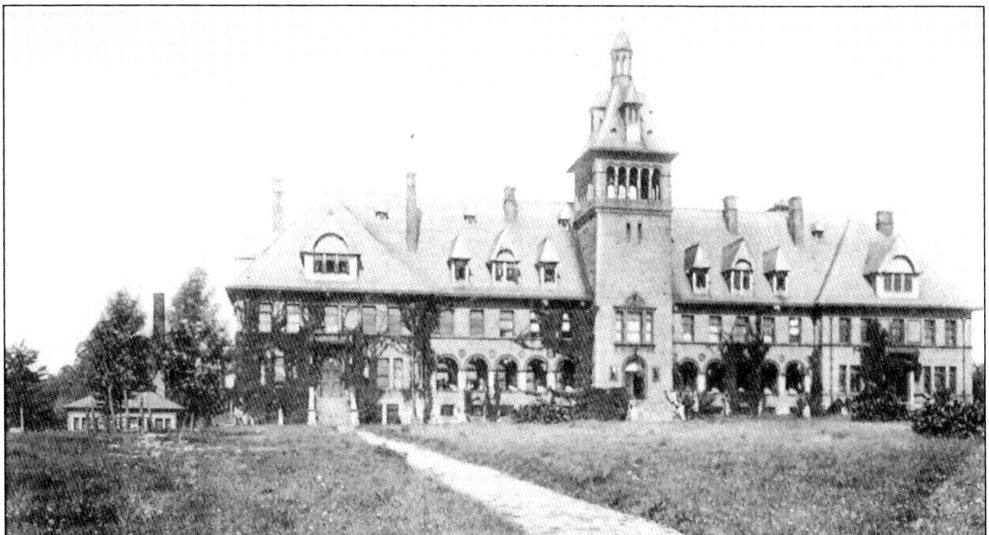

Mount Aloysius Academy. The academy relocated from Loretto to Cresson in 1897 because the new site was accessible to the railroad. The construction took five years; bricks were made on the property and the surrounding woodlands provided much of the interior woodwork, particularly oak, maple, and cherry wood. The commencement of 1897 was the initiation of ceremonies at Cresson.

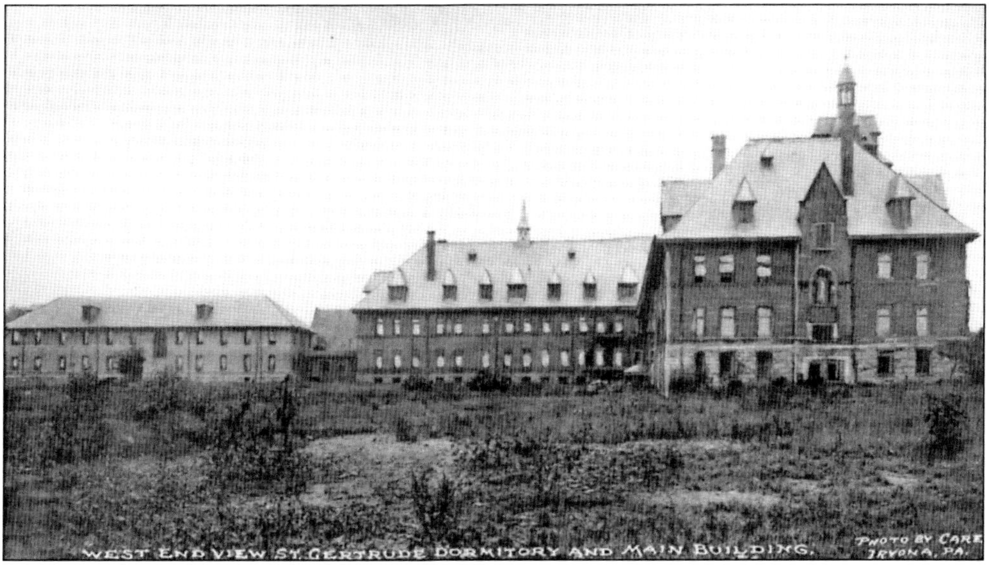

Looking north in 1906 at St. Gertrude Dormitory (a 1904 addition), Alumnae Hall, and the L-shaped main building.

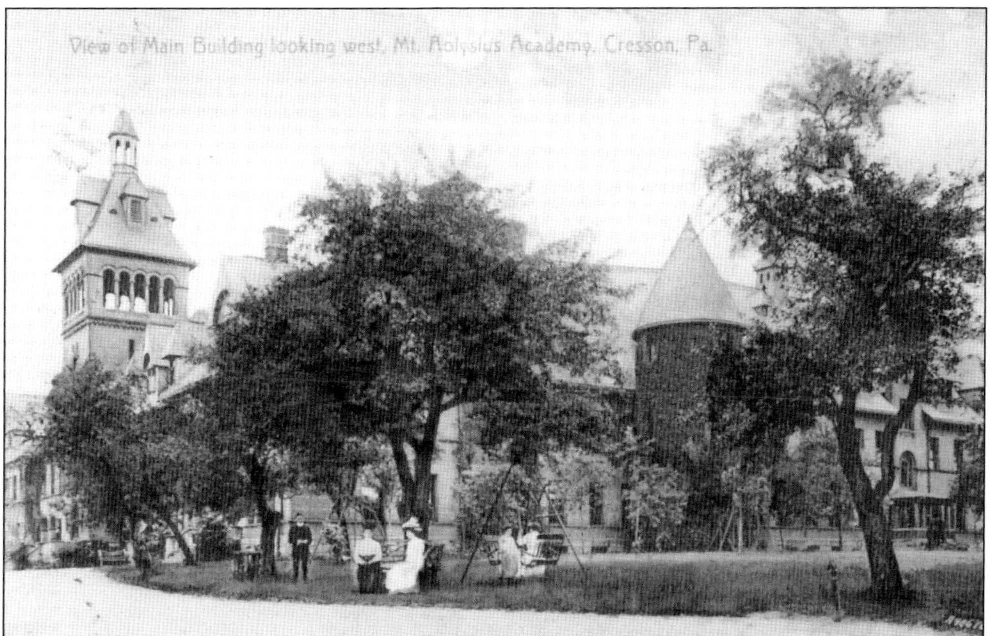

The ivy-covered rotunda and after-class activities, in a 1908 photograph taken facing south from the main gate.

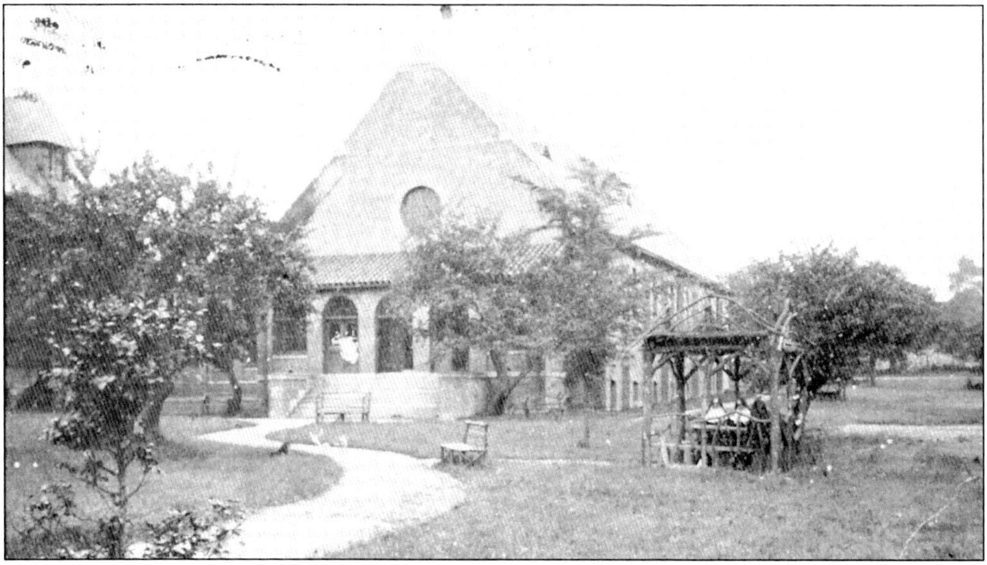

Alumnae Hall, erected in 1902 with the aid of alumnus Charles Schwab. This provided a recreation facility, music hall, and entertainment center.

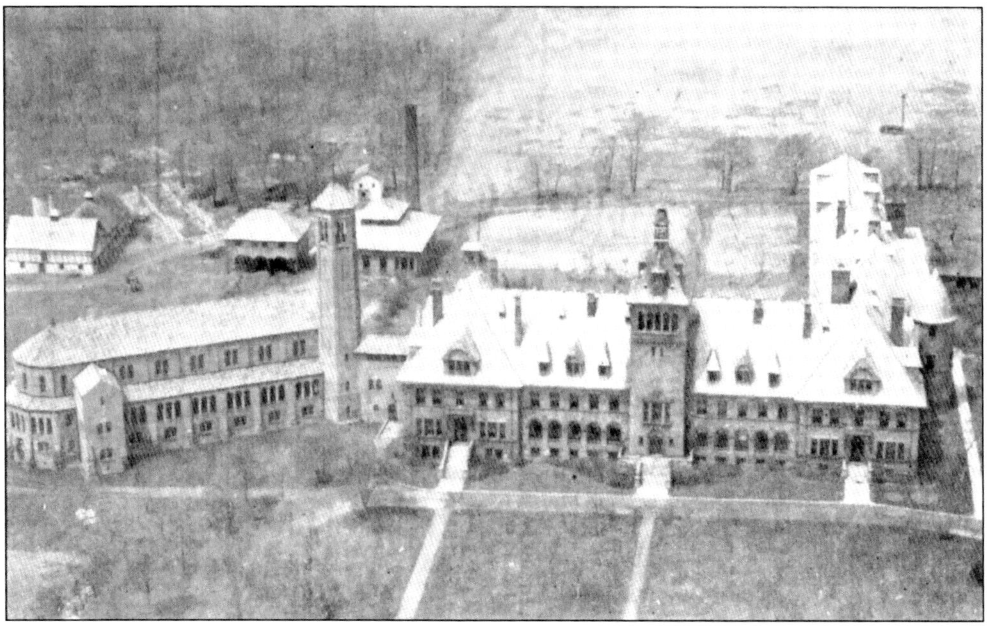

The Mount Complex, after the chapel building was completed in 1923. The barn is in the the far left background, and the three-door garage is still in use! The boiler house, with its skyscraper smokestack, was long the sole source of heat for the complex.

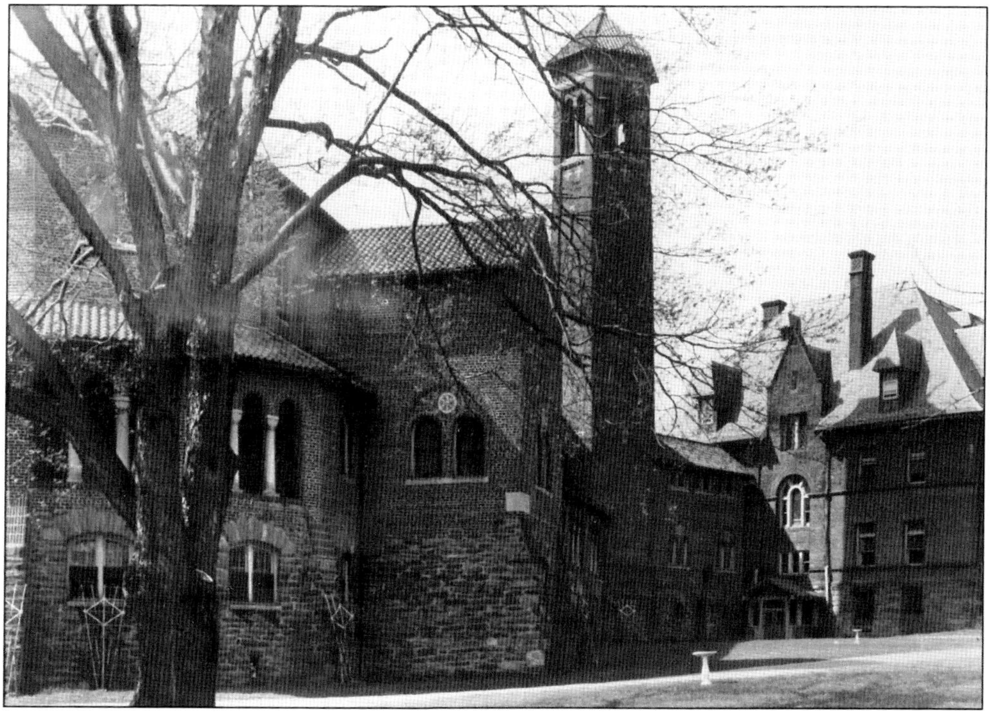

The chapel wing, which housed the convent. This was a welcome addition in 1923. The stone foundation and superstructure merge so that the edifice of variegated brick seems to grow out of the base. Designed in Lombardy Roman style, the rugged base of foxford stone is enhanced by the cloistered arches, creating a monastic effect. The loggia has been enjoyed for many years and the tower has become a landmark.

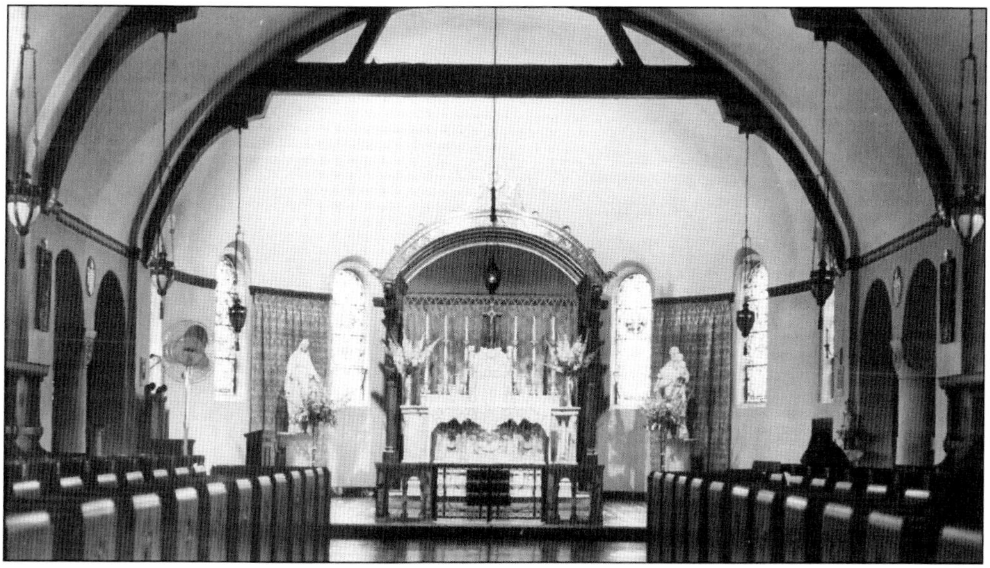

The chapel interior. The Siena marble main altar and railing in the academy chapel were sent from Italy as a gift from Bishop Richard Phelan of Pittsburgh when the area was still part of that Diocese. Spaciousness dominates the sanctuary! Carved oak and vivid stained-glass windows create a meditative, prayerful atmosphere throughout the chapel.

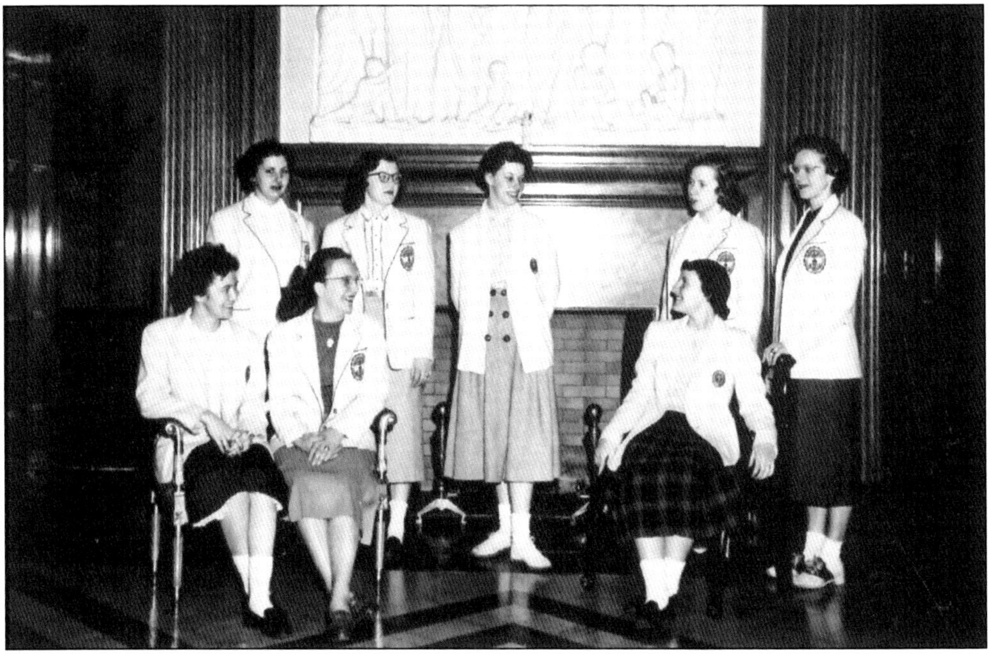

The student council in the main hall at the fireplace, *c.* 1940s. The council has gathered beneath Luca Della Robbia's Singing Gallery, done in bas relief.

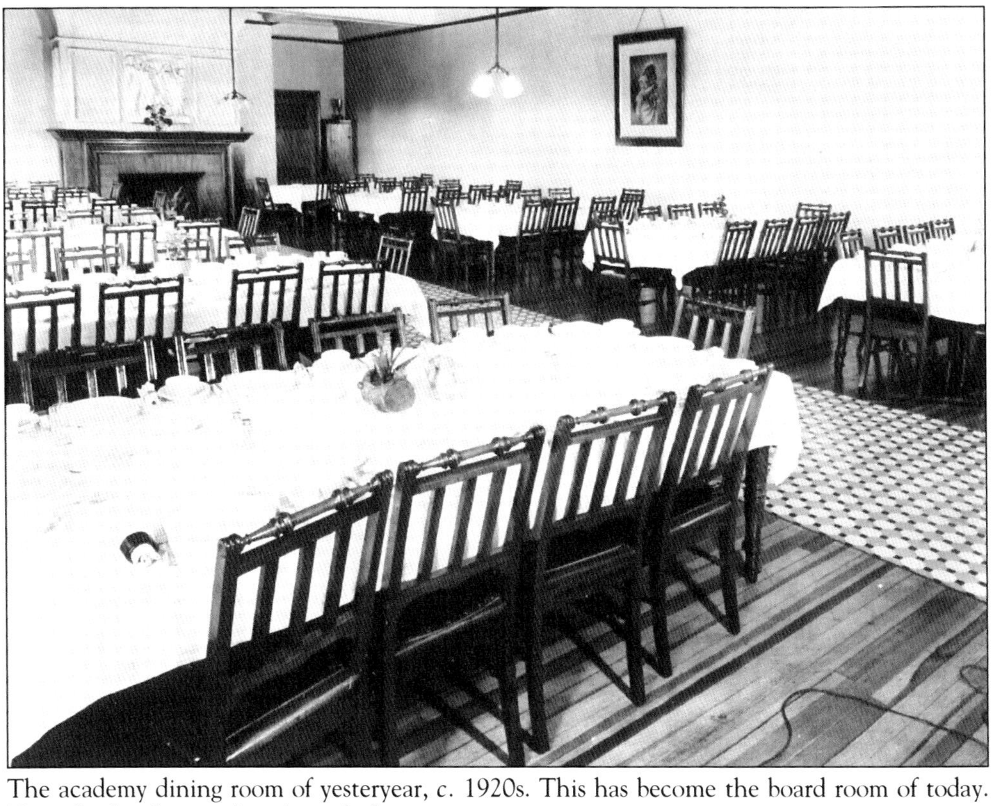

The academy dining room of yesteryear, *c.* 1920s. This has become the board room of today. Note the fireplace with its bas relief.

The class of 1946 choir, sing beneath the stained-glass window of Our Lady of Mercy, brought from Munich by Fred Ihmsen. The singers are, from left to right, as follows: (front row) Helene Sorrentino, Celeste Favoccio, Kitty Lou McGough, Nadine Zugfa, Jane Trexler, and Loretta McCartney Yarnish; (second row) Connie Litzinger Eger, Helen Miller, Margaret Mary Beirlair, Anne Spearing, and Mary Catherine Galbraith.

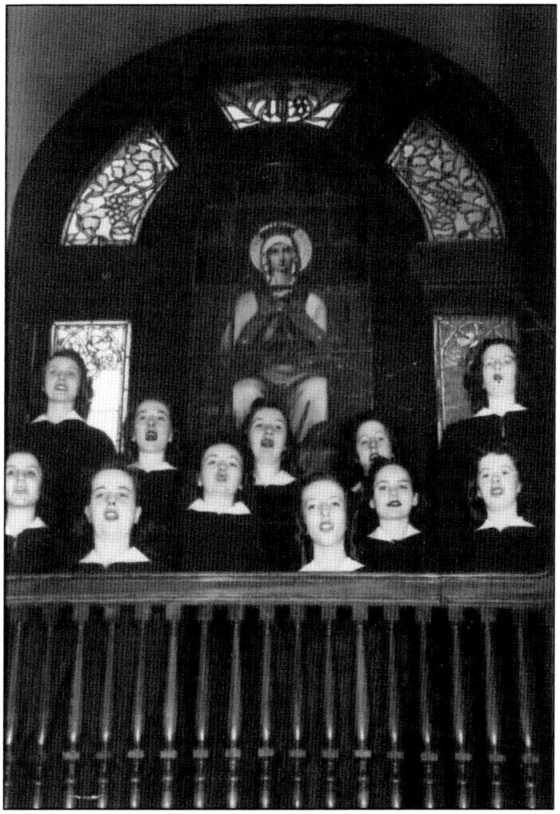

A c. 1940 volleyball game in Alumnae Hall, which doubled as a gym for many years!

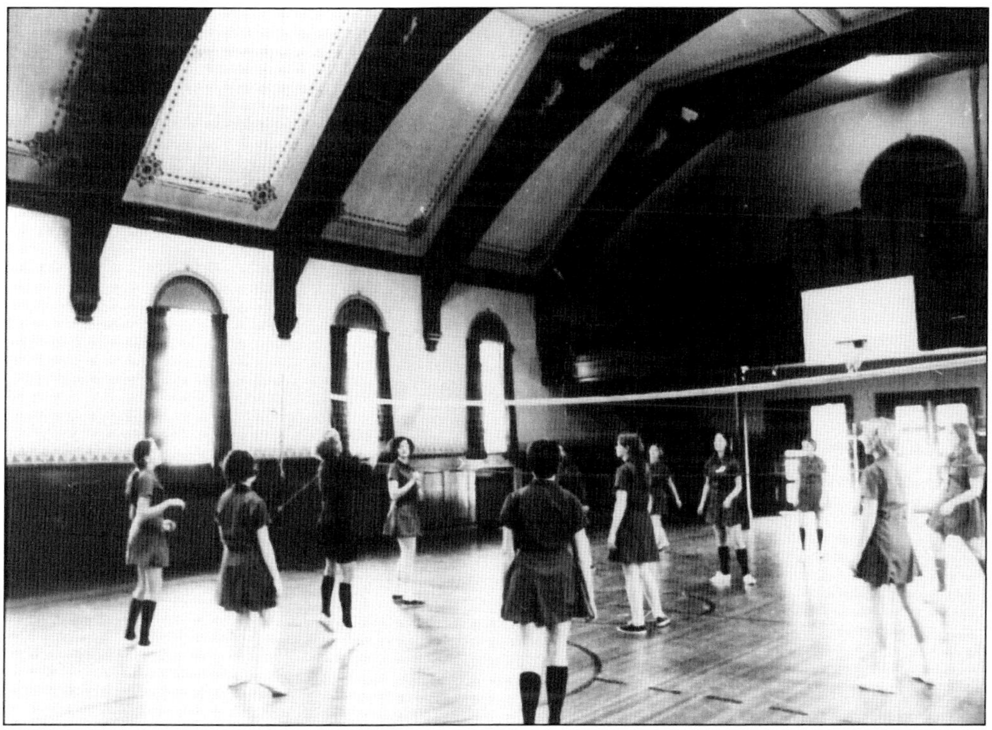

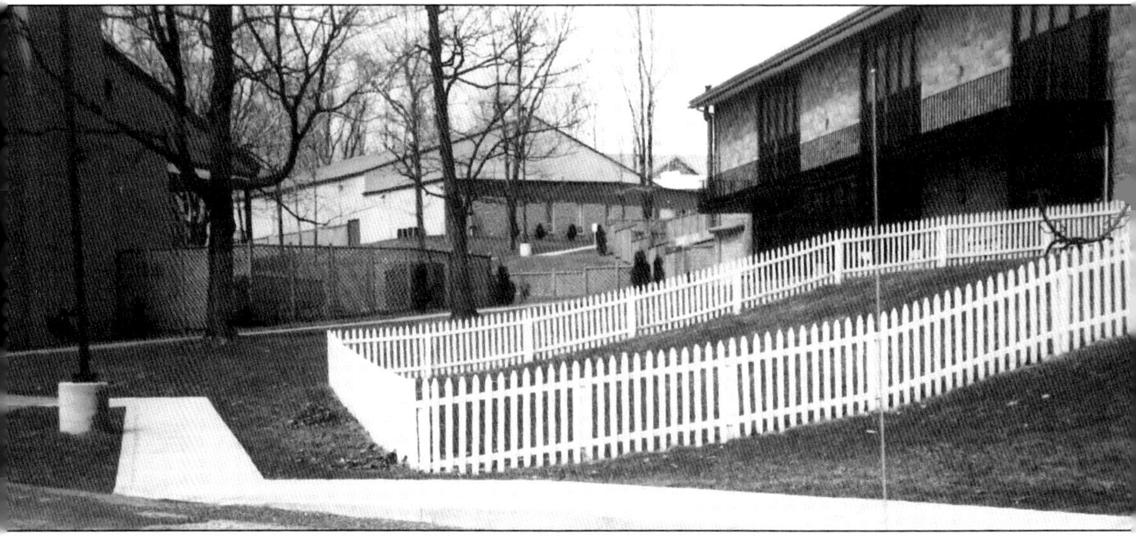

College expansion. Several important additions to the campus can be seen here, including Academic Hall (1992), built to provide much needed classroom space; the Fitness Center (1990), which can accommodate up to three thousand people and features a jacuzzi; the Mt. Aloysius College Library (1995); and the Cosgrave Student Union Center, which features a cafeteria, bookstore, and the "Little Peoples Place," where parents may bring small children while in class.

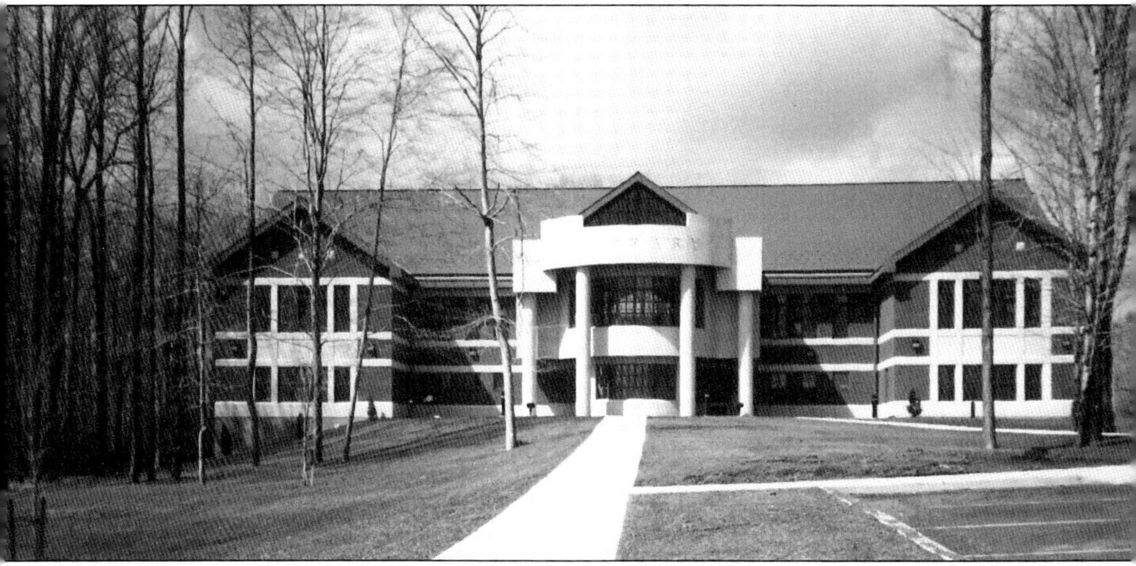

The library. Located on a scenic hilltop overlooking the college complex, it features state-of-the-art equipment, meeting rooms, classrooms, and a law library, while retaining an unique spaciousness and beauty.

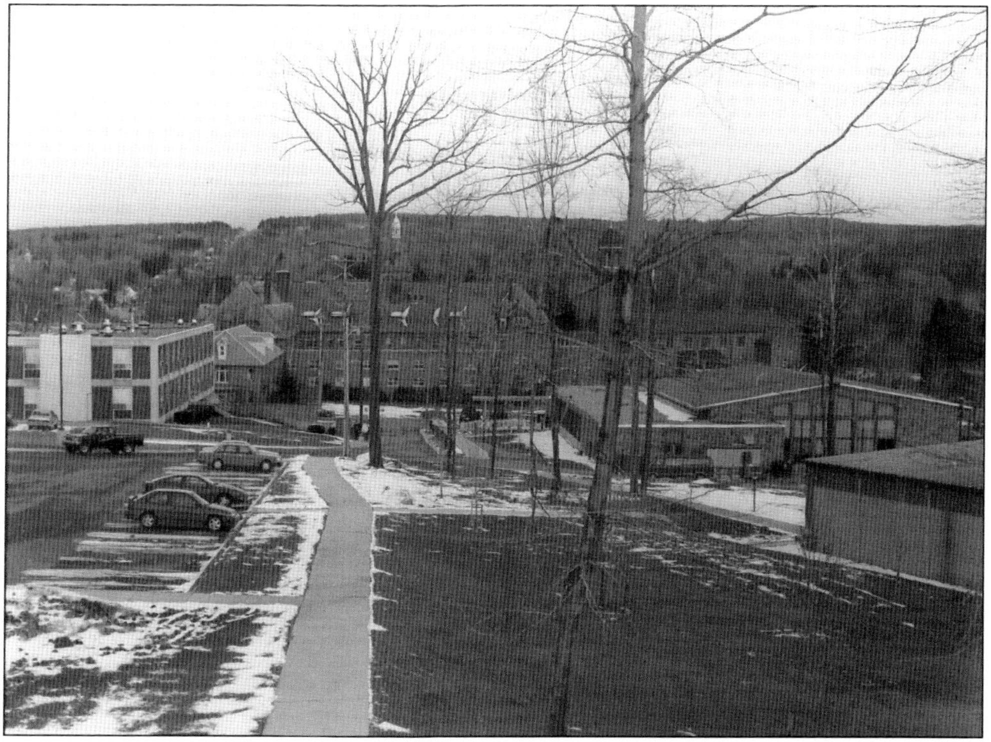

Looking east toward Cresson Mountain and the Summit from a window of the library in March 1996. Ihmsen Hall (left) with its artistic breezeway can be seen, along with St. Gertrude's Dormitory, the main building, the chapel wing, Cosgrave Center, and the Fitness Center.

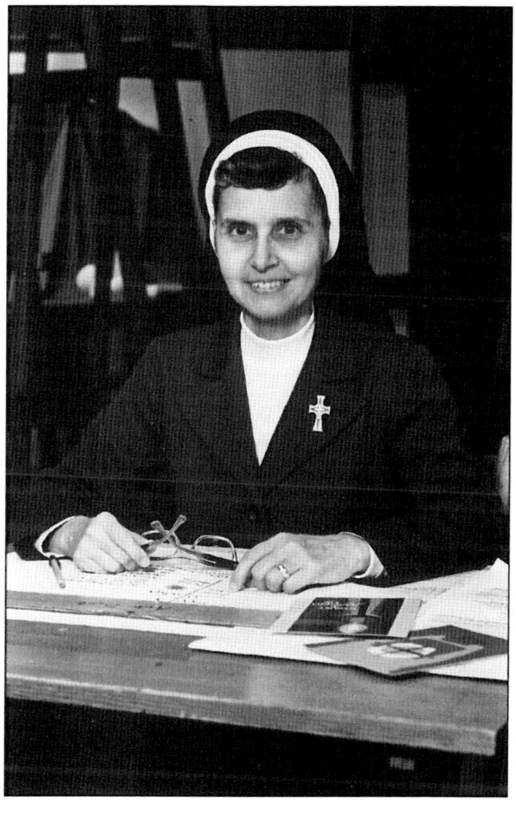

Sister Maria Josephine D'Angelo, wears the international symbol she created in Cresson. Following the Second Vatican Council, religious attire underwent transformations, and artists throughout the country were requested to submit what they envisioned as an appropriate symbol to identify the Sisters of Mercy. Numerous designs were submitted and this one was chosen! It has become an international symbol in all parts of the world where Sisters of Mercy serve.

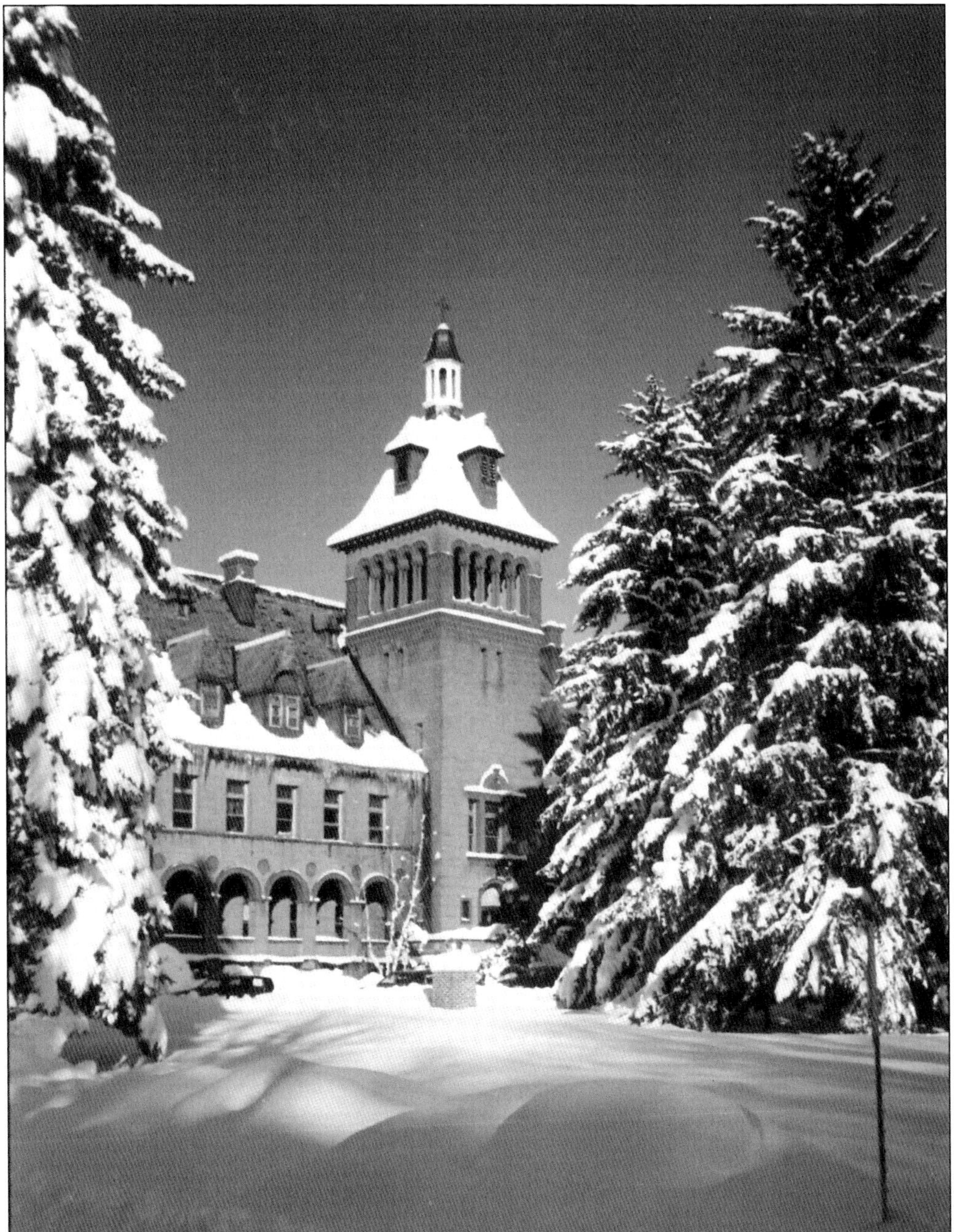

A snowy glimpse of the Mount Aloysius College main building in its centennial year on the Cresson campus. The Sisters of Mercy were founded in Dublin, Ireland, in 1831. The first group to leave their homeland for the American missions came through Loretto in 1843 en route to Pittsburgh. Five years later, in 1848, The Sisters of Mercy were invited to Loretto, thus forming the first religious community of women in what is now the Diocese of Altoona-Johnstown. One century ago (1897) it was deemed advisable to provide greater accessibility to the railroad, and the Mount relocated to Cresson. The sturdy building with its stately towers evolved into a junior college in 1939 and a four-year college in 1990. Enrollment is now in the thousands.

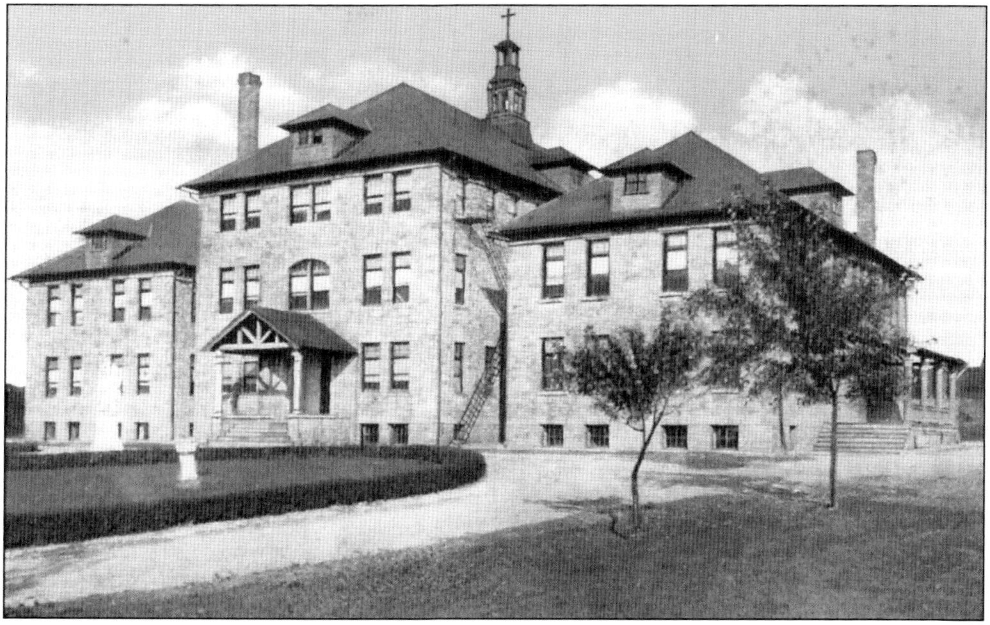

St. John's Orphanage for boys, established on Country Club Road in 1909 and staffed by the Sisters of The Immaculate Heart of Mary. The building, destroyed by fire in 1968, is the site of present Veteran's Park. St. Mary's Orphanage for girls was opened in 1917 on land now occupied by Skills of Central Pa. It was razed in 1983. Both facilities were sponsored by the Diocese of Altoona-Johnstown and closed in 1963.

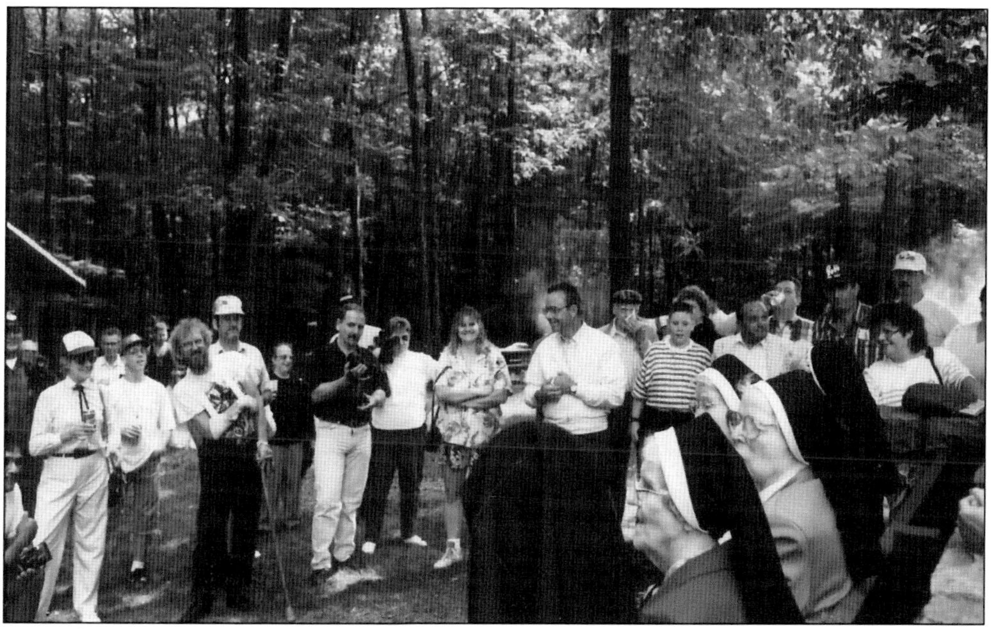

An orphanage reunion. A singular, most unique reunion on August 22 and 23, 1992, brought together many former residents of the orphanages for a weekend of nostalgic memories. Spearheaded by Jack Santucci, who first conceived of the reunion, and aided by his buddies, it dispelled any myths about orphans. In the group of over two hundred members all professions were represented!

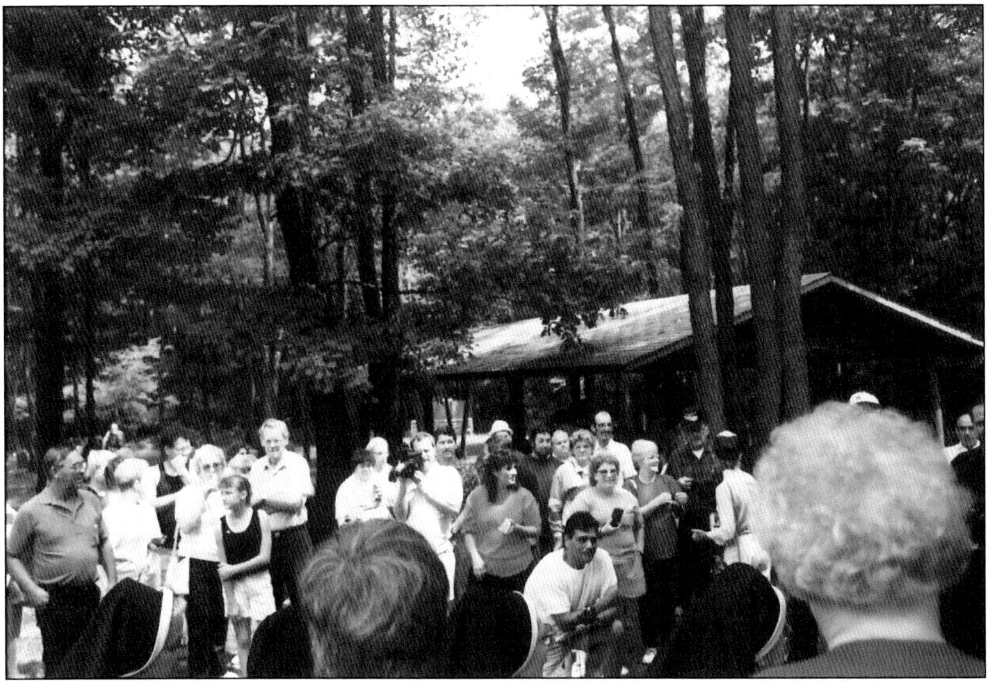

The first-of-its-kind reunion at St. Aloysius Hall, near the site of the former orphanage. An afternoon was devoted to renew old acquaintances and reminisce about childhood days. This was followed by a dinner at St. Aloysius Hall and a dance at the American Legion in Cresson. On Sunday, a picnic at the Allegheny Portage Railroad Picnic Grounds completed the reunion.

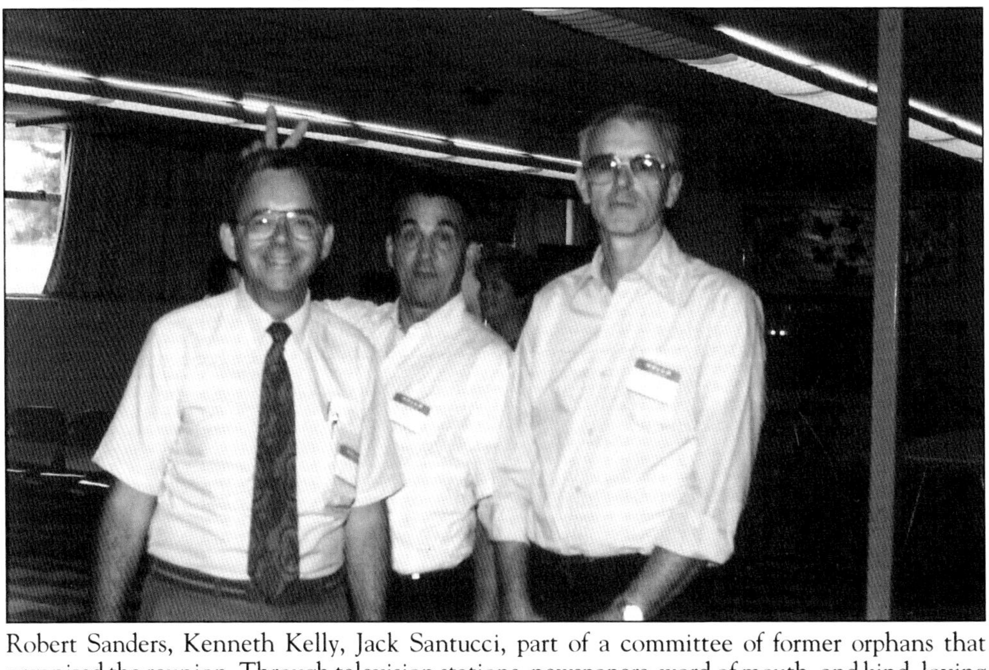

Robert Sanders, Kenneth Kelly, Jack Santucci, part of a committee of former orphans that organized the reunion. Through television stations, newspapers, word of mouth, and kind, loving people they were able to locate 250 former residents representing 18 states and 87 different zip codes, some as distant as California.

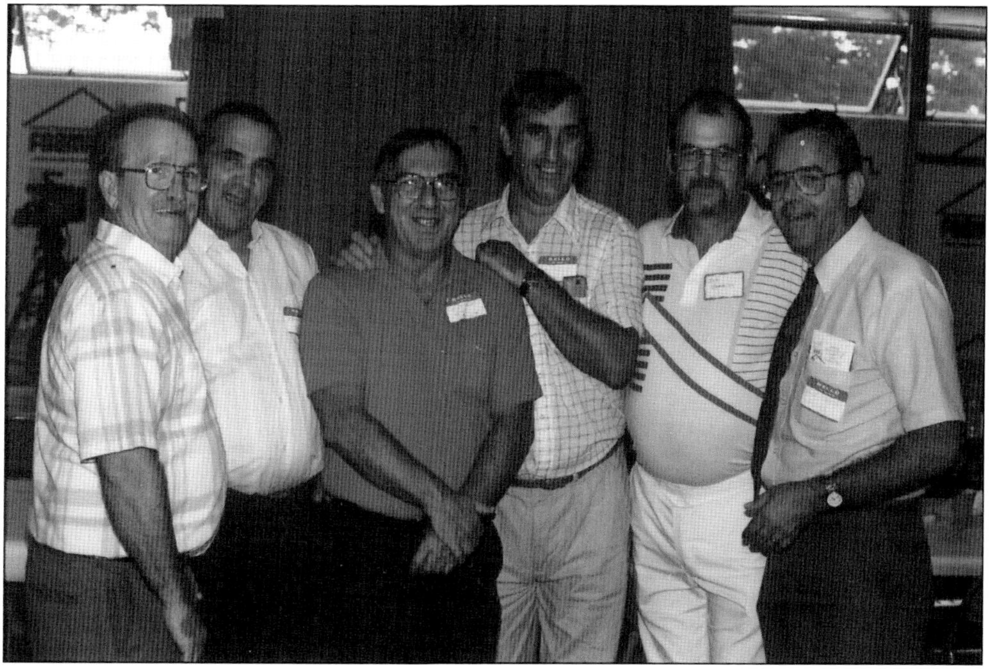

Boyhood days. B. Parks, Kenneth Kelly, Michael Kelly, Ray Cherico, Joe Parrish, and Robert Sanders renew old friendships and share memories.

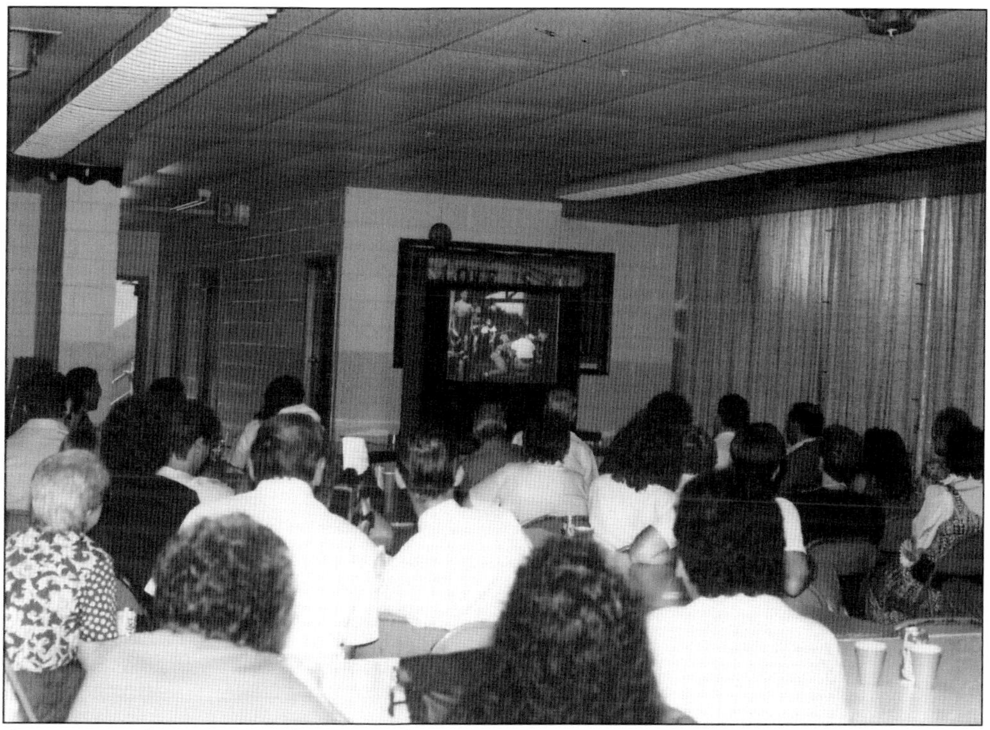

A montage of memories. The group shared a video of old photographs put together for the occasion. Many were intrigued as they saw themselves thirty or forty years ago. The reunion afforded a reacquaintance with a large family, reclaiming a past that seemed exotic.

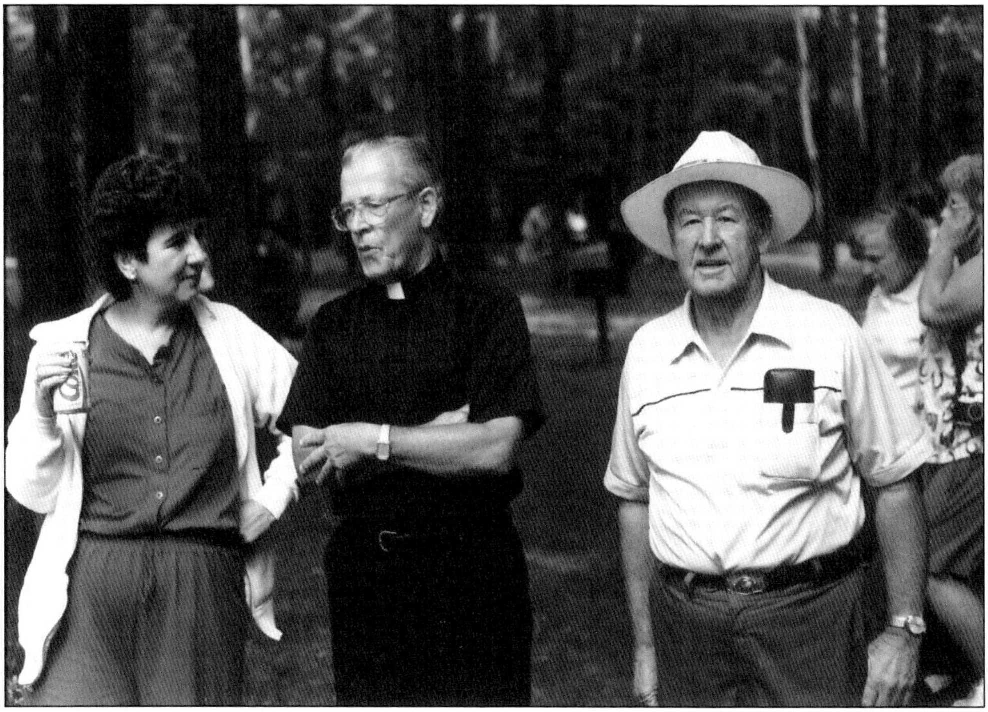

Fr. Gerald Glass and a friend. Fr. Glass, who spent his boyhood days at the orphanage between 1930 and 1942, is the only known priestly vocation among young residents of St. John's. Fr. Glass currently lives in Arizona. He is remembering when . . . and sharing memories with a friend.

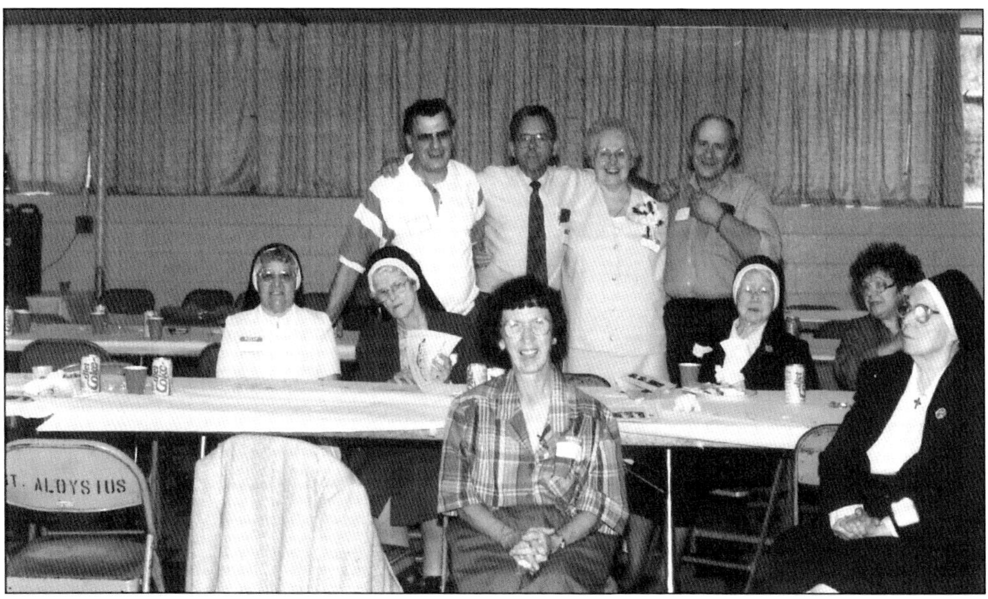

The days of yore. George Swode, Robert Sanders, Sr. deRicci, a friend, Sr. Magaline, Sr. Colombo, Flora Wessner, Sr. Leonella, Louise Hafford, and Sr. Eustace share memories of long ago. The Sisters, many now retired, all served at the orphanage and traveled from Scranton for the reunion.

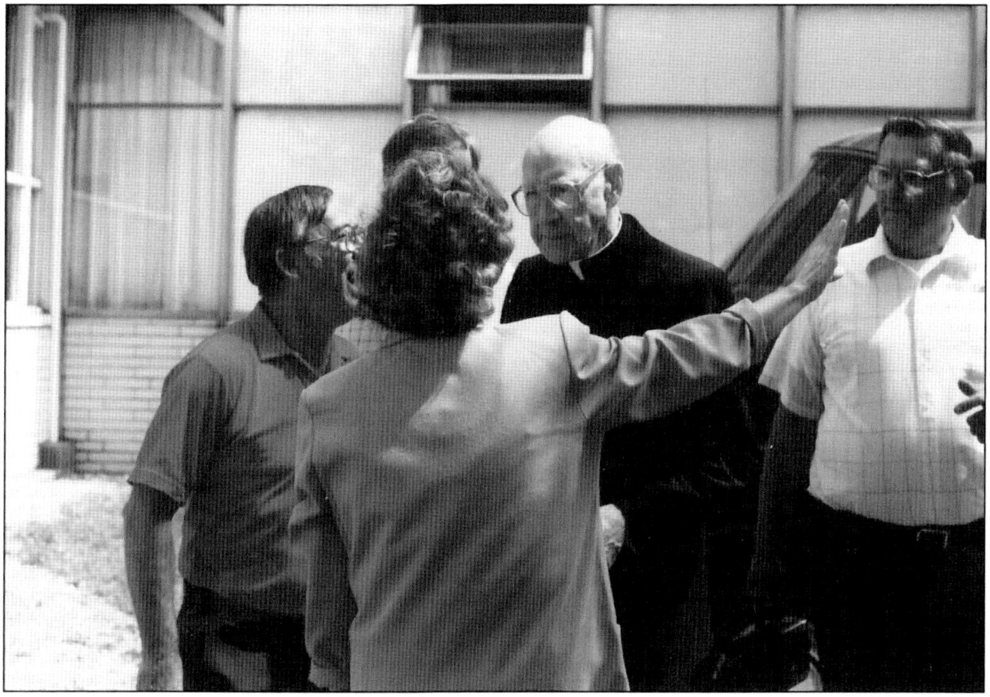

Msgr Francis Ackerson with friends. Msgr. Ackerson spent twelve years as chaplain of the orphanage.

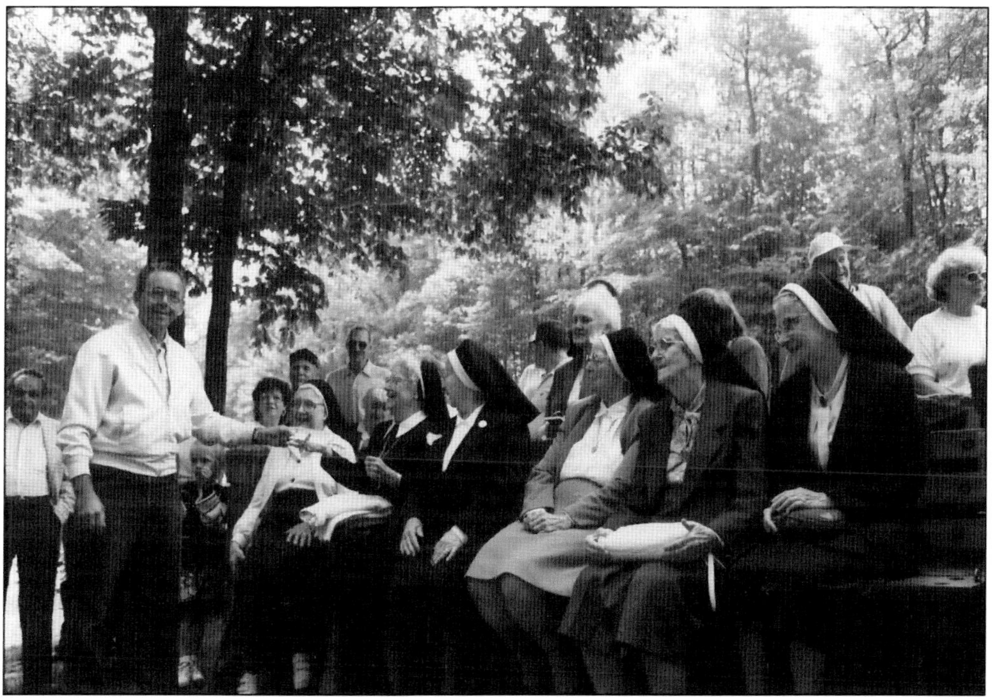

Robert Sanders and Sr. Marie Bernadette IHM. Sanders presented a check to the Sisters Retirement Fund, on behalf of all his fellow orphans, which was accepted by Sr. Marie Bernadette IHM.

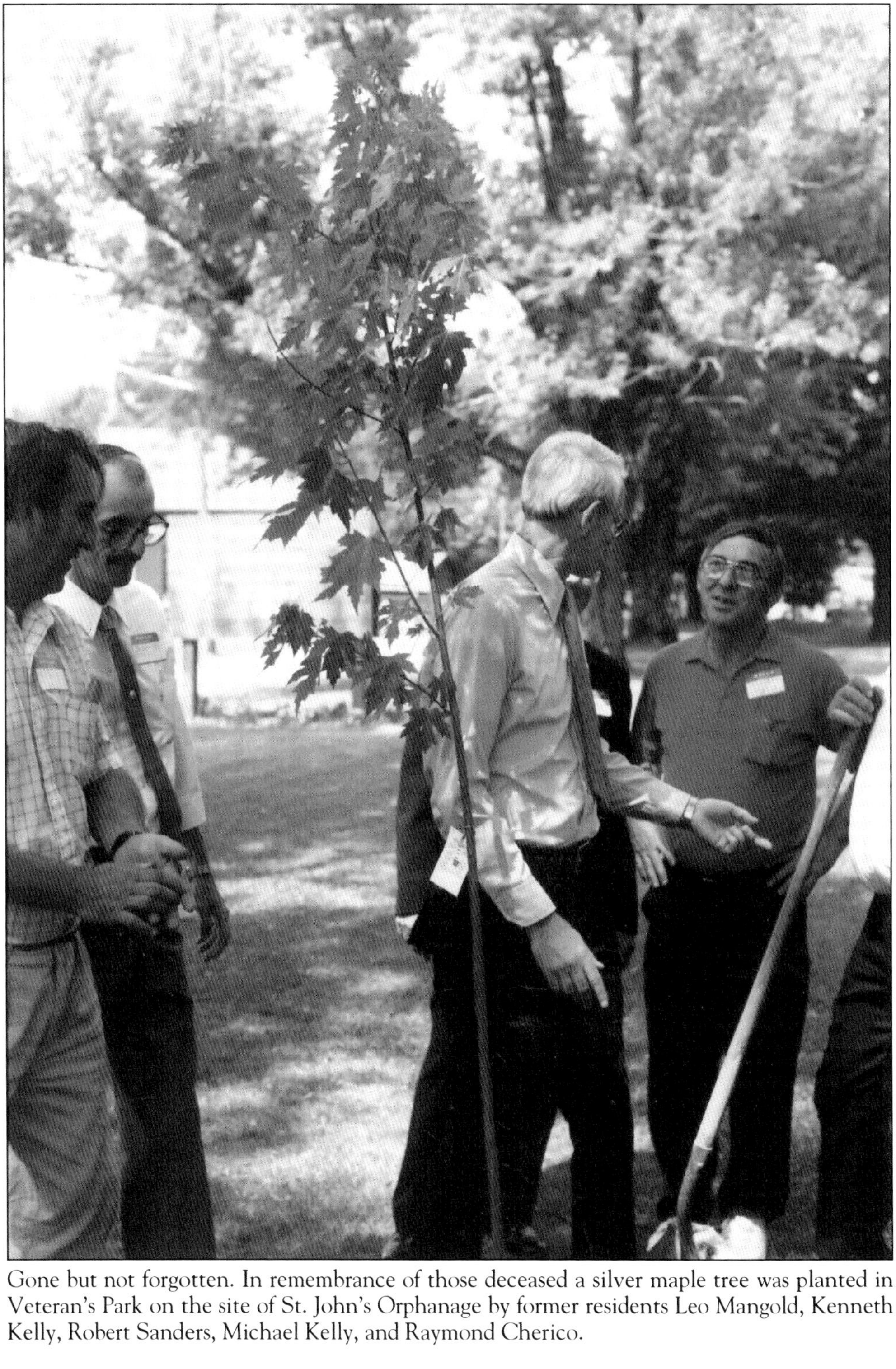

Gone but not forgotten. In remembrance of those deceased a silver maple tree was planted in Veteran's Park on the site of St. John's Orphanage by former residents Leo Mangold, Kenneth Kelly, Robert Sanders, Michael Kelly, and Raymond Cherico.

Six

Meet Our Neighbors

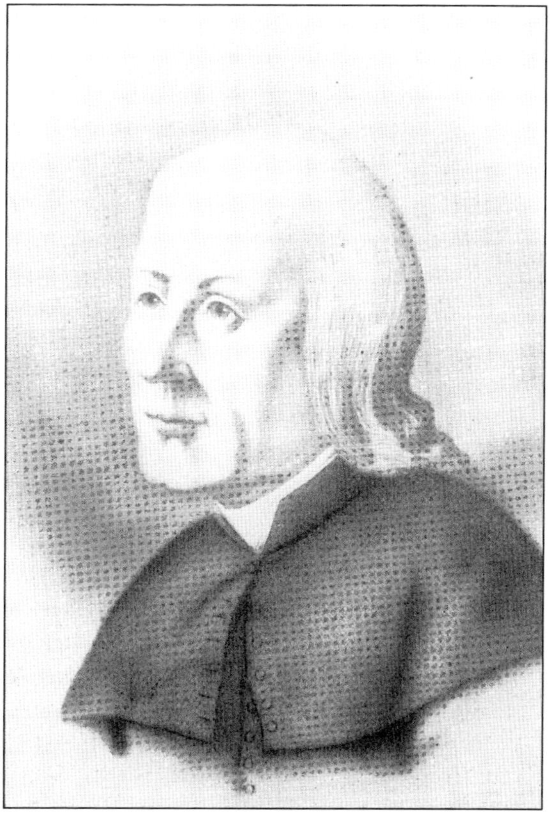

Prince/priest Demetrius A. Gallitzin, "The Apostle of The Alleghenies." A prince of noble birth, Gallitzin was the son of a Russian diplomat and a Prussian countess. He was commissioned in the Russian Army at an early age and sent to travel in the United States in the 1790s. Aspirants to military or diplomatic careers were expected to better themselves through travel. When he recognized the need for priests, he entered St. Mary's Seminary in Baltimore, and was ordained to the Priesthood in 1795. Gallitzin came to these mountains, in 1799, sacrificing his princely inheritance and career to serve the Catholic Church, as a missionary in the American wilderness. His career spanned four decades. He died herein 1841.

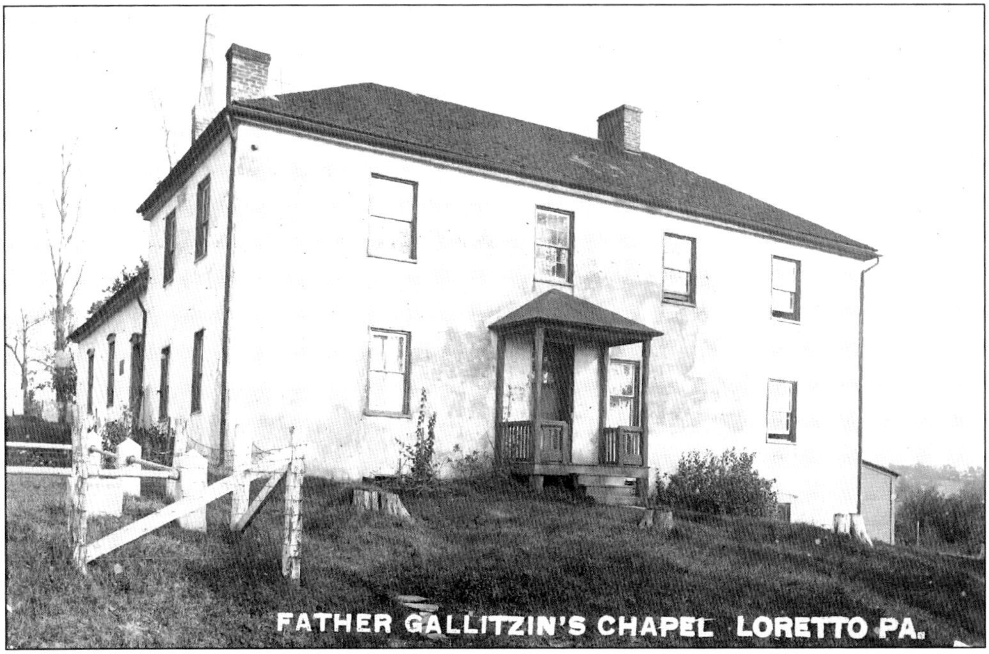

The Gallitzin Chapel House. This building was built in 1832 as a chapel and residence, replacing an original log edifice. It has become a historic landmark on a picturesque hillside and has not changed much since the days of the prince.

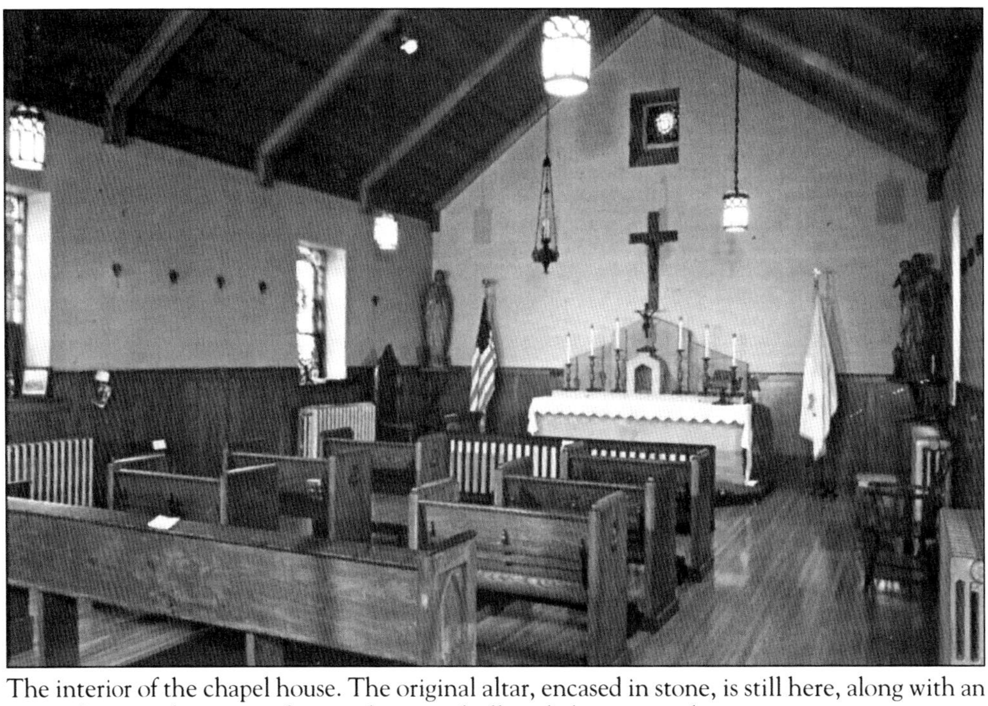

The interior of the chapel house. The original altar, encased in stone, is still here, along with an original pew and many artifacts and personal effects belonging to the prince.

Prince Gallitzin, Apostle of the Alleghenies. This crypt, in front of St. Michael's Church, Loretto, contains his mortal remains. The statue was a gift of Charles Schwab commemorating the centenary of Gallitzin's arrival in Loretto.

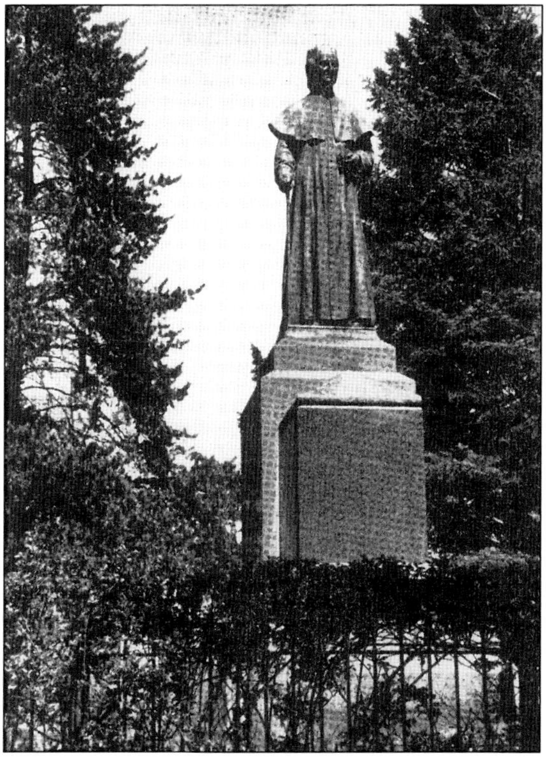

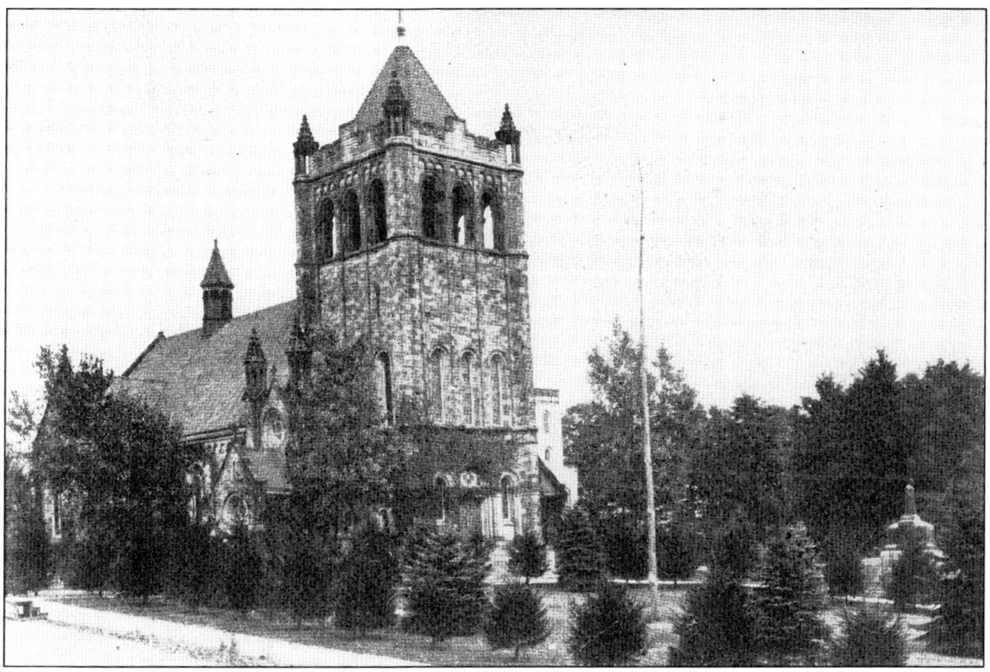

The Basilica of St. Michael the Archangel, originally a gift of Charles Schwab to the people of Loretto following the centennial celebration of 1899. Note the monument, tomb, and statue of Prince Gallitzin on the right. This historic church was granted the status of a Minor Basilica by Pope John Paul II in September 1996.

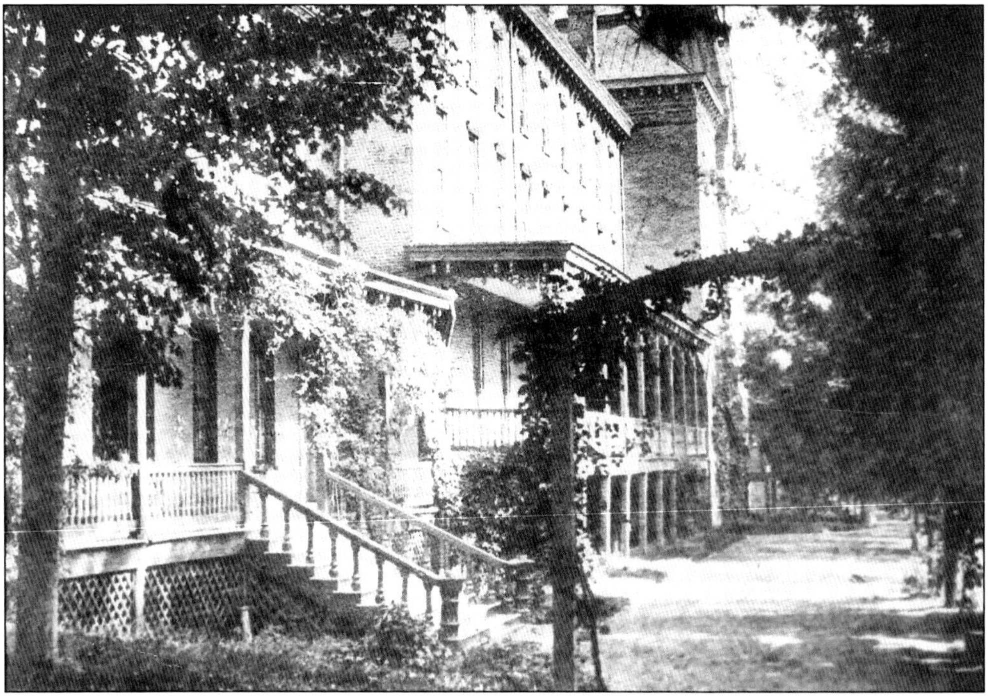

Mount Aloysius Academy, established in Loretto by The Sisters of Mercy in 1848. The academy, situated at the present site of the Our Lady of The Alleghenies Shrine (between the Chapel House and St. Michael's Church), flourished here for over four decades. The Loretto Academy consisted of grades nine through twelve! Elementary grades would be added later.

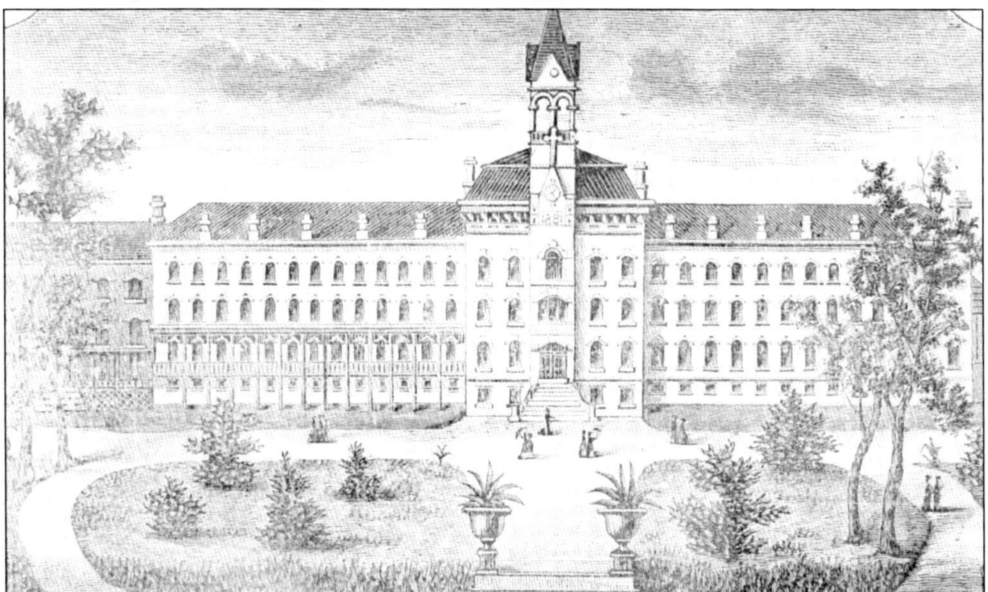

The old academy building. In 1897, when the Mount relocated to Cresson, the building became a children's home. It was destroyed by fire in 1904, but bricks were salvaged and used in the present convent, located behind the old academy. Stately pines of Loretto flourished in this area, creating a grove which is where the Diocesan Shrine was later established.

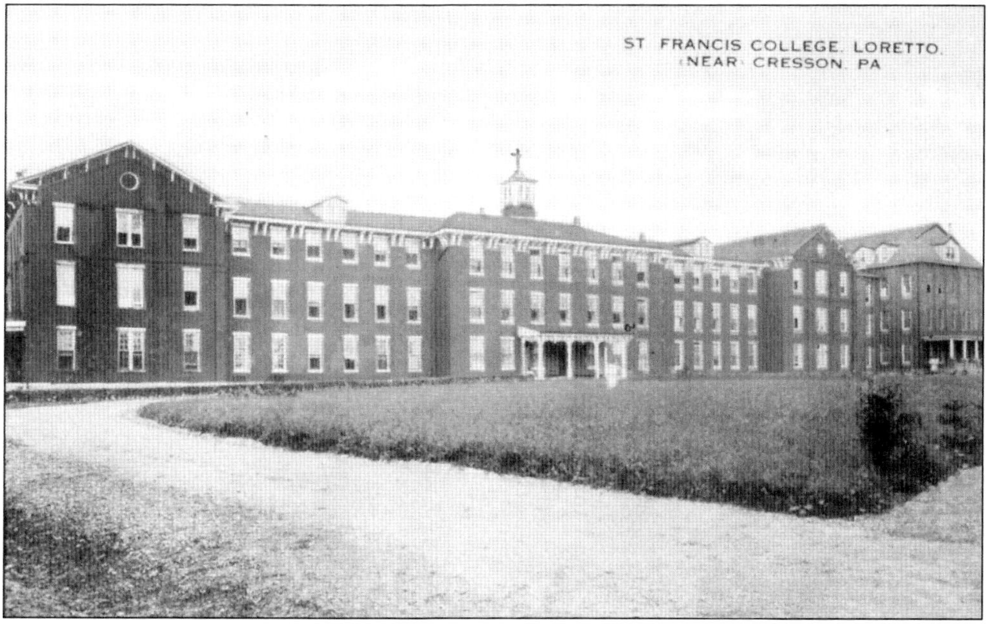

"Old Main." In 1847 six Franciscan Brothers established the beginnings of St. Francis College, which expanded as its enrollment increased. In 1942 it was destroyed by fire; however, the Franciscans, through faith, courage, and confidence in God, rebuilt the college from the ashes of Old Main. For several years barracks and quonset housing served as classrooms.

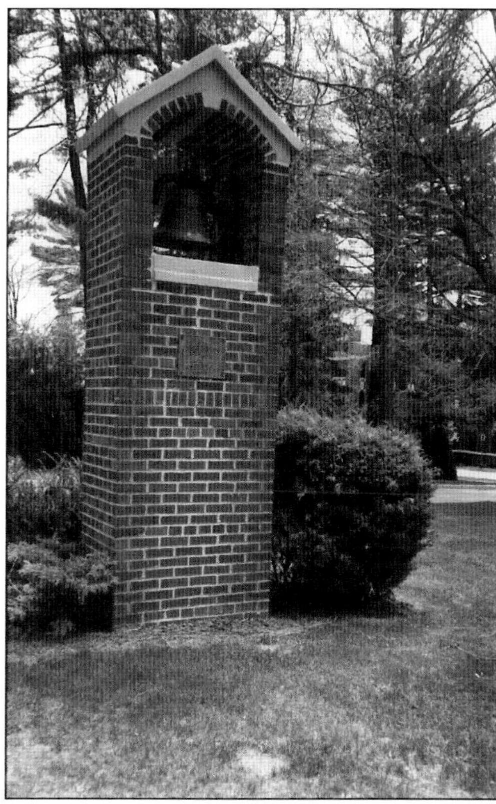

The bell tower, a nostalgic memento on the southern end of the college mall where Old Main once stood. The St. Francis College campus has been reestablished around the commons.

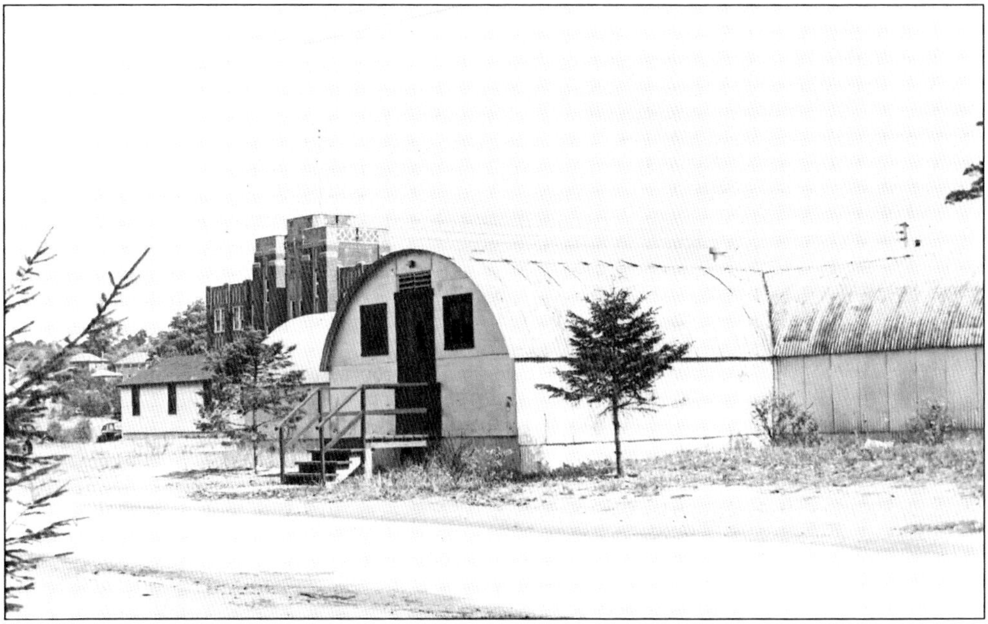

Quonset housing. These pre-fabricated shelters, set on foundations of steel with semicircular arching roofs of corrugated metal, served as a chapel and dormitories for several years following the fire in Old Main.

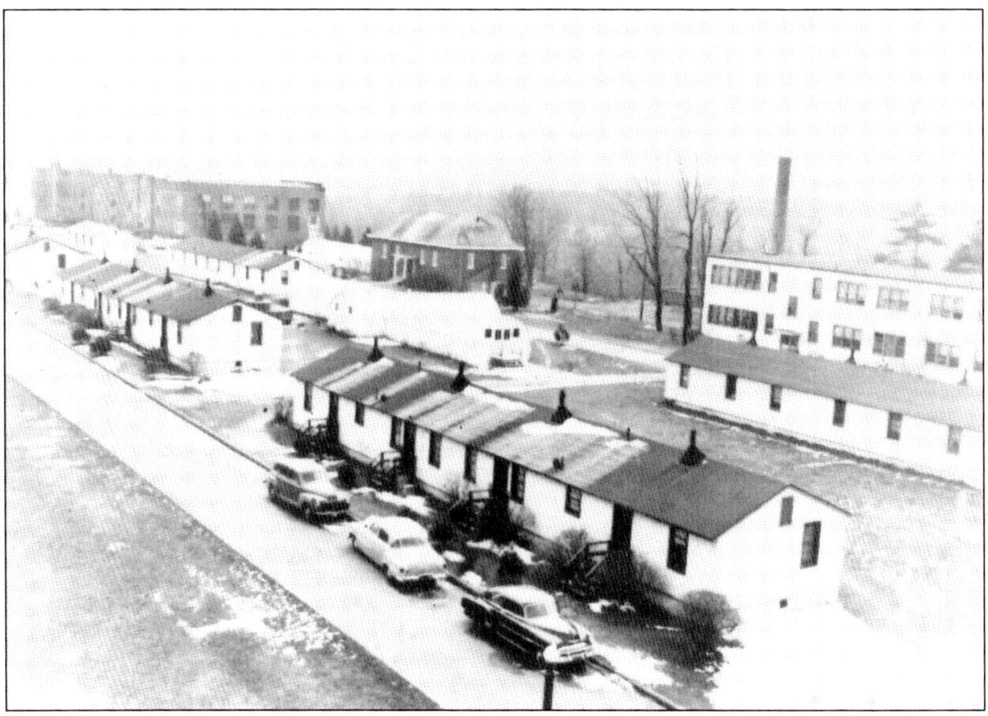

Pre-fabricated barracks. These structures were set up as classrooms and dormitories while new college buildings were being constructed around the commons. The gym, administration building, and library are in the background, the white chapel is in the center, and dormitories are in the foreground

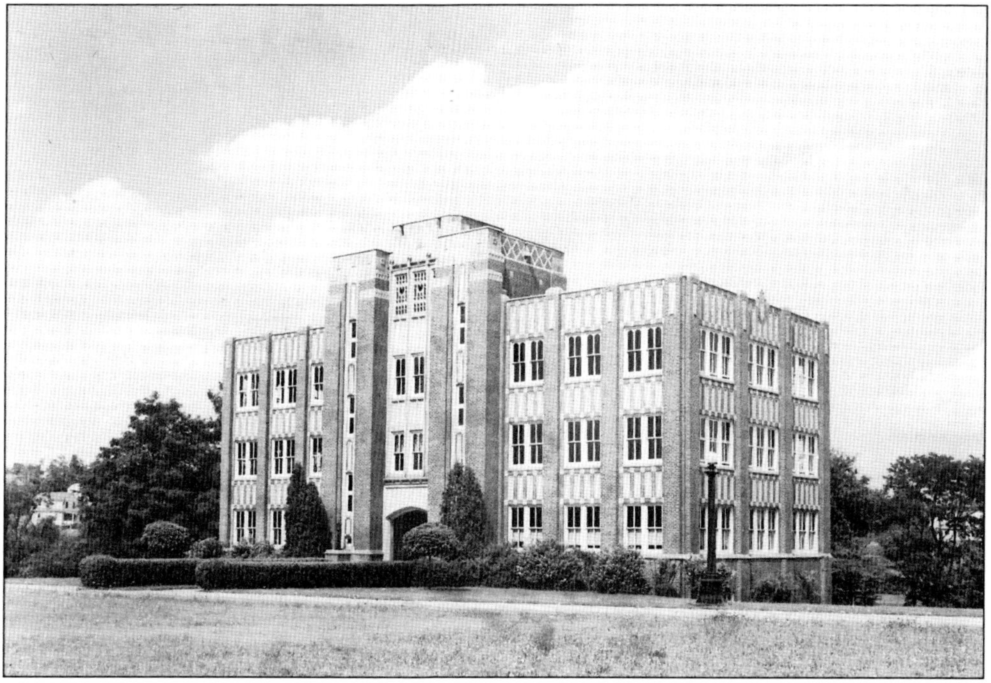

The Schwab Science Hall, donated by Charles Schwab to his alma mater in 1930. It contains laboratories and acid-proof tile floors. Evergreen trees were replanted to complete the hall.

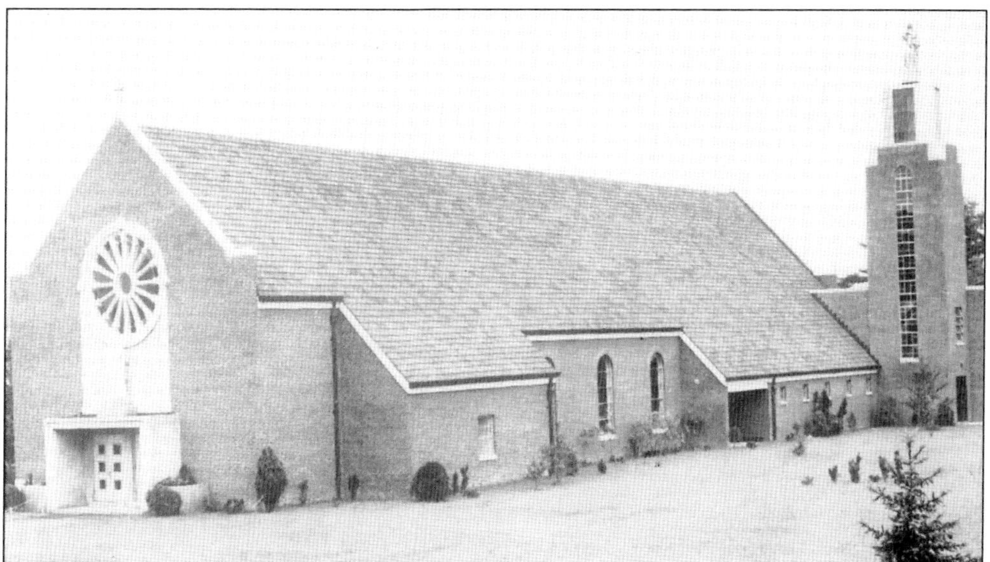

The Immaculate Conception Chapel on the St. Francis College campus, dedicated on May 4, 1957. The Monastery is on the right.

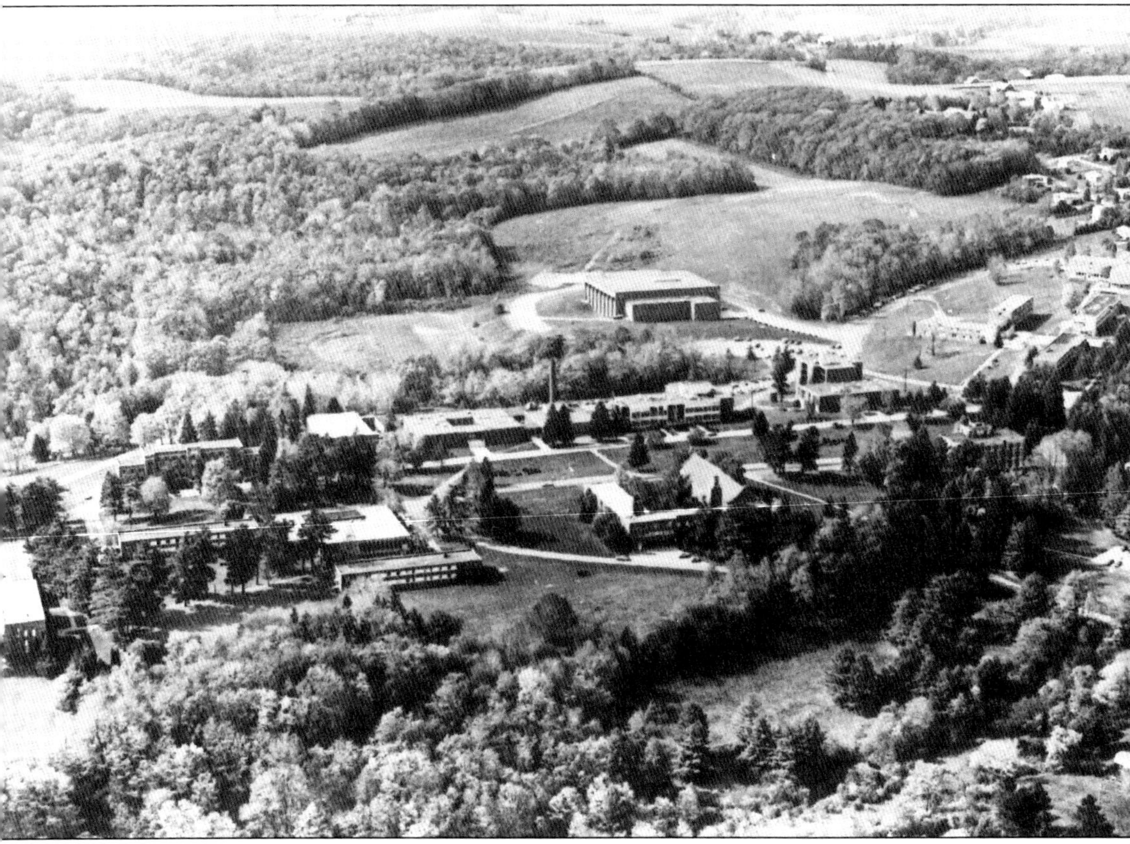

"The College Among The Pines," as it celebrates 150 years on the Loretto hillsides. The buildings, erected around a rectangular esplanade, include Raymond Hall, the Southern Allegheny Art Museum, Scotus, Padua, the Sullivan Complex and Pasquerilla Library, The Louis and Amici Halls, the Torvian Dining Hall, Giles Hall, the Friary, the Chapel, and Schwab Hall. Dorms and the JFK Student Complex are on the right. Stokes Gym is in the background, as is College Heights.

Charles Michael Schwab. Schwab was born in poverty in 1862 and completed his education while working as stagecoach driver. In 1879 he obtained a position with Carnegie Steel of Pittsburgh, where his photographic mind, retentive ability, and positive attitude were recognized. By age thirty-five he was appointed president of Carnegie Steel and later was instrumental in the development of U.S. steel. Immgrund was his palatial estate and summer retreat. He died in 1939.

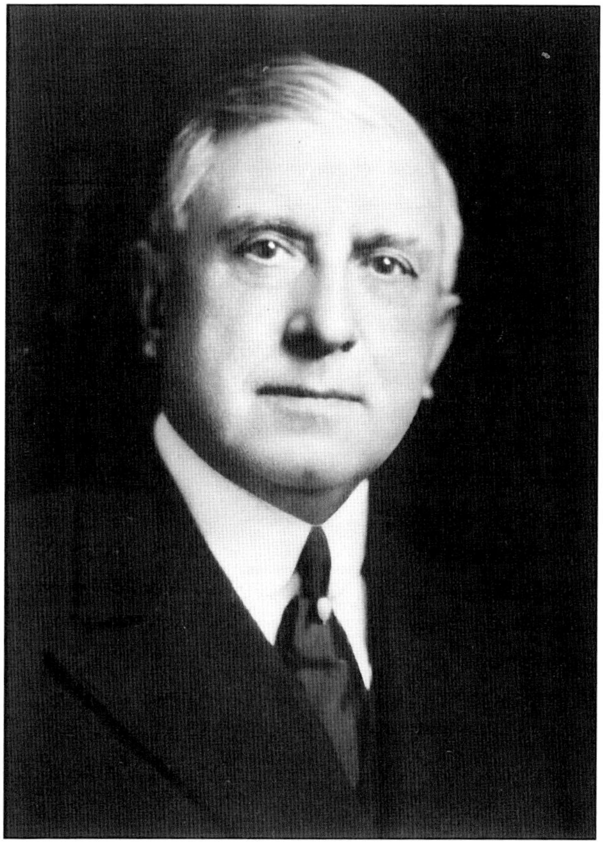

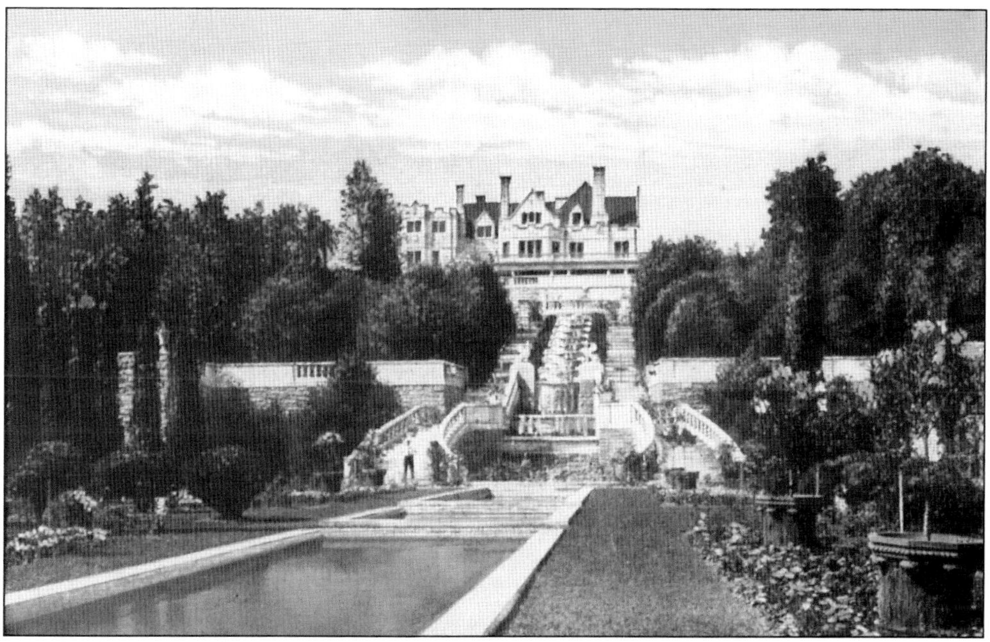

"Jewel of The Alleghenies." Schwab's estate includes an Italian garden and a magnificent cascade down to the Sunken Gardens, which contain trees and shrubs from around the world.

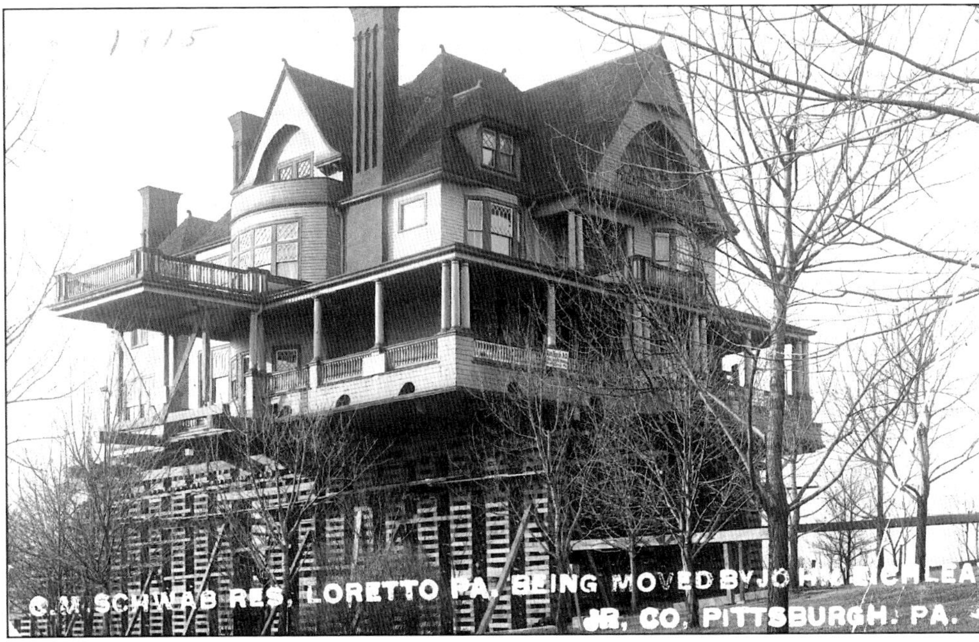

Charles Schwab's original mansion, now Bonaventure Hall. This building was lifted 37 feet over the treetops on November 26, 1915, and relocated a distance of 1,500 feet to make room for a new, more elaborate structure. It is now a house for candidates to the Franciscan Friars.

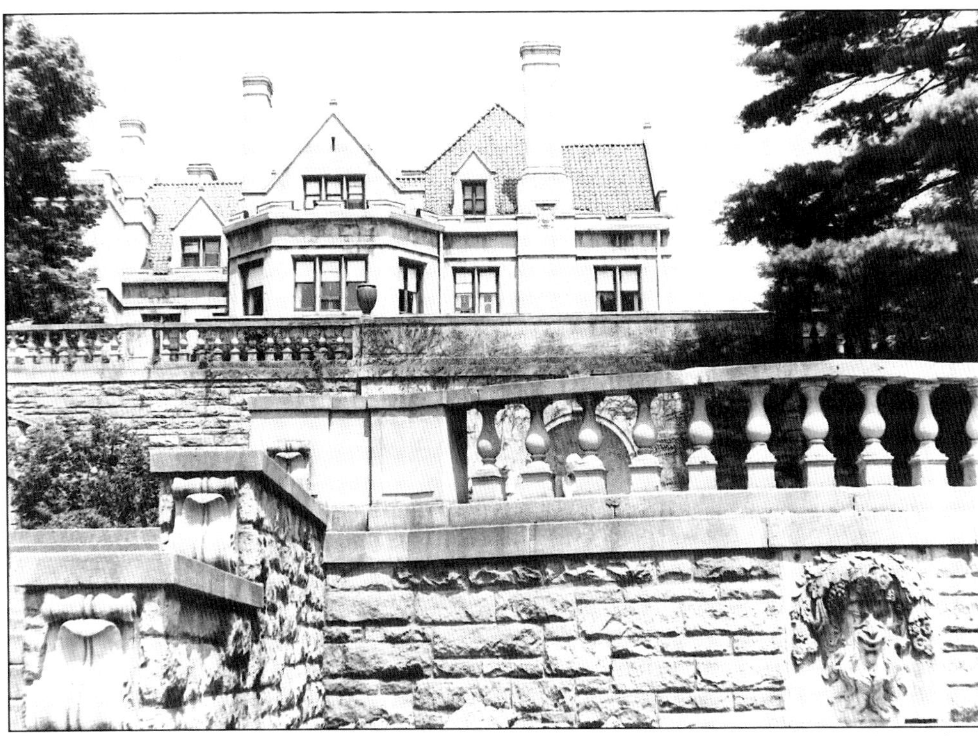

The new structure. A fortress emerged on the hilltop overlooking the Sunken Gardens, where Schwab spent many summers following his philanthropic pursuits.

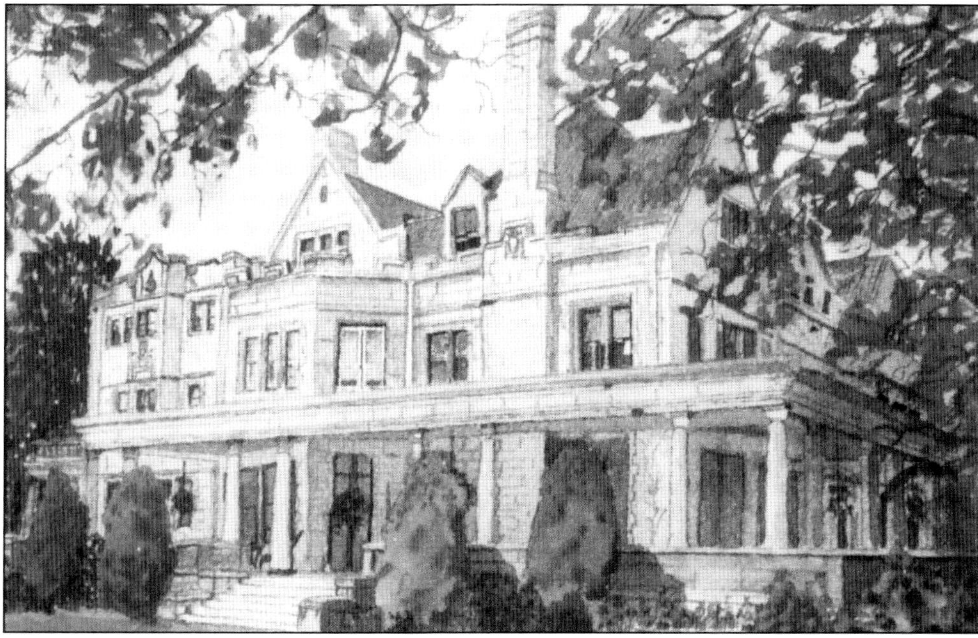

Schwab's forty-four room Renaissance mansion, completed in 1919. This building reflects the grandeur and splendor Schwab brought to Loretto, as captured by native artist Mary Itle Lessard, a nurse and housewife with four children, who had just reached a half century when a latent talent suddenly blossomed! The mansion would eventually become the Mount Assisi Monastery, and now houses Franciscan Priests (TOR) of The Sacred Heart Province.

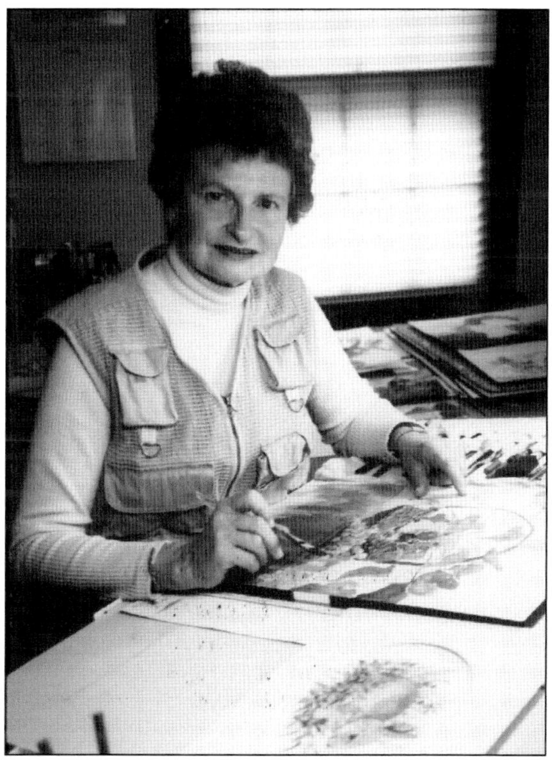

Mary Itle Lessard. On Christmas 1988 Mary's husband presented her with watercolor materials. She was amused because she considered her expertise in this vein non-existent. After reviewing the January bills, she decided to enroll in art classes! Watercolor became an obsession in which she delights. Commissioned by the Franciscans, her 1996 Mount Assisi Collection is a series of four watercolor paintings capturing the charm and beauty of the estate and its environs.

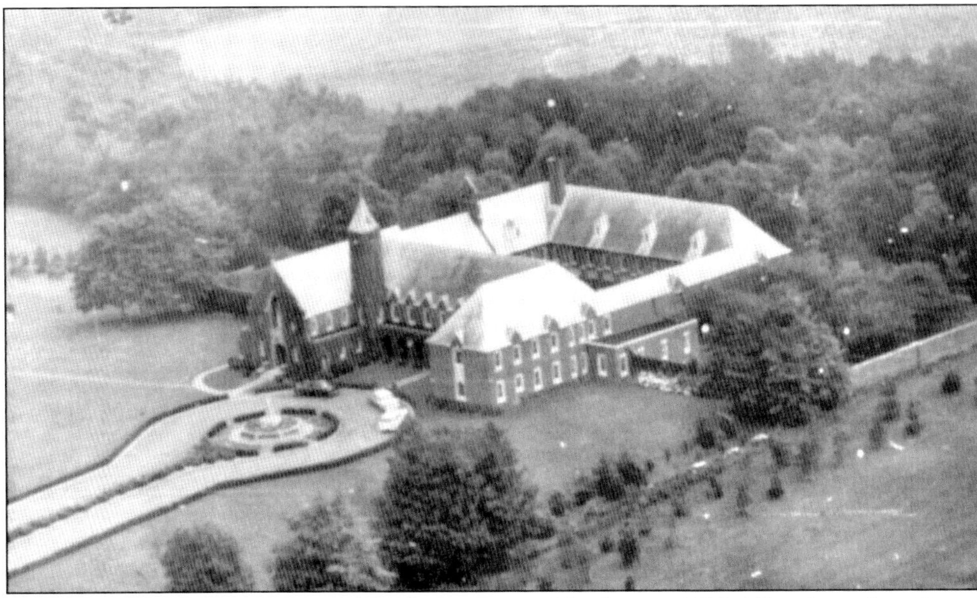

The Carmelite monastery, established on Loretto Heights in 1930. The Carmelite Sisters, along with many other religious groups, were exiled from France following the World War I. Charles Schwab's sister Cecila joined the Carmelite congregation and he assisted in financing the monastery.

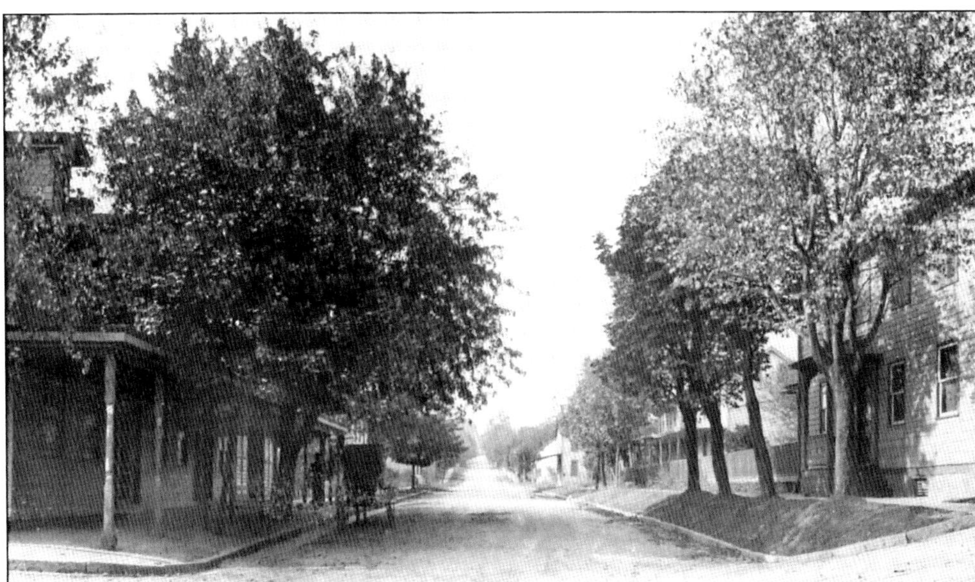

A Loretto street scene looking north in 1923. The hamlet, originally called McGuire's Settlement after a Revolutionary War veteran, was renamed Loretto in 1803 for the Shrine of The Holy House in Loretto, Italy. Note the horse and buggy waiting outside Schwab's Store.

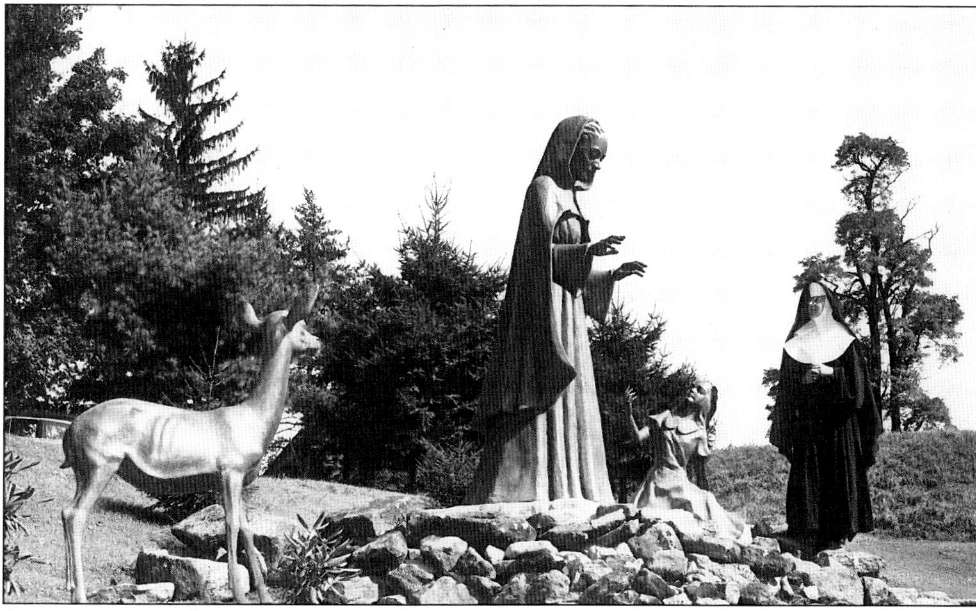

Sister Mary Benedicta San Antonio. The Sister is surveying her work as the designer of the Shrine of Our Lady of The Alleghenies. It was dedicated on September 8, 1951. She developed the art department at Mt. Aloysius College and initiated a Certified Occupational Therapy Assistants (COTA) program. She was instrumental in the design of many area churches of various faiths.

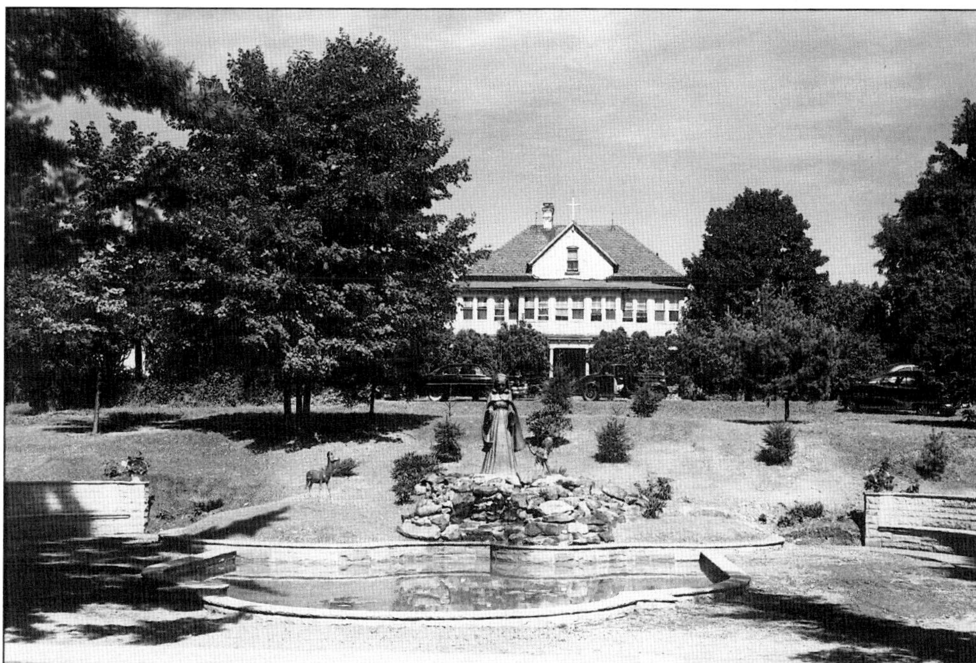

The Shrine of Our Lady of the Alleghenies, situated on the site of the original Mount Aloysius Academy in Loretto. The child represents humankind, the hart symbolizes nature's response, and the lily pond signifies baptism. The Convent of the Sisters of Mercy is in the background.

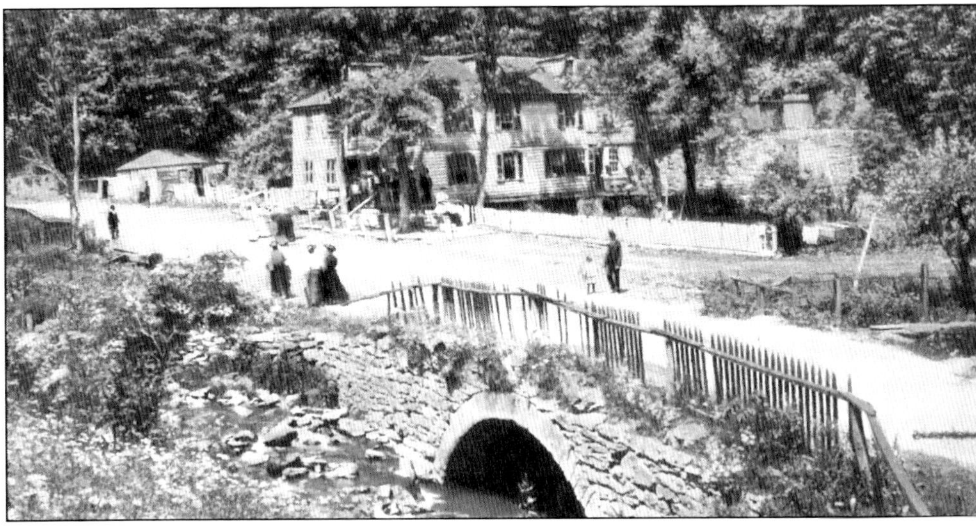

Fountain Inn, located along the stagecoach line at Muleshoe curve. Pioneers crossing the mountains rested here, on the eastern slope of the Alleghenies.

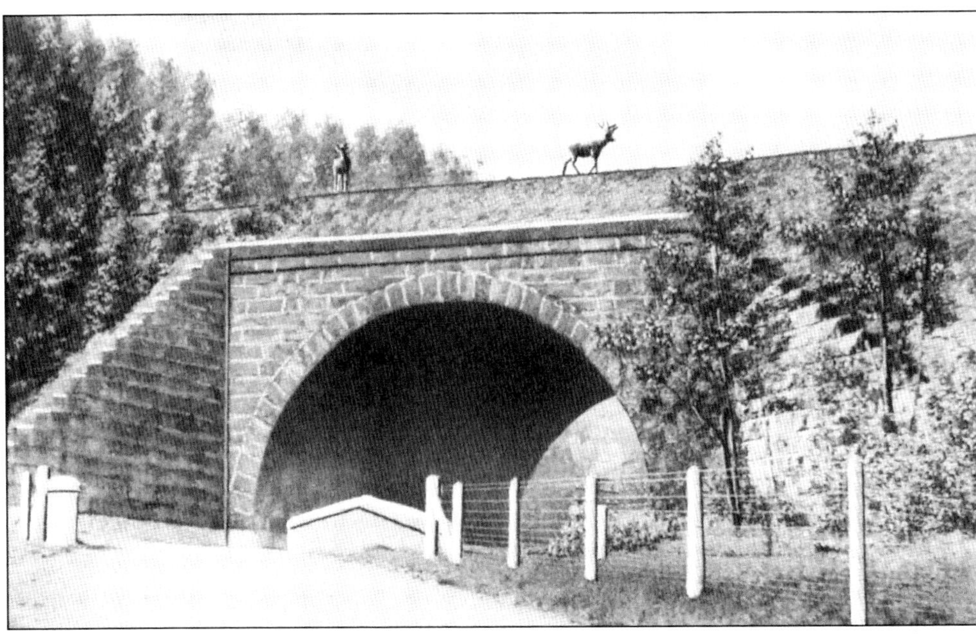

Looking west toward the Allegheny Ridge. Elk ramble across Muleshoe culvert, which once carried the APRR. The culvert still stands along "The Pike."

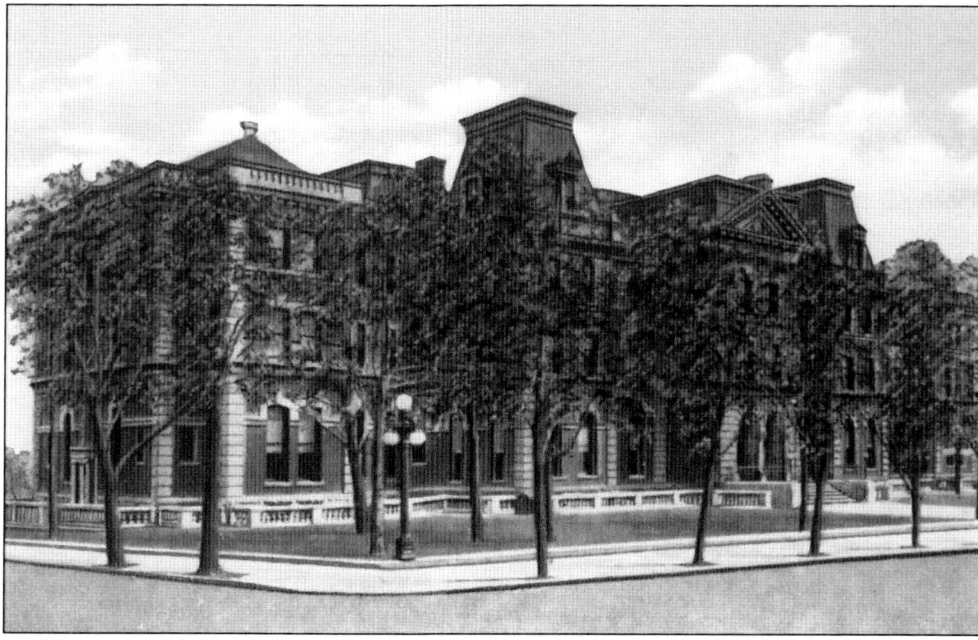

Ebensburg. This settlement was designated the county seat of Cambria County in 1804 by Reverend Rees Lloyd, who donated property for public buildings. The present courthouse was erected in 1880. Originally a Welch settlement, Cambria County was named for the Cambria Mountains of Wales.

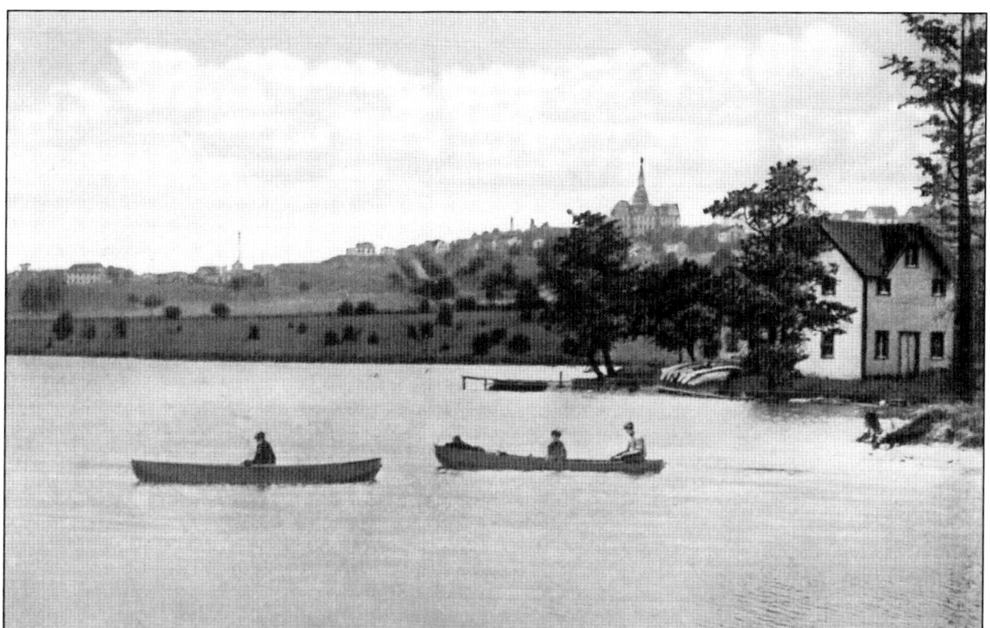

Lake Rowena, situated just below Ebensburg. The lake affords plenty of opportunity for boating and fishing. The courthouse rises in the distance; its spire has since been removed.

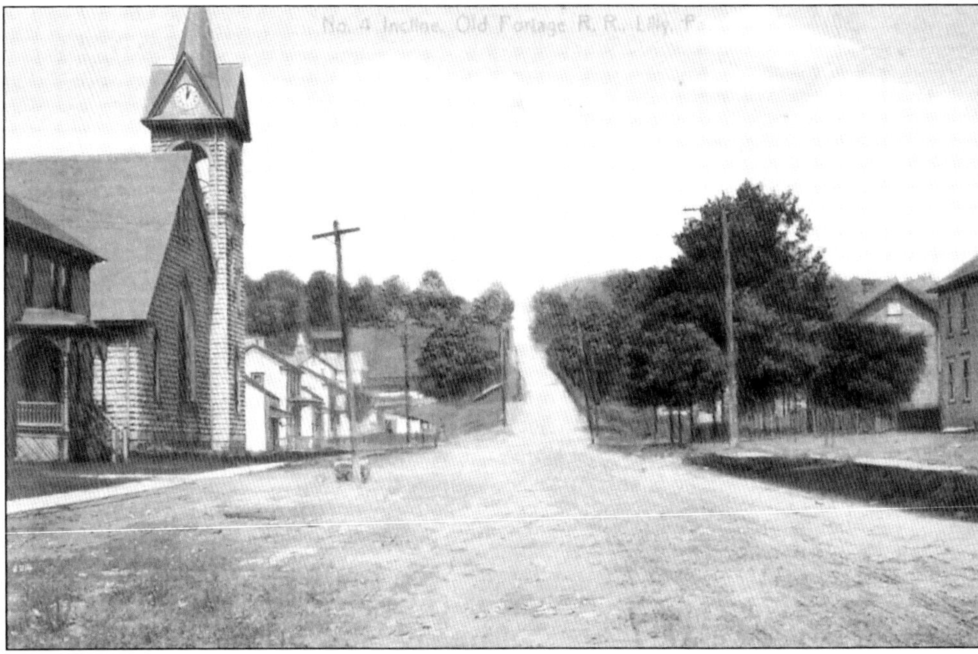

Looking north along the roadbed of the Allegheny Portage Railroad and Plane #4 in Lilly. St. Luke's Luthern Church (c. 1783) is on the left. Lilly was named for Richard Lilly, the son of an early pioneer.

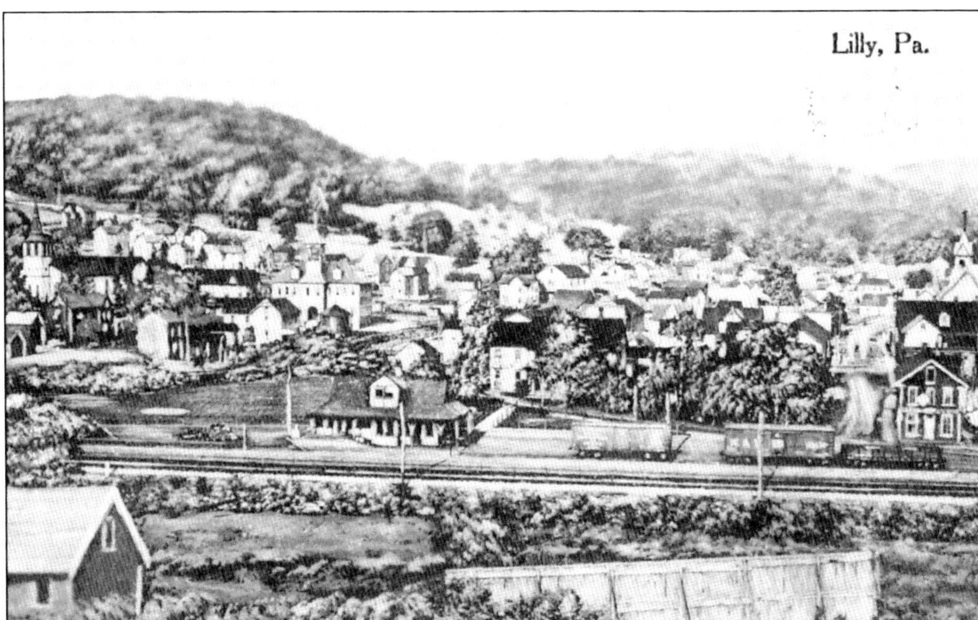

Lilly in 1911. The railroad station is in the foreground, and St. Brigid's Church and School are on the left. Dense forests of hemlock and oak created not only a fragrant aroma but a rapid rise in sawmills that supplied timber for the APRR.

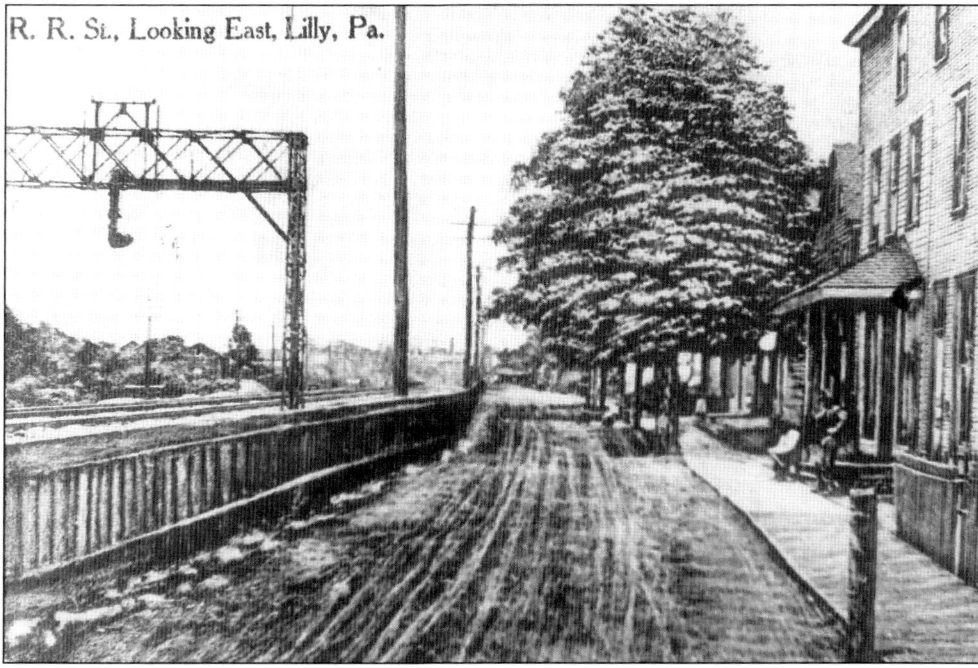

The timber-loading platform. Trains frequently stopped at Lilly for lumber as well as passengers. This huge platform was erected across from the Sokol Building to load timber.

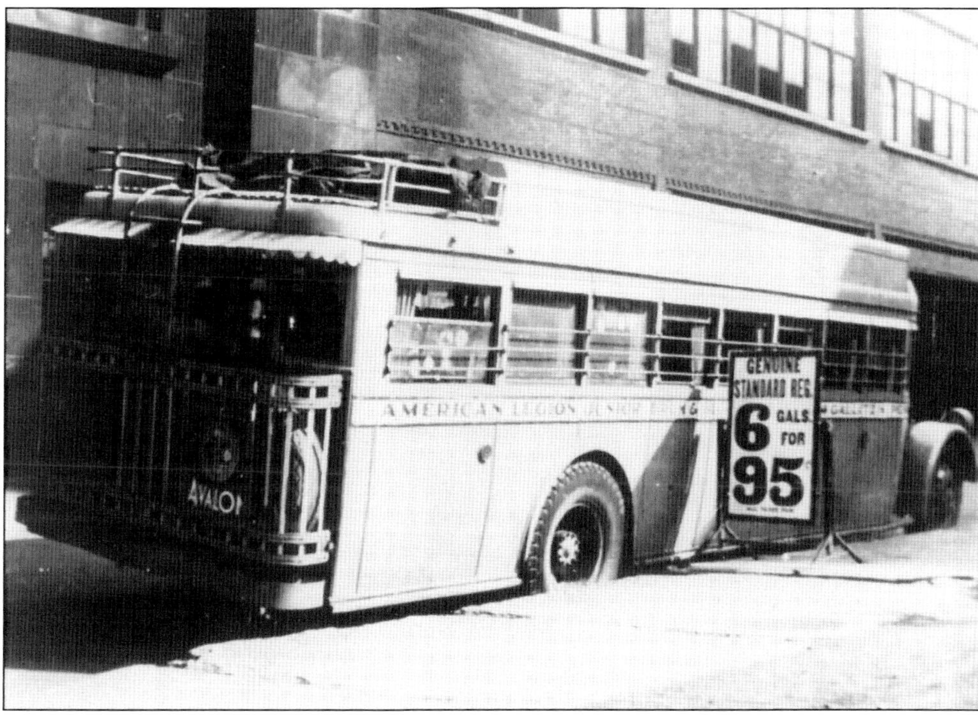

Transportation for the American Legion Drum & Bugle Corps of Gallitzin. Sponsored by Dr. Alfred Bergstein and directed by Bob McCaa, this drum and bugle corps was awarded the National Championship in 1936 and 1937. Note the price of gas during that era!

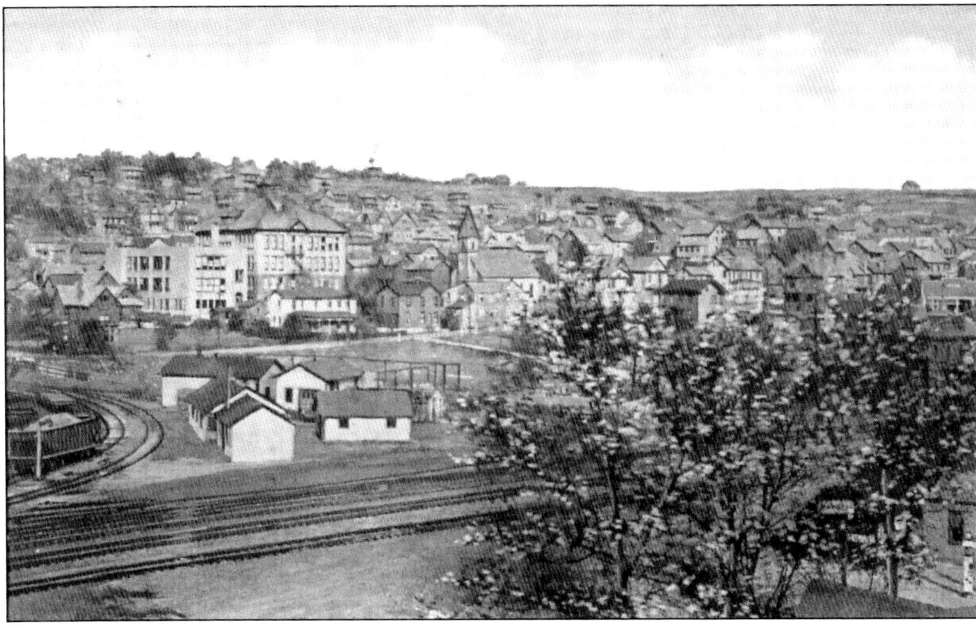

The coming of the railroad. Gallitzin became a thriving, fast-growing area when the railroad arrived. The inhabited area over the tunnels on the left became Tunnellhill.

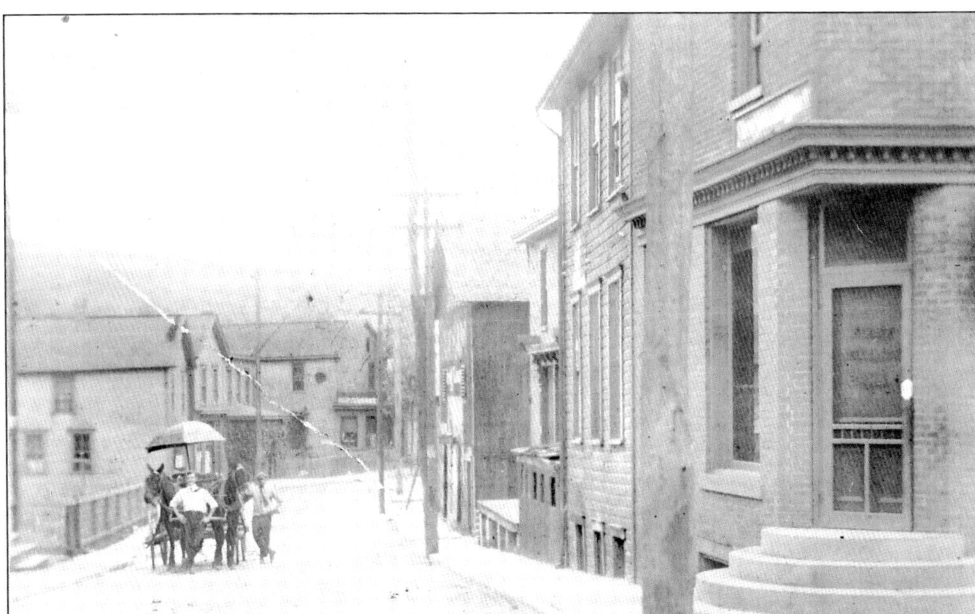

A street scene in Gallitzin on September 29, 1911. The First National Bank is in the foreground.

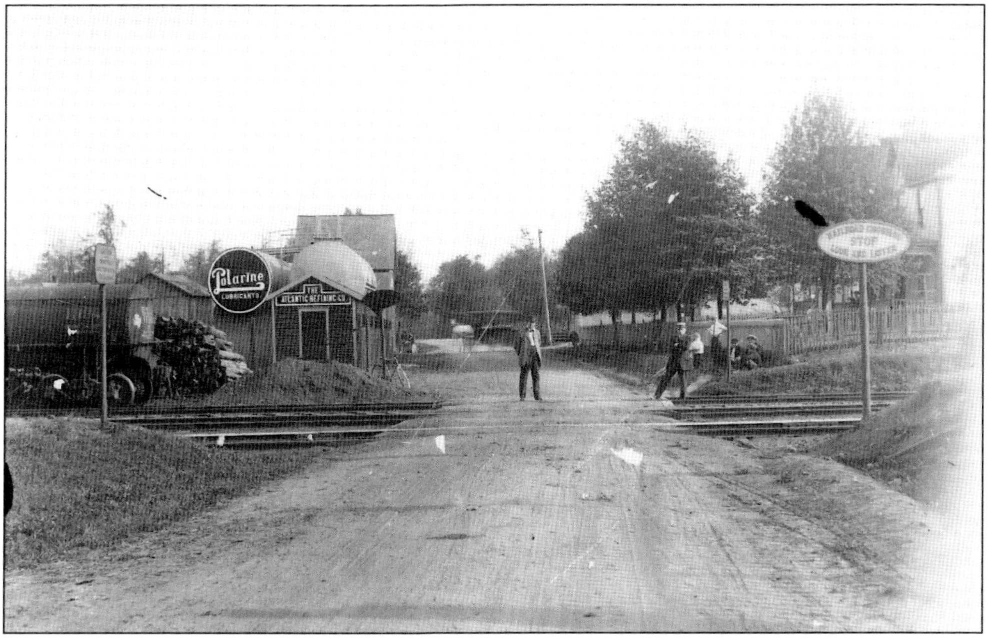

The Hoguetown railroad crossing facing south toward Cresson in 1915. An overhead culvert now carries the trains over this roadway, along what is often called "The Loretto Road."

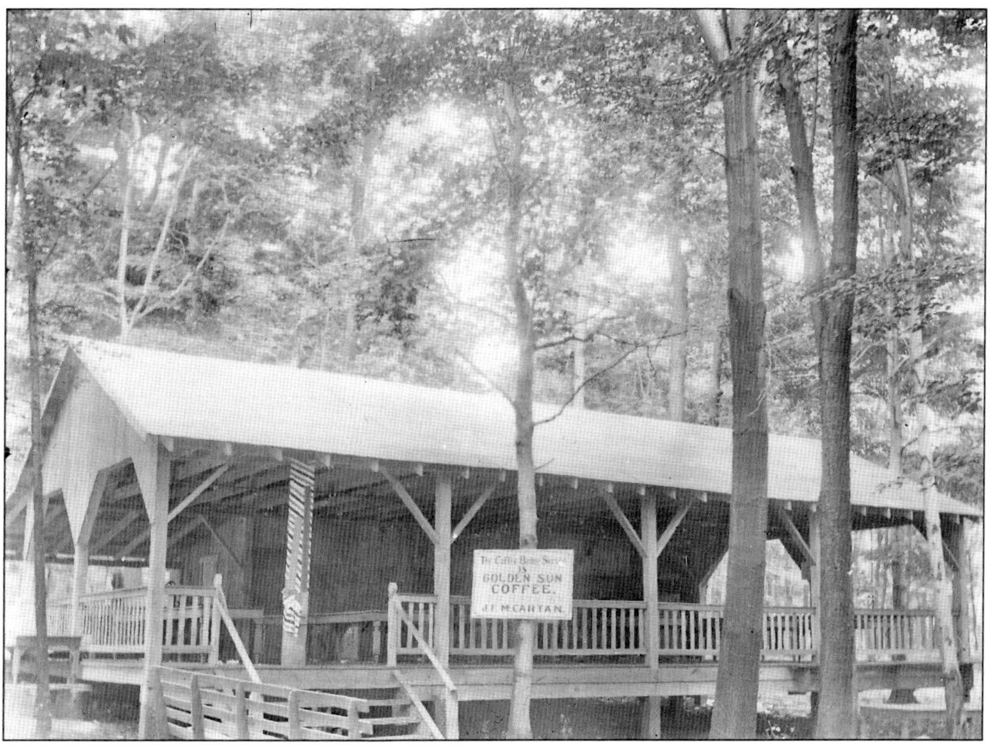

A 1915 Golden Sun Coffee advertisement on the Maplewood Park Pavilion. The pavilion was located at the west end of Penn Avenue in Sankertown.

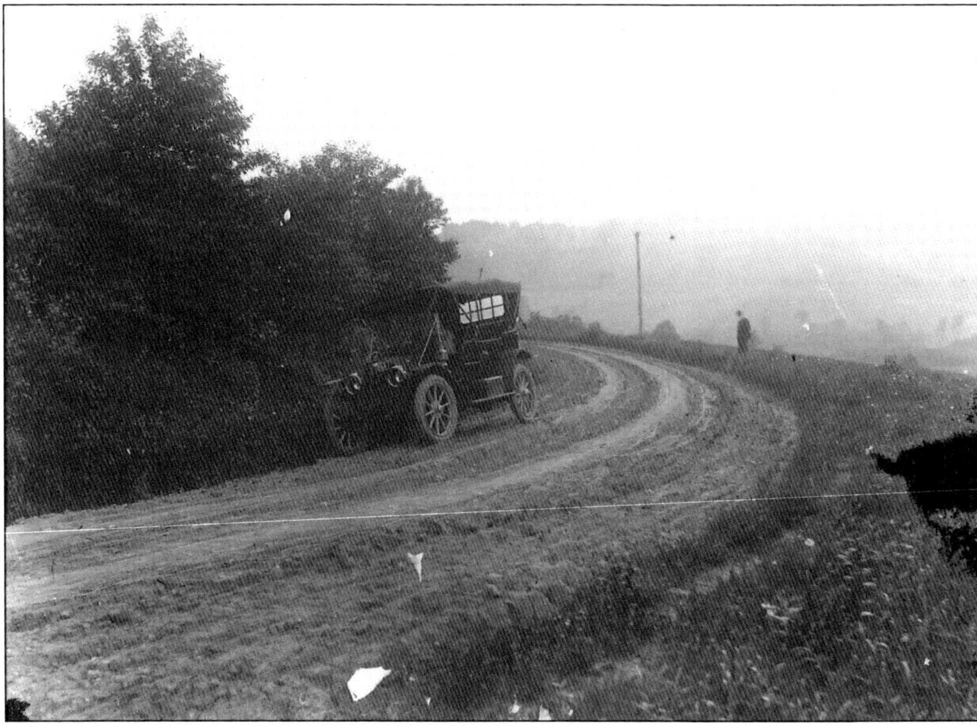

Parrish Curve in 1915 looking north toward Loretto. The federal prison is now on the left and the belfry of St. Michael's Church can be seen in the background. There are twenty-eight picturesque bends in this mountain road on the four-mile trek between Loretto and Cresson.

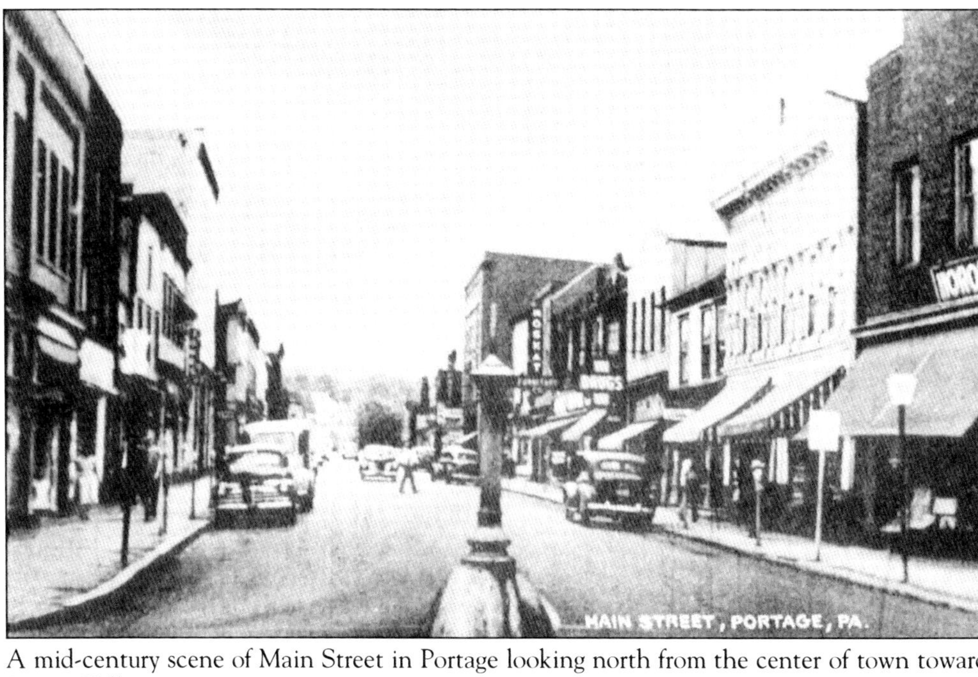

A mid-century scene of Main Street in Portage looking north from the center of town toward Spring Hill.

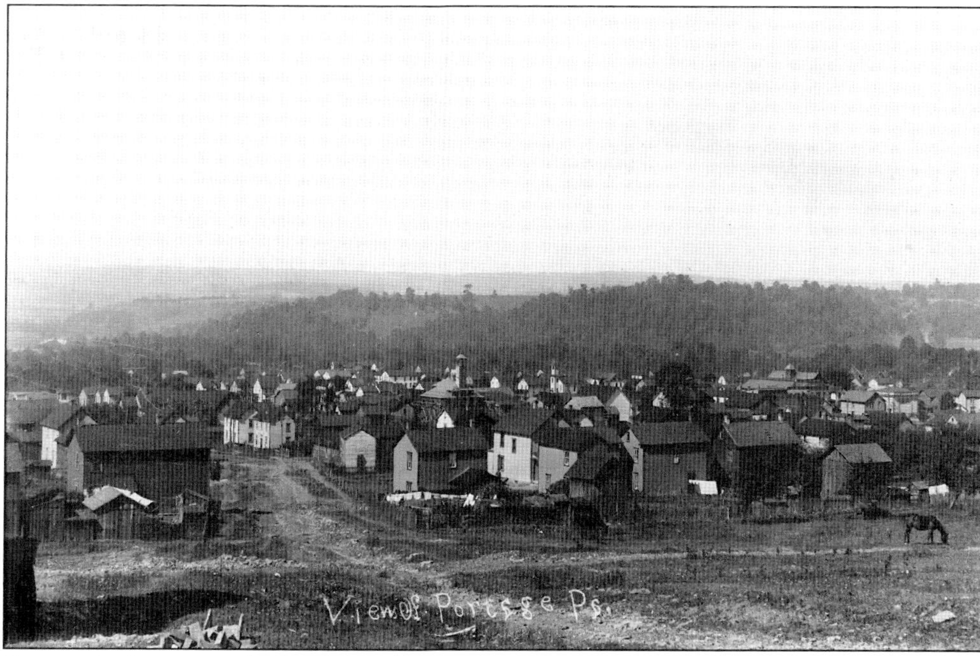

Portage, looking west along Mountain Avenue, prior to 1913. The fire tower is in the center and Troxel's home is in the left foreground. Located along Plane #2 of the Allegheny Portage Railroad, Portage was once called "Hemlock Mills" because of its dense forests and numerous sawmills. Coal mining eventually became prominent and drew immigrants from many parts of Europe. The name Portage derives from the famed railroad—"portage" means to transport.

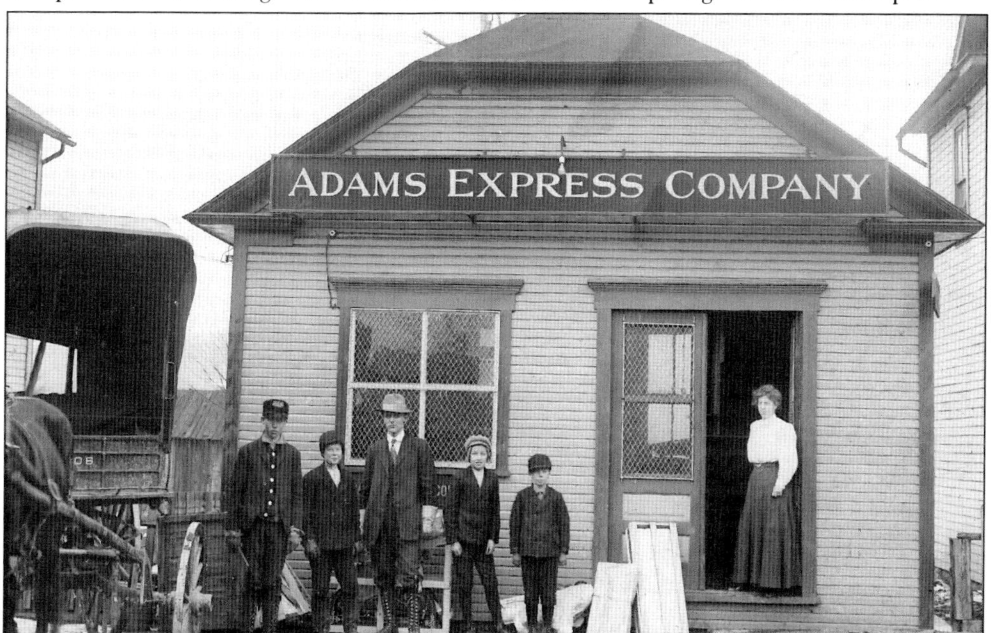

Adams Express of Portage. Miner's checks were distributed from this building, located north of the railroad. Adams Express served the early pioneers in an era when railroading was the fashionable and fastest mode of travel. The horse and buggy wait to make a delivery.

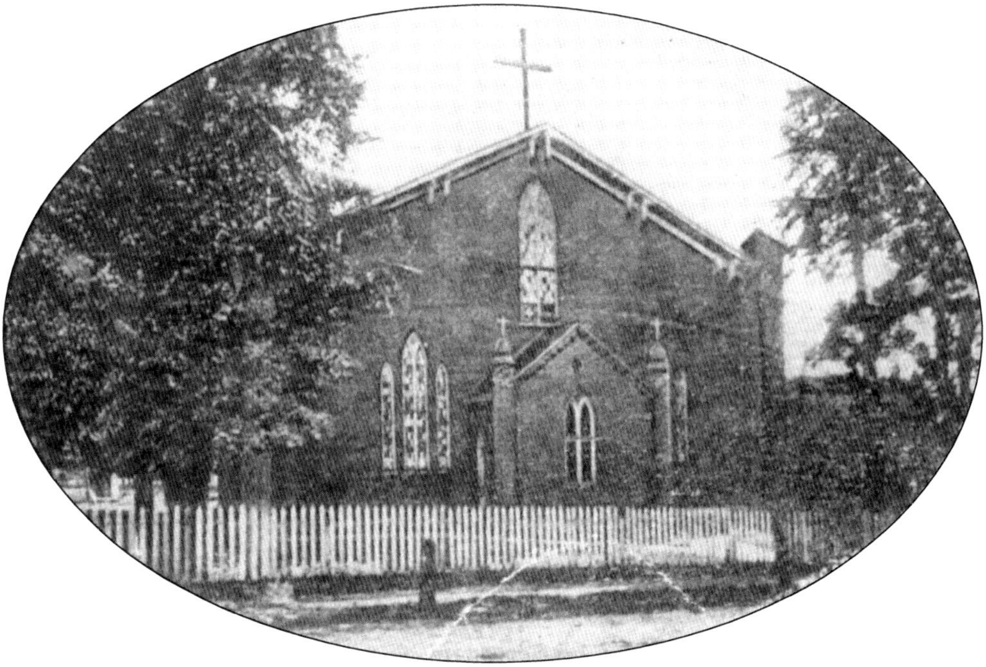

The St. Aloysius Roman Catholic Parish, established by Prince Gallitzin at the Summit of the Allegheny Mountains in 1838 on land donated by Ignatius Adams. Located along the Pike near the intersection of the Allegheny Portage Railroad, the two main thoroughfares gave rise to a thriving settlement. The original church was a simple, devotional structure built by pioneers.

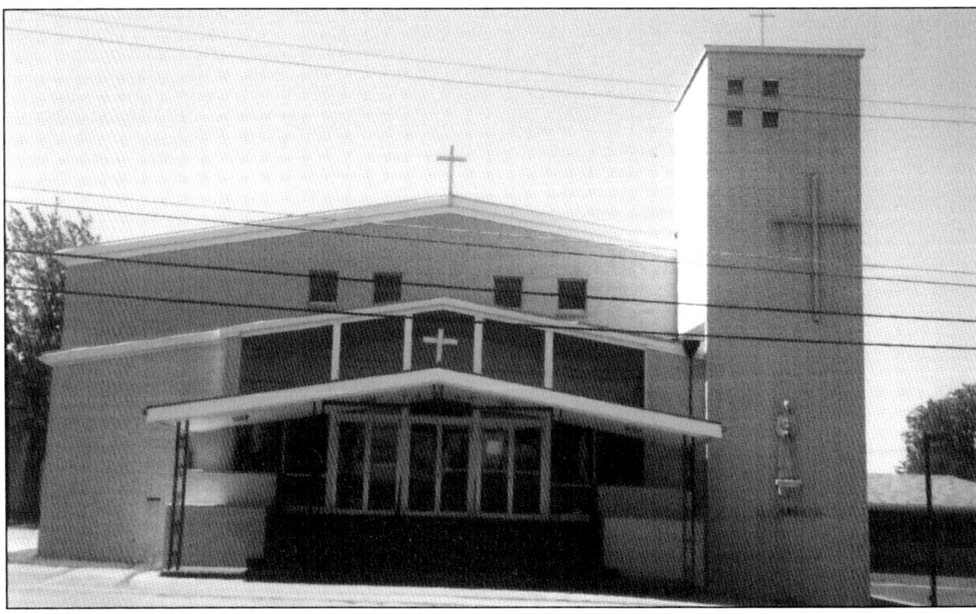

The present-day St. Aloysius Roman Catholic Church, located on the same site. Subsequent structures had been erected over a fifteen-decade period. In 1925 a windstorm demolished the church and a basement church served for three decades. In 1956–57 parishioners gave their time, talent, and labor in the erection of the new edifice, which was dedicated in December 1957.

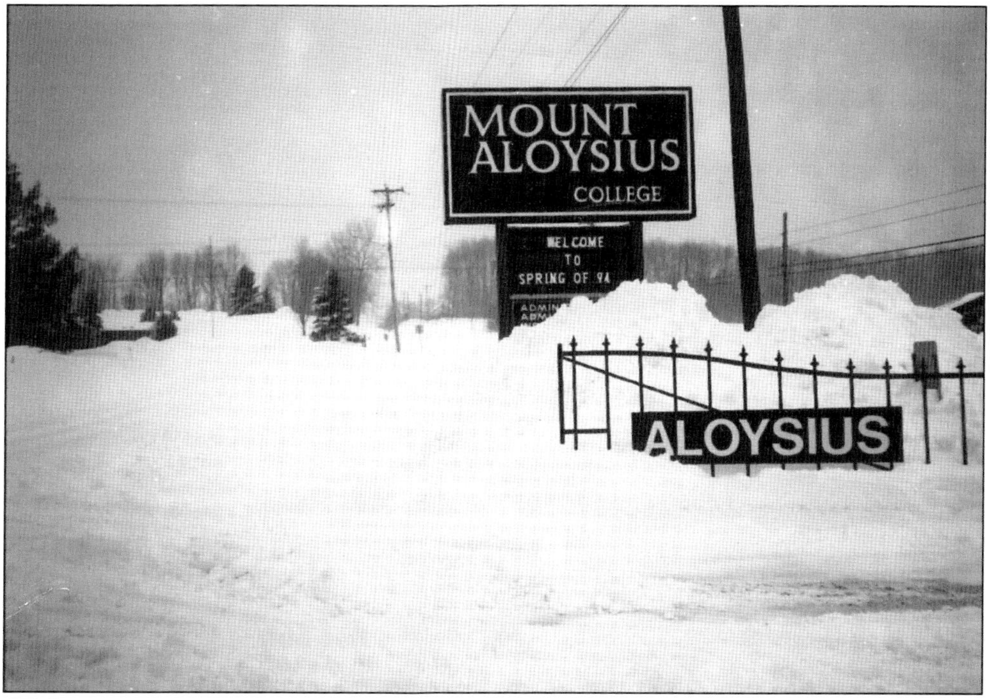

"Welcome to Spring Semester," March 1994. Snow is an abundant natural resource found throughout the region.

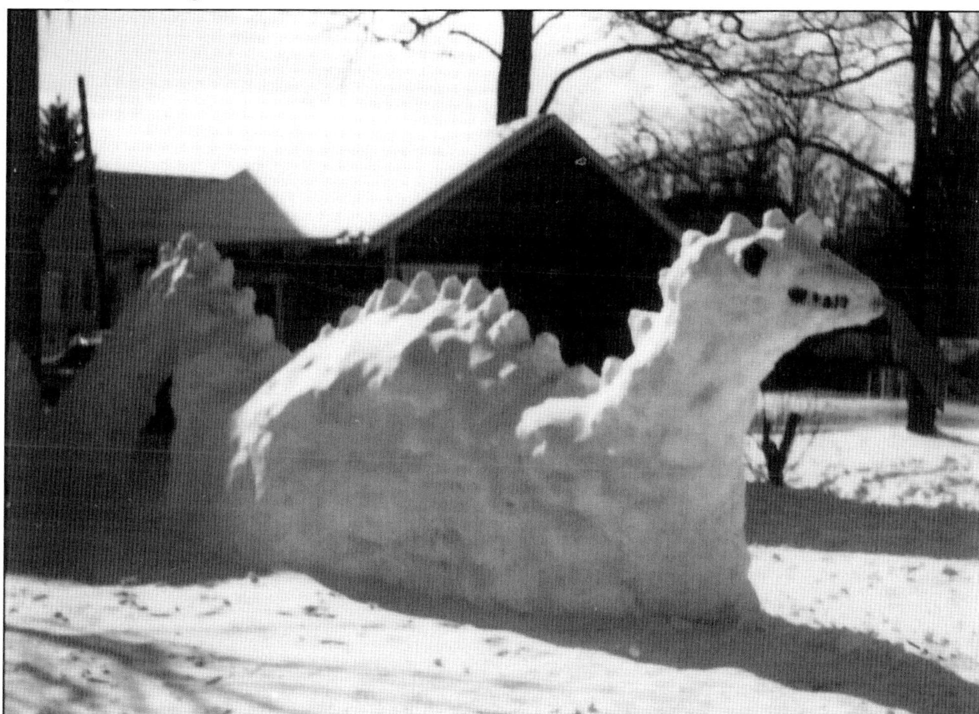

An ingenious, creative sculpture, February 1976. J. Dewey Adams transformed a natural resource into a 25-foot dinosaur on Keystone Avenue.

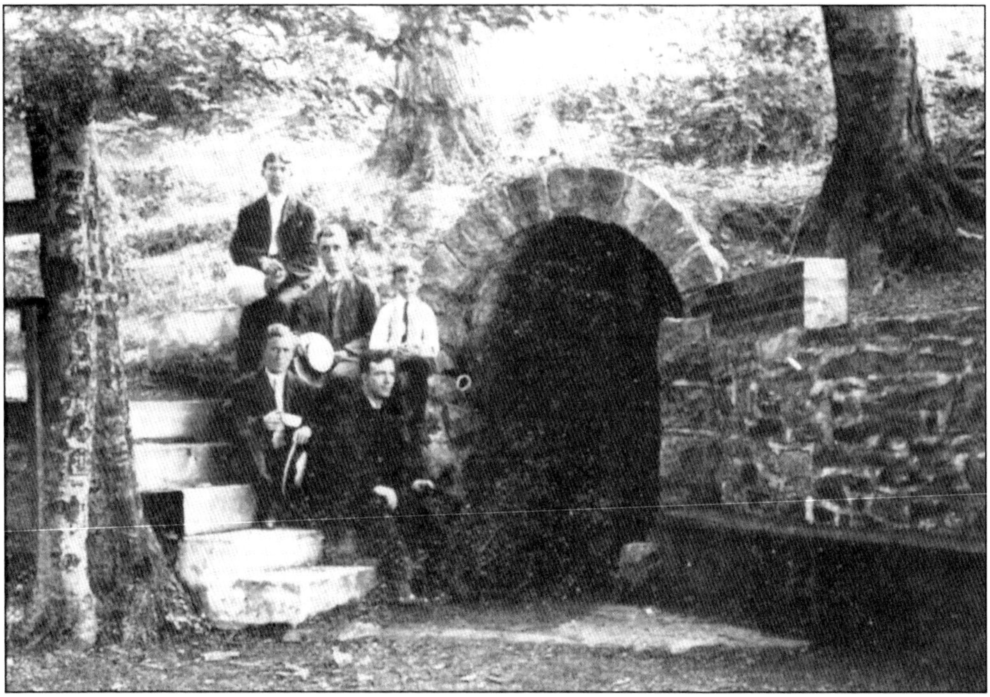

The spring, always a popular gathering place for folks of all ages. This was the forerunner of bottled water and soda pop. Cups and flasks are held by the unidentified group. Sharing utensils was a necessity.

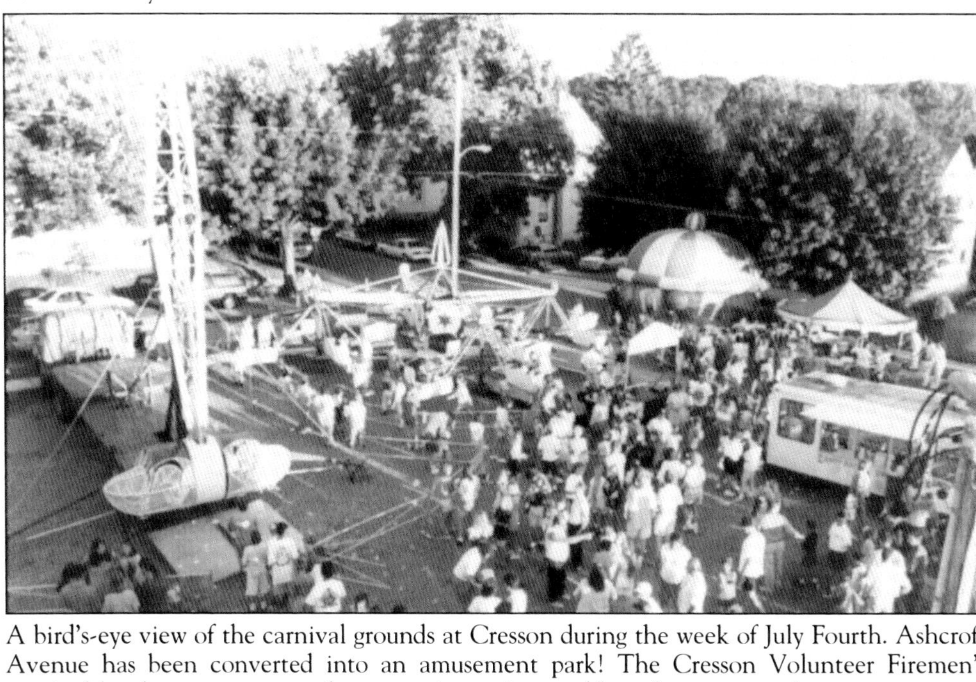

A bird's-eye view of the carnival grounds at Cresson during the week of July Fourth. Ashcroft Avenue has been converted into an amusement park! The Cresson Volunteer Firemen's carnival has become an annual community project and has always enjoyed great community support. Calandra Industries supply a flatbed trailer which is converted to a bandstand, Vale Wood farms provide a refrigerator truck, and businesses are most helpful.

The Garbrick Wheel. Unlike the Ferris wheel of Coney Island fame, the use of hydraulics permit Garbrick's rides to fold up. This is one of the most thrilling and popular rides as it takes one over the rooftops!

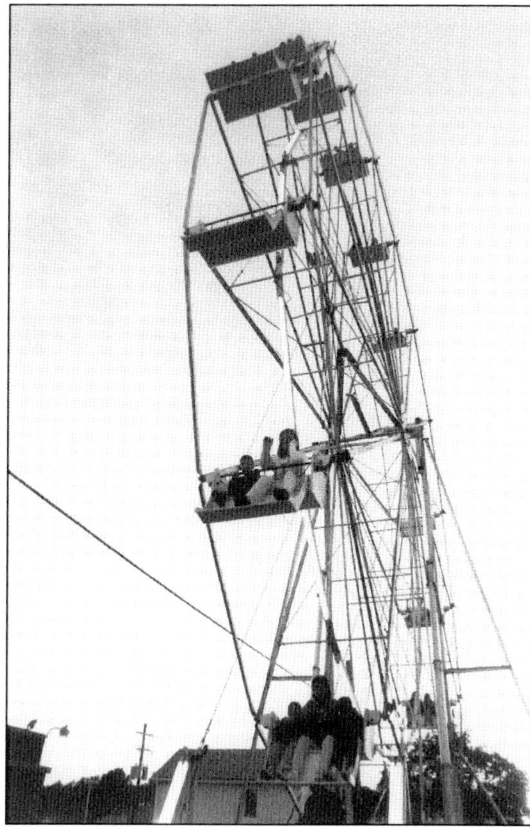

The Cresson Volunteer Firemen's Carnival. This celebration has become an annual homecoming for many former residents. Distance does not deter faithful carnival patrons. It provides an opportunity to visit family and renew old friendships in a setting of fun and excitement. Garbrick provides the rides and the fire company has its own game booths and kitchen staffed by local volunteers.

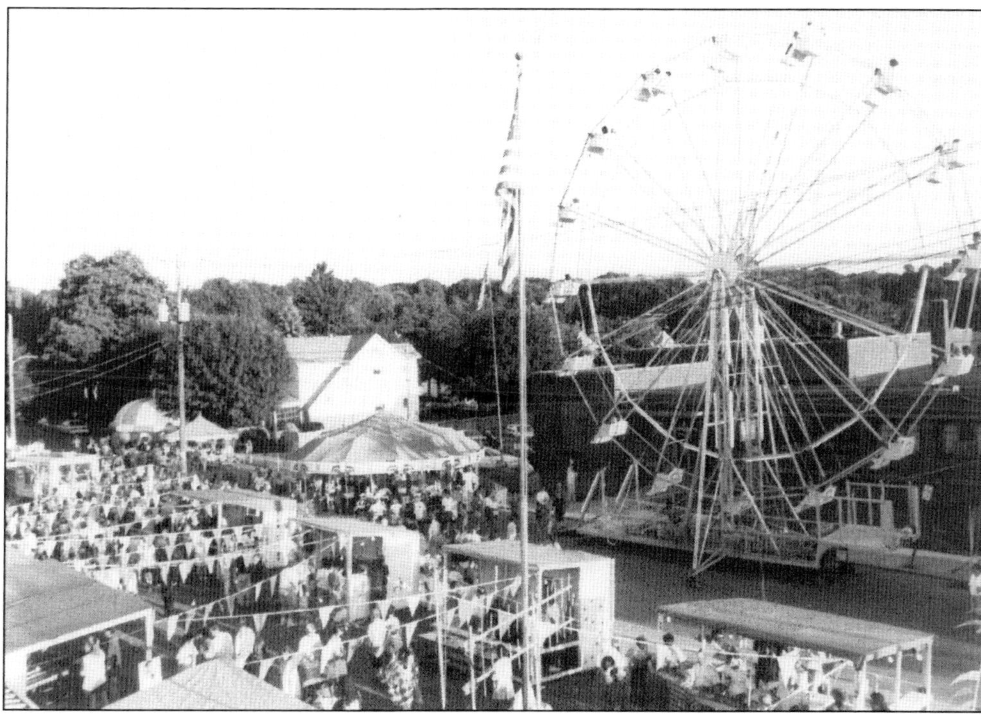

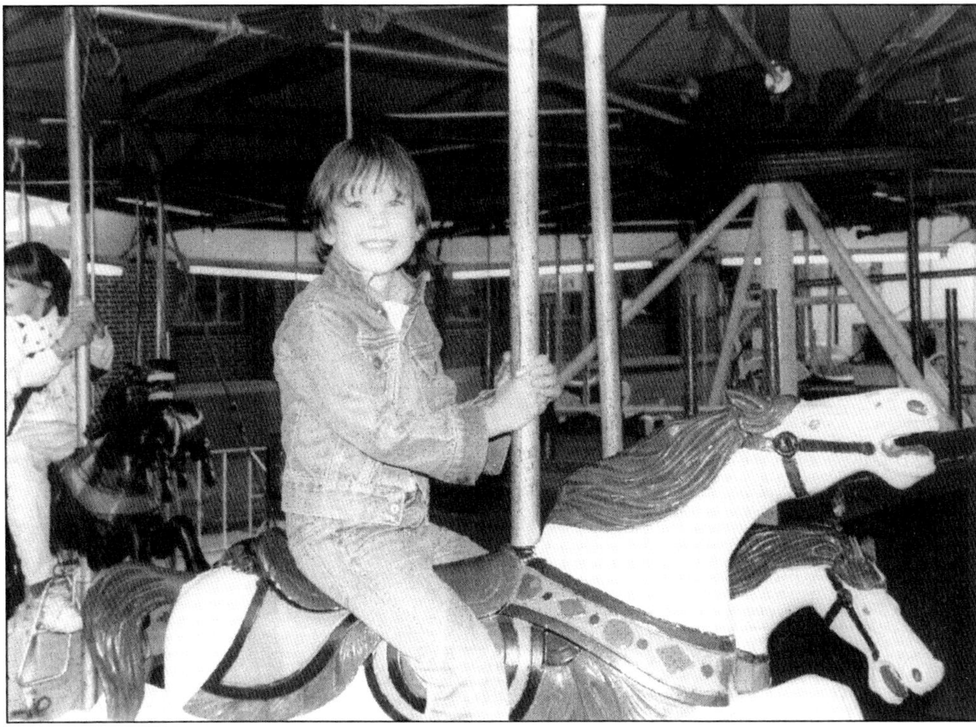

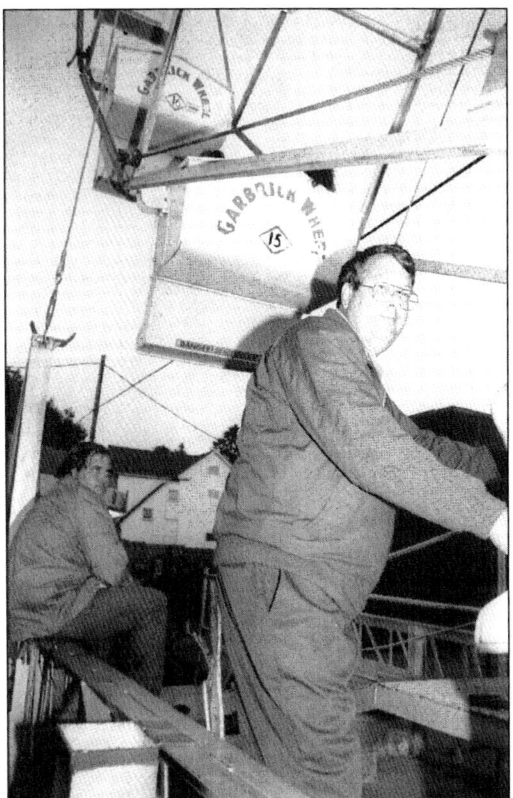

Five-year-old George Reed, of Lilly, on the carousel—a favorite of the youngsters.

Henry Garbrick at the helm of his Ferris wheel. Garbrick has been providing thrill and excitement to carnival seekers in Cresson since 1969. The firehouse was a lumberyard when the carnival was initiated as an offshoot of the County Firemen's Convention, which has been held in Cresson since 1968. The Merry Mixer provides a fun-filled experience on a ride Garbrick designed.

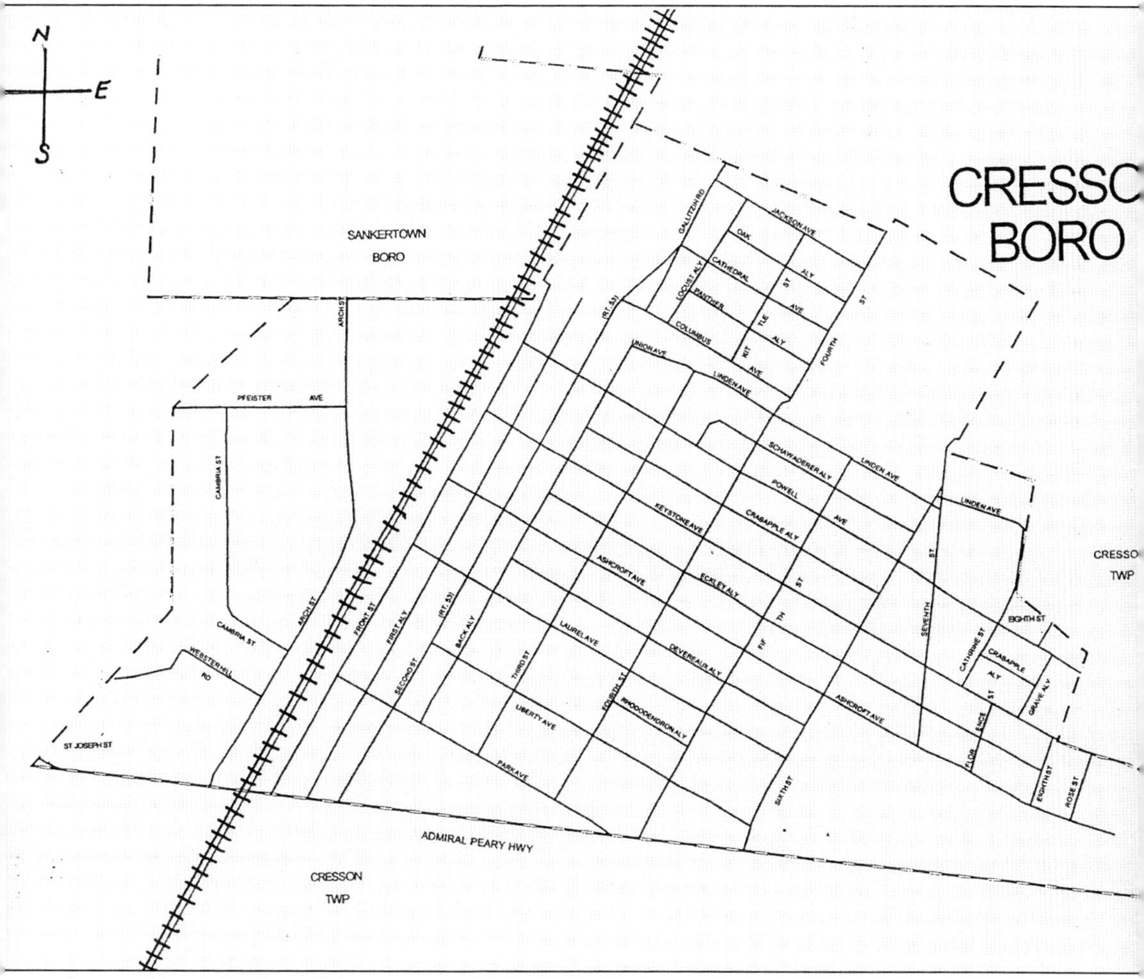

Cresson Borough. Carved from Cresson Township, the borough was officially incorporated on June 7, 1906.

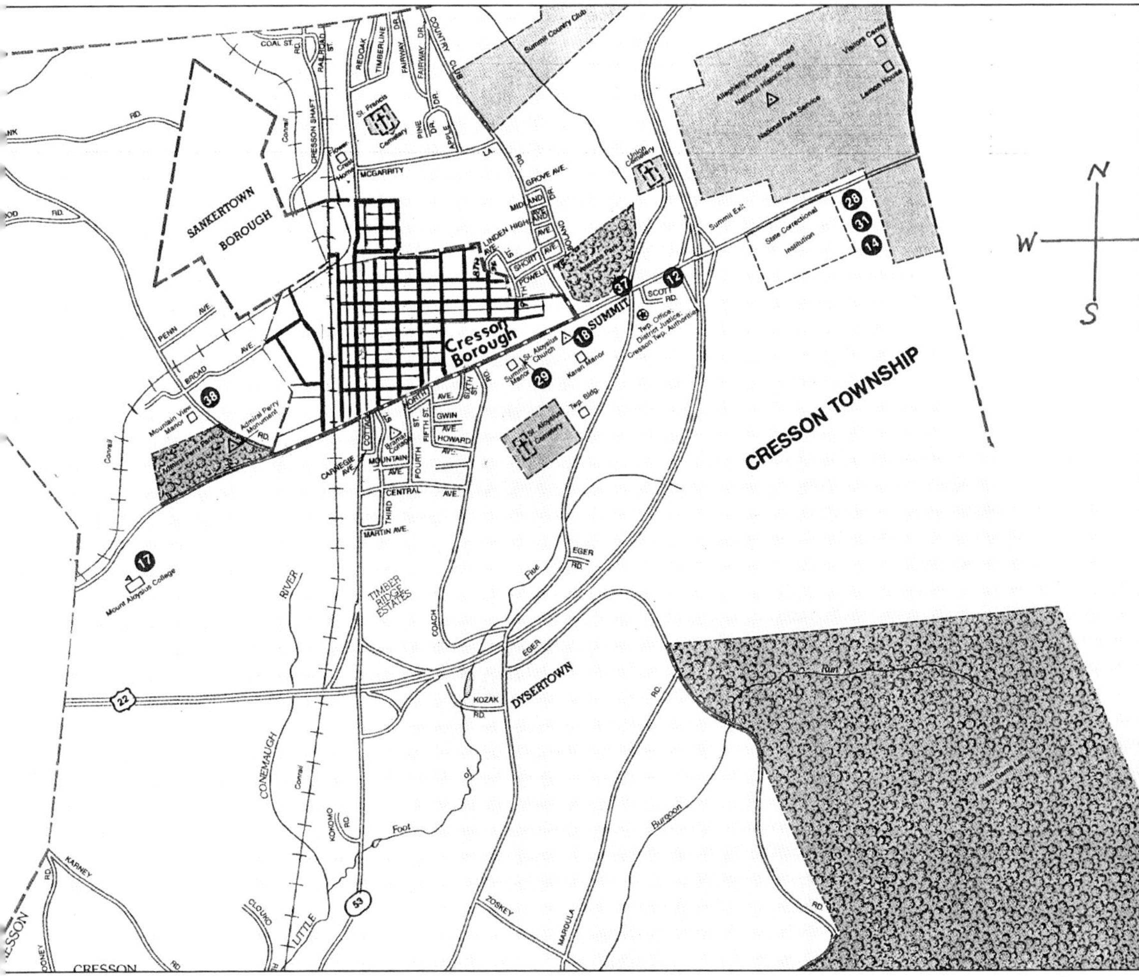

Cresson Township. A land of swamps, glens, laurel-dotted hillsides, and silent splendor, the township was officially organized on December 4, 1893.